Praise for *Resource Discovery for the Twenty-First Century Library*

'As someone who has been watching the discovery space with interest for years, I read this book with interest and it did not disappoint. Blending case studies of state-of-the-art projects such as the National Library of Singapore's OneSearch interface - which does data harmonisation to combine multiple GLAM sources in Singapore together to be seamlessly searched, with practical chapters such as one on investigating the resource needs of the University of Oxford, it has something for everyone. The more speculative chapters on semantic search prototypes and futures, in particular, also intrigued me on what the future might bring. I recommend this book to all professionals who are interested in the art and future of library discovery.'
Aaron Tay, Library Analytics Manager, Singapore Management University, and author of the Musings about librarianship blog

'The impressive roster of contributors gives an enormously valuable overview of current advanced practice and future directions for discovery. With occasional acknowledgements back to Diderot and Ranganathan, these chapters illuminate the present and propel us forward into a linked data near-future and towards a next-generation environment of repeatedly executable research publications and AI personal discovery bots.'
Neil Grindley, Head of Resource Discovery, Jisc

Resource Discovery for the Twenty-First Century Library

Resource Discovery for the Twenty-First Century Library

Case studies and perspectives on the role of IT in user engagement and empowerment

EDITED BY
Simon McLeish

facet publishing

Published by Facet Publishing
www.facetpublishing.co.uk

Facet Publishing is wholly owned by CILIP: the Library and Information Association.

British Library Cataloguing in Publication Data
A catalogue record for this book is available from the British Library.

ISBN 978-1-78330-138-6 (paperback)
ISBN 978-1-78330-139-3 (hardback)
ISBN 978-1-78330-140-9 (e-book)

First published 2020

MIX
Paper | Supporting responsible forestry
FSC www.fsc.org FSC® C013604

Every purchase of a Facet book helps to fund CILIP's advocacy, awareness and accreditation programmes for information professionals.

The manufacturer's authorised representative in the EU for product safety is Logos Europe, 9 rue Nicolas Poussin, 17000 La Rochelle, France (contact@logoseurope.eu, www.logoseurope.eu).

Typeset from editors' files by Flagholme Publishing Services in 10/13pt Myriad Pro and Minion.
Printed and bound by CPI Group (UK) Ltd, Croydon, CR0 4YY

Contents

Figures and tables

Figures

Tables

Contributors

Simon McLeish, Resource Discovery Architect, Bodleian Libraries, University of Oxford (editor)

Dr Simon McLeish has been the Resource Discovery Architect at the Bodleian Libraries since the post came into existence in 2013. He is responsible for running the discovery service SOLO (Search Oxford Libraries Online; http://solo.bodleian.ox.ac.uk), advising across the libraries and beyond on discovery questions and researching discovery initiatives to enhance the services offered to readers.

Prior to this, Simon had 15 years' library IT experience as a consultant, and at the London School of Economics. He worked on projects such as pioneering the development of Shibboleth in the UK; creating a 1998 web portal, which incorporated elements that later surfaced in social media sites and virtual learning environments; and identity management for universities. This last was the topic of an earlier book published by Facet Publishing (Garibyan, McLeish and Paschoud, 2013).

Chris Awre, Head of Information Services, University of Hull

Chris Awre is Head of Information Services at the University of Hull, where he previously worked as Integration Architect following posts at Jisc, working on discovery service development, and at Imperial College, London, as a member of the systems team. He was a founder member of the Hydra Repository Project (now known as the Samvera Community and has sat on the Steering Group since 2008.

Chris was a member of the BEIS Open Research Data Task Force (2017–18) and currently sits on the Jisc Collections Management Community Advisory Board.

Tamir Borensztajn, EBSCO (Elton B. Stephens Co.)

Tamir Borensztajn has served as EBSCO's vice president of software-as-a-service strategy since 2014. In this role, he helps inform and present EBSCO's software strategy while working with libraries worldwide to understand their systems and software needs. Before joining EBSCO, Tamir served as Executive Director, Public Sector Innovation for Europe, the Middle East and Africa at Infor. He is a graduate of Hebrew University of Jerusalem and holds a Master of Library Science from Simmons College in Boston.

Lorcan Dempsey, Vice President and Chief Strategist, OCLC

Lorcan Dempsey began his career in public libraries in his native Dublin, Ireland. Before moving to OCLC, he managed the UK higher education national investment in information services for Jisc. Lorcan currently oversees research and membership at the Online Computer Library Center (OCLC), and is Chief Strategist. He has worked for library and educational organisations in Ireland, the UK and the USA. His influence on national policy and library directions is widely recognised. In 2010 he received the highest award from the National Federation of Advanced Information Services, the Miles Conrad Award. He is an honorary doctor of the Open University in the UK and has twice received a presidential citation from the Association for Library Collections & Technical Services for his work with OCLC colleagues.

David De Roure, Professor of e-Research, University of Oxford

David De Roure is Professor of e-Research at University of Oxford and a Turing Fellow at the Alan Turing Institute. He focuses on advancing digital scholarship, and works closely with multiple disciplines including humanities (studying digital musicology), engineering science (cyber security and the internet of things), social sciences (developing the concept of social machines) and computer science (large-scale distributed systems and social computing). David is also closely involved with libraries and collections, and developing the infrastructure for future scholarship.

David's career has followed an e-science path, looking at the affordances of digital infrastructures and methods to enable new research, and simultaneously web science, where large-scale citizen engagement enables democratisation and empowerment. He has extensive experience in hypertext, multimedia archives, semantic web, web science, social machines and the internet of things. His research today focuses on the relationship between humans and machines, especially around creativity and algorithms, with music as a powerful interdisciplinary thread. David is a frequent speaker and writer on the future of digital scholarship and scholarly communications, when he draws on this broad interdisciplinary background.

David is based in Oxford's world-leading Department of Engineering Science and is responsible for digital humanities within the Oxford Research Centre in the Humanities. He was previously Director of the Oxford e-Research Centre and, before moving to Oxford in 2010, Professor of Computer Science at the University of Southampton, UK. He was closely involved in the UK e-science programme and a founding member of the UK Software Sustainability Institute. From 2009 to 2013 David was the UK National Strategic Director for Digital Social Research for the Economic and Social Research Council, and subsequently a strategic adviser. He is a Fellow of the British Computer Society and of the Institute of Mathematics and its Applications.

Ed Fay, Deputy Director of Library Services, University of Bristol

Ed Fay is currently responsible for library collections, digital scholarship services and strategic planning at the University of Bristol. He has a decade of experience in library innovation and has developed a consciously user-centred approach to digital community and product development. He has been variously responsible for collection development, digital library infrastructures, scholarly communication and research data management, user experience and learning environments, and open source digital preservation.

Masha Garibyan, Librarianship and Information Science Consultant

Masha Garibyan has worked on a number of cutting-edge national and international initiatives in library access and identity management, online resource discovery, research data management, information literacy and open scholarship. In 2016, she represented Jisc on Knowledge Exchange, a collaboration between six European national organisations committed to advancing open scholarship and access. In 2015, she undertook an extensive consultation with libraries and museums in the UK and abroad for the resource discovery project at the University of Oxford. Prior to that, Masha had worked on several library identity and access management (IAM) projects and initiatives, helping UK institutions and service providers to move towards using federated IAM solutions, such as Shibboleth. Masha is one of the authors of *Access and Identity Management for Libraries* (Garibyan, McLeish and Paschoud, 2013), as well as a number of articles, briefings and papers.

Richard Green, Consultant to Library and Learning Innovation, University of Hull

Richard Green is an independent consultant who has worked with the University of Hull's repository team for many years. He was a founder member of the international Hydra Repository Project (now known as the Samvera Community – http://samvera.org) and was Chair of their Steering Committee for 2018/19. Among other related activities, Richard has also served as Vice Chair of the Open Repositories conference.

Wolfram Horstmann, Director of Göttingen State and University Library

Wolfram Horstmann has been Director of Göttingen State and University Library since 2014. Prior to this, he was Associate Director at the Bodleian Libraries of the University of Oxford. He is also Professor at the Information School of the Humboldt University in Berlin, teaching electronic publishing, open access and open science. He is biologist by training and worked in the field of computational neuroscience before turning his attention towards scholarly communication and libraries, working as head of publishing services at the academic library centre in Cologne and as Chief Information Officer at Bielefeld University.

The State and University Library is one of the most extensive university libraries in Germany and is closely involved in regional, national and international innovation processes. Wolfram is currently leading several strategic initiatives, for example those establishing agile library organisation, new models for collaboration between libraries and academic computing on campus for e-research services, for the federated Data Infrastructure in Germany (NFDI), the Research Data Alliance, Digital Research Infrastructure for the Arts and Humanities (DARIAH), Open Access and science (OpenAIRE) and future library networks (LIBER). He advises several bodies and initiatives, e.g. the European Commission, the Alliance of Science Organisations in Germany or the German Research Foundation and Rectors Conference.

Megan Hurst, co-founder and principal consultant, Athenaeum21

Megan Hurst is co-founder and principal of Athenaeum21 Consulting (www.athenaeum21.com). She works with clients to create and improve organisations, systems and services through a human-centred, data-driven, experience-design approach. Before co-founding Athenaeum21 in 2015, she defined the user and product requirements for web systems and services at EBSCO Information Services, where she most recently served as Director of Product Management for Open Web and Mobile Initiatives. Prior to EBSCO, she was the architect of Harvard University Library's first comprehensive digital assessment and user research programme for the Open Collections Program, and worked with non-profit, venture-funded start-ups and Fortune 100 companies as a management consultant for MIDIOR Consulting. She holds an MLIS from the University of Rhode Island, an MFA in integrated media from Massachusetts College of Art and Design, and graduated from Smith College.

Haliza Jailani, Deputy Director in the Resource Discovery and Management Division, National Library of Singapore

Haliza Jailani is a deputy director in the Resource Discovery and Management Division of the National Library Board of Singapore. She is responsible for the resource discovery portfolio of cataloguing and metadata creation, knowledge organisation systems and ontology, and information discovery using metadata. She is currently overseeing work on exposing the collection of National Library Board (NLB) metadata to Google using structured data and various aspects of open data work, including sharing of NLB's local name authorities with Singapore's government agencies. She is a member of the Linked Data Sub-Committee at the International Federation of Library Associations and Institutions (IFLA).

Kate Lawrence, User Experience Director, Research, Akamai Technologies

Kate Lawrence was appointed Vice President of User Research at EBSCO in 2014, having joined in 2011. She has over 25 years' experience as a User Experience (UX) practitioner.

Christine Madsen, co-founder and principal consultant, Athenaeum21

Dr Christine Madsen is co-founder and principal of Athenaeum21 Consulting (www.athenaeum21.com), where she works with universities, libraries, museums, research and information organisations around the world on strategy and innovation. She is expert in designing and building large-scale systems that use technology to connect people with the information they need. Her background is in digitisation and digital scholarship, understanding how to digitise and why we should. Previously, she has worked as Head of Digital Programmes at the Bodleian Libraries, University of Oxford, and led the Open Collections Program at Harvard University.

Roxanne Missingham, University Librarian and Chief Scholarly Information Officer, Australian National University

Roxanne Missingham is University Librarian and Chief Scholarly Information Officer, Australian National University. She was previously Parliamentary Librarian and Assistant Director General, Resource Sharing Division, National Library of Australia. She has had a long career in libraries and IT focused on the development of digital delivery and digital services. Formerly President of the Australian Library and Information Association (ALIA), she is a Fellow of the Association. She is currently a member of the Board of the Council of Australian University Librarians. She is also a member of a number of national and international committees including the OCLC Metadata Managers Focus Group and ALIA International Relations Advisory Committee.

Oliver Pesch, Chief Product Strategist (Information Services), EBSCO

Oliver Pesch works as Chief Product Strategist for EBSCO Information Services where he helps set direction for EBSCO's resource management and access products. He is currently co-chair of the National Information Standards Organization's (NISO's) Standardized Usage Statistics Harvesting Initiative (SUSHI) Standing Committee, and chair of the COUNTER (Counting Online Usage of Networked Electronic Resources) board of directors, serves on the COUNTER Executive Committee and Technical Advisory groups, and chaired the COUNTER Release 5 Technical Working Group.

Carl G. Stahmer, Director of Data Digital Scholarship, UC Davis

Carl G. Stahmer, PhD, is the Director of Data Digital Scholarship at the Shields Library, University of California, Davis (UC Davis), and an Associate Professor in the UC Davis department of English and faculty member at the Rare Book School, University of Virginia. He also serves as the Associate Director for Humanities for the UC Davis Data Science Initiative; Associate Director of the English Broadside Ballad Archive (http://ebba.english.ucsb.edu); is lead developer for the ongoing Mellon-funded initiative to re-design the English Short Title Catalogue (http://estc.bl.uk) as an exemplar 21st-century library catalogue; and is technical director for the Advanced Research Consortium (http://arc.dh.tamu.edu/). He has been working in the digital humanities and digital library fields since the early 1990s when he co-founded the Romantic Circles website (www.rc.umd.edu) for which he served as the technical lead and co-general editor for the following ten years. His work has been funded by the National Endowment for the Humanities, the Institute of Museum and Library Services, the University of California Humanities Research Institute, the Andrew W. Mellon Foundation and the British Society for Eighteenth Century Studies.

Carl's current research focuses on developing and implementing digital bibliographic tools and methods, including descriptive strategies for linked open data catalogues, digital analysis and description of historical printed materials and physical media (paper, parchment and typeset), and tools for content-based image recognition. For more information, please visit his website at www.carlstahmer.com.

Chris Tang, senior manager, National Library of Singapore

Chris Tang is a senior manager from the Content and Services division of the National Library of Singapore (NLS), where he oversees digitisation works and digital content management matters. He has previously presented on one of the NLS's digital projects, the Singapore Memory Project, at the IFLA World Library and Information Congress in 2013, and on the NLS's digital strategy at the 2015 IFLA World Library and Information Congress. Since joining the NLB in 2005, Chris has also been involved in business reference work and managing the National Library Office and donor collections' policies and operations.

Julie Zhu, Senior Manager, Discovery Partners, IEEE

Julie Zhu has been working in the publishing industry for over 17 years. As the Senior Manager, Discovery Partners at the Institute of Electrical and Electronics Engineers (IEEE), she cultivates and manages working relationships with Discovery Service, Link Resolver, proxy service and search engine providers, as well as libraries and consortia, to maximise IEEE content findability, visibility and accessibility in multiple discovery channels. She serves in NISO's Information Discovery and Exchange Topic Committee, Open Discovery Initiative standing committees and KBART (knowledge base and related tools) Automation Working Group. She has published and presented on topics such as complying with publishing standards, reducing content gaps in discovery services, publisher–vendor–library collaborations and metadata enhancement projects. Julie has a PhD in English from Marquette University and an MBA from Stony Brook University. Read more about Julie on LinkedIn (https://www.linkedin.com/in/julie-zhu-29901a4/) and ORCID (http://orcid.org/0000-0002-2005-2719).

Reference

Garibyan, M., McLeish, S. and Paschoud, J. (2013) *Access and Identity Management for Libraries: controlling access to online information*, Facet Publishing.

Foreword: library discovery directions

Lorcan Dempsey

Introduction

The variety of topics and perspectives represented in this collection is clear evidence of the diverse scope of library discovery. In only a few years the emphasis has shifted from consideration of the development of a particular library service (the evolution from catalogue to metasearch to discovery layer) to a broader consideration of user behaviours and service development in a complex network ecosystem of offerings from libraries and third-party providers. A full appreciation of discovery and discoverability in a library environment now involves thinking about much more than the discovery layer.

(In writing this short piece I was interested to trace this evolution in two earlier pieces I have written about similar themes (Dempsey, 2006, 2012). Considered alongside this one, the three pieces are written at approximately six year intervals.)

For a sense of the diversity of the current ecosystem, consider the various current roles of Wikipedia, Google Scholar, reading lists, the library discovery layer, resource guides, Scopus and Web of Science, WorldCat, Goodreads, ResearchGate and Mendeley, ArXiv and PubMed Central. These and other resources are used by library users to find specific resources of interest to them, for serendipitous discovery and for exploration. They are used alongside library resources, and sometimes in combination with them. The transition from Google Books to a library catalogue via WorldCat, or the transition from Google Scholar to a licensed article via a registered library knowledge base, or the serendipitous discovery of special collections in Google or Wikipedia are all examples of such combinations.

In this environment, three broad related trends are of interest. First, 'discovery often happens elsewhere'. We know that library users now search for and find materials of interest in many places. These include the network level services that are now so much a part of our network lives (Wikipedia, Google, Amazon) and more specialist resources (arXiv.org, for example). The discovered resources may be books or journals, software, research data, learning materials and so on. We also know that people may 'discover' materials of interest in non-library services and then turn to the library to 'locate' particular instances of those resources, whether these are on a shelf, licensed by the library, or potentially requestable from elsewhere. So, a user who spends time on ResearchGate, say, may turn to the library if a copy of a discovered article is not available there.

Second, while the library collection may be a part of the library's information universe, it is not necessarily central, nor the first used. This is a natural outcome of a shift from an environment of information scarcity (where the library acquired materials for local use, and was the only place to get them) to one of information abundance (where the network environment is rich in relevant resources).

And third, we are observing a reconfiguration of workflows. In a print world, or a world of information scarcity, the learner or researcher had to build their workflow around the library. In a network world, many people expect library resources to fit into a user's network workflows, which may comprise multiple resources (citation management, network discovery services, and so on).

These changes are important, because historically library discovery and library collections went hand in hand. However, both our sense of discovery and our sense of collections are changing in different ways in the current network environment.

In this context, two important trajectories seem to me to lie just under the surface of much of the discussion in the following papers, and perhaps to provide an integrating pattern:

- the peeling away of library discovery from the local collection
- the peeling away of library discovery from the local audience.

Collection and audience boundaries are blurring, placing different requirements on discovery. Each of these has very much co-evolved with changing research and learning behaviours in a rich networked, discovery ecosystem, so at the same time we can see a variety of other service and technology directions emerge, and I make notes about some salient areas in subsequent sections.

In this brief foreword, I can only say a little about such directions, which can then be traced with more detail and nuance in the contributions assembled here.

The peeling away of discovery from the local collection

The facilitated collection and the collective collection

In a print world of scarce resources, assembling a collection close to the user made sense. And indeed, 'goodness' was associated with the size of that local collection. This model extends into the electronic world, where resources were licensed for local use. Increasingly, we are seeing that the centrality of the acquired collection to the library service and identity is an artefact of a particular phase of library development, which we are now moving beyond. By 'acquired' I mean the collections that the library has purchased (often in print) or has licensed (usually electronic), and makes available to a local audience.

But researchers and learners inhabit a network environment rich in information and workflow resources – for research, communication, archiving, social sharing, and so on. These are general purpose (GitHub, Wikipedia) or specialised (Amazon, arXiv, PubMed Central, Google Scholar, etc.). 'Localness' is no longer a determining influence in information use. The acquired library collection is now actually only one resource among many of potential interest.

In this context, we see a progressive shift in library interests from the locally acquired just-in-case collection to the 'collection as a service', facilitating access by researchers to resources of potential interest wherever they are. Figure 0.1 shows how a variety of services have been added successively over the years to the resources the libraries offer.

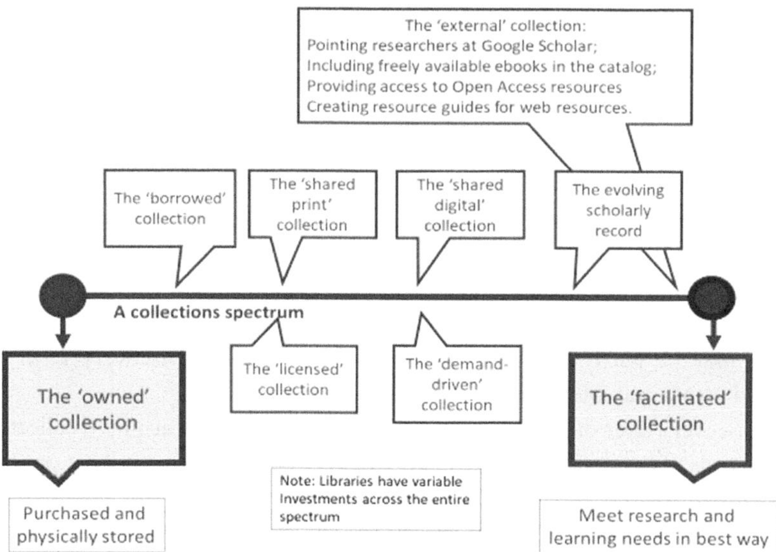

Figure 0.1 *The evolution of library services*

Historically the library had a 'purchased' or 'owned' print collection. This was supplemented by the 'borrowed' collection as libraries grouped together to share materials through interlibrary lending. Then the licensed collection emerged, first with abstracting and indexing services and then with the journal literature itself.

More recently we have seen demand-driven collections emerge. Narrowly, this relates to demand-driven acquisition. More broadly, we see more reliance on data-driven decision making around acquisition choices. In this context, there is an interesting flip. Previously, collections drove discovery; in a more demand- or data-driven environment, discovery may drive collections.

As research and scholarly network resources have proliferated, we now see greater reliance on external, freely available resources. A library may proxy access to Google Scholar, may add metadata for free e-book collections or open access collections to the discovery layer or knowledge base, and is developing resource guides based on broad user interests rather than on what is solely available in the collection.

One aspect of this facilitation is the 'collective collection' where collections are managed in some way at a shared level above the institution. This is becoming more common, as libraries group together for resource sharing, shared print initiatives, a shared library system, or some other group activity. In the USA resource sharing consortia are common; in other countries there may be national or regional groups (e.g the Library Hub services in the UK, Sudoc from ABES in France, or Libraries Australia). The level of co-ordination may vary. For example, as an example of strong co-ordination, the Research Collections and Preservation Consortium (ReCAP) manages a physically consolidated print collection on behalf of its research library members. (This is also interesting from a discovery point of view, as members add an index of the ReCAP shared collection to their discovery layers, which has resulted in significantly increased use of the shared collection – it would be worth exploring how scalable an approach this would be across more libraries.)

There are now also collective collections comprising shared digital collections (such as those made available by Europeana, for example) or shared scholarly materials (such as the Australian Research Data Commons).

As a result the library interest in discovery has broadened. However, the extent of the shift may be partly obscured by organisational issues. Discovery is in fact supported across multiple library divisions or specialties.

So, a discovery layer may be managed to provide access to the acquired collection, and this tends to be seen still as the main 'discovery' support. Typically, it provides access to the catalogue (and maybe to WorldCat or another union catalogue), to licensed article data (and works with resolver or knowledge base infrastructure), and maybe to unique local digital materials (from a local repository or repositories). As noted above, various additional freely available resources may be added. In fact, management of the discovery layer has become more complex, as access to resource sharing groups is added, and as it is supported from a variety of metadata streams.

Direct access may also be provided to Google Scholar, WorldCat, PubMed Central, Scopus or Web of Science, and core disciplinary databases (PsycINFO, for example), among others. A knowledge base may be configured in Google Scholar to ensure transition from that discovery environment to resources licensed by the library. As noted, a discovery layer may be created in some way with a union catalogue for access to a collective collection of which the library is a part (as is the case with our neighbours here in Ohio, for example, who have access to the shared resource of OhioLINK alongside their local collections).

A major outcome of this shift to facilitated collections is the rapid development of resource guides, which guide users to resources of potential interest to them, inside and outside the local collection. To meet the strong interest in open access, services have emerged which may be integrated with a discovery layer, a knowledge base, resource sharing, or may be deployed as browser plug-ins. And new areas of interest continue to emerge, research data management and open educational resources in recent years for example, where, again, the library may wish to provide discovery options.

In this way, we can see that the library is guiding users to resources in multiple ways, and librarians may be advising their users on finding and using resources in a much broader discovery ecosystem, as discussed below.

Full library discovery

In current services, a library user is usually presented with a collection search, and a range of web pages about other library services or expertise. The two are separated in the website experience, but may not actually be separate in the user expectation of the library. If I am interested in demographics, for example, why not find a curated resource guide or the name of a subject specialist as well as relevant articles or books when I do a search?

And, indeed, we have seen discovery environments which provide a layer over not only the collections, but also potentially over the library website, library staff and expertise, resource guides, and so on. In other words, we are seeing approaches to 'full library discovery' emerge.

The steps which have been taken include a search over the website generally; over events, exhibitions or specialist services; over people and expertise (sometimes associated with resource guides); and over resource guides (as discussed above). Indeed, in the absence of dedicated services (for events, for example), resource guides are often used as a simple content management framework for various types of information about the library, and not only for lists of information resources.

Although collections are still key for libraries, as library services continue to evolve beyond the collection and there is a focus on deeper engagement with user communities, it makes sense for discovery services to represent more of what the library does and can provide.

This is of interest in academic libraries and of special interest in public libraries where event and meeting management are an important part of outreach.

We can see some systems development alongside this. One is the use of Drupal, Blacklight and other frameworks to deliver unified results across several resources including website, and other elements of library operation. In public libraries we have seen the use of events management software, customer relationship management systems and other systems for engagement. BiblioCommons is interesting here. OCLC's system Wise puts community engagement at the centre of its operations, rather than the collection.

We may not have thought of this as 'discovery' in the past, but it is an important part of the 'discoverability' of the library's capacity and potential value. And this is increasingly important for libraries of all types.

The peeling away of discovery from the local audience

The inside-out collection

Much of the discussion of discovery has been about the acquired collection, the materials bought and licensed and assembled for local use. This is an outside-in collection – the materials originate outside the institution.

However, in a network environment, institutions are important producers of cultural and scholarly resources of potentially broad interest to different external audiences.

In this context, think of the scholarly workflow. Historically, the final product of research, the book or article, was published and it was the main research output. However, as workflows are digital and as they are supported by various workflow tools, there is more interest in other outputs – software, methods, preprints, research data. This is encouraged by policy mandates (at national, funder and institutional levels), by changing norms of science and research, by an interest in reproducibility, and so on. Research outputs appear across the research lifecycle.

A related scholarly activity involves the creation of expertise and research profiles. Institutions may have their own systems for this, which pull together data about researchers, including bibliographic data. One aim is to improve the discoverability of local faculty for various reasons. And many researchers are very interested in managing reputation and visibility through Google Scholar, ResearchGate or other services. The library may advise here, or encourage the use of ORCID iDs, which again support discoverability in the scholarly ecosystem.

Or think also of special collections and archives. These tend to be assets which are unique to the institution or are rare, which have reputational value, and where the institution may accept a preservation responsibility as part of the broader scholarly or cultural record. There is growing interest in digitising distinctive materials and making them more broadly available. This is to integrate them more effectively in local learning and research activities. However, it is also important to disclose them to a wider audience outside the institution, or to allow them to be placed alongside related materials from elsewhere.

In each of these cases, there is a growing interest in 'discoverability' by an audience outside (and inside) the institution. In this sense, these are 'inside-out' collections (Dahl, 2018). The discovery dynamic is very different. While it makes sense to make sure they are represented in local discovery systems, it may be more important that they are represented effectively in external discovery systems used by potential audiences. So, care may be taken that they are indexed effectively by Google, or metadata for them may be marked up with additional links to improve chances of crawling, indexing or ranking. Metadata may be provided to aggregators of cultural, scholarly or open access materials. Links may be added to Wikipedia. And so on.

The library has a role in improving discoverability for audiences outside the institution, to enhance reputation, to increase the impact of local scholarship and research, and to share awareness of distinctive scholarly or cultural materials.

Attention here is diffuse: it has no single organisational focus within the library. It is not entirely clear how much effort libraries are putting into this area, and this will certainly vary across types and scale of library. But supporting discoverability more directly in this way clearly represents a different and important orientation.

Some technology directions

Several technologies and techniques are important, and are discussed in later contributions. Here I discuss some interesting directions.

Linked data

Important intellectual work has been undertaken by library staff on describing people, subjects, works and other entities and an extensive apparatus of authority files exists. That work is now being mobilised in a new environment. Our bibliographic infrastructure is evolving towards a more entity-based approach, as we think about modelling and exposing data about structured entities of interest (graphs of works, authors, places, for example), rather than only shipping around bundles of data about titles (records). Work on data modelling, entity backbones and data augmentation is being carried out by staff in multiple agencies, including national libraries, publishers and individual libraries, as well as OCLC. This is part of a more general trend, of which Google's knowledge graph and Wikidata are important examples. As the volume and variety of links grows, and as those links resolve to metadata about 'things', it becomes possible to match and merge data more easily at scale, to build greater navigation and context into interfaces, and to build relationships across the web. The work on these is at an early stage, but shows promise in improving discovery and discoverability.

Data science and machine learning

Discovery is a data-intensive field, and will benefit from advances in data science and machine learning. For example, it is likely that discovery in the journal literature will be facilitated by programmatic analysis of bodies of literature assembled by publishers, researchers and others. As large amounts of data are assembled in this way and transaction or 'intentional' data are collected from users, machine learning will increasingly be mobilised to develop scalable approaches to extract insights. There is an interest in entity recognition, topic modelling, summarisation, plagiarism detection, recommendation, ranking, personalisation and identifying patterns that may support new findings or directions. This raises issues about privacy, algorithmic transparency, authority and appropriate use, and libraries are stepping up to a critical role as advocates for the interests of users and researchers.

Presentation

When the discovery layer was introduced into libraries, there was a lot of discussion of a 'Google-like experience' and the 'simple search box'. However, not even Google does a 'Google-like experience' any more. There is a simple search box, but a huge amount of work goes into presenting the results. There is no longer a single ranked flow. There is the now familiar knowledge card summarising what Google knows about an entity. It may pull out images, news items, scholarly articles or other elements for highlighted presentation. Different entities have different elements presented. A literary work has book covers of various editions, various fulfilment options, maybe works in the same genre. For organisations, a map may be presented. In some cases, a carousel of similar or related items is presented at the top of the page. And so on. Libraries rely on a small number of suppliers for their discovery layer systems (one of which is OCLC). Some then layer different presentation environments over them (e.g. Blacklight). There has also been some experiment with the so-called 'bento box' display, where results from different sources (e.g. resource guides, article index, catalogue) are presented in different sections of the screen. As discussed in later contributions, there is some discussion how best to present results given these options. However, given the full range of the discovery experience I have described here, it seems to me that we are at an interesting point in the evolution of library discovery where richer options for co-ordinated presentation of discovery results will evolve. I have focused on presentation here, what is generally presented for direct interaction. We may also see a renewed interest in more push technology, or alerting approaches, views of the facilitated collection customised to particular group or individual perspectives.

Some service directions

The evolving library consultative role

The shifts I have spoken about are mirrored in the consultative role of the library. It is evident in the evolution from subject to a wider liaison role, and in the progressive broadening of the 'literacy' role – from bibliographic instruction, to digital literacies, to a more reflective consultation around the complexities of the emerging information environment. Barbara Fister writes nicely about the transition (Fister, 2019).

One could think about two aspects of this, echoing the discussion above. The first is an outside-in one, where consultation about the use of discovery and other information resources in a complicated environment becomes more important. This encompasses thinking critically about a complex evolving network information environment, understanding the structure of disciplines, thinking about relevant network resources, and advice abound surveillance, algorithmic retrieval and #fake. Again, this parallels the move from use of a defined local collection to more nuanced facilitation of information discovery and use in a network ecosystem.

The second is an inside-out one, where it becomes increasingly important to advise researchers and others about their informational lives as creators. One important aspect of this is to understand more about the discoverability of people and their work and how to optimise this in a network world, especially where systems and services increasingly measure, rank, recommend and cluster work algorithmically. Advice about the assignment of persistent identifiers, such as the ORCID iD for researchers, or DataCite for data sets, has become interesting here, as has advising about use of consistent names for organisations and people to improve discoverability and matching. Areas of interest include researcher profiles, copyright, publishing choices and open access, data consultancy, advice about mandates and best practices, and so on.

These twin aspects are connected in a network environment as we are both creators and consumers of resources. Indeed, for some, the boundaries between workflow, content and online identity have become blurred (think of the use of ResearchGate or Mendeley for example).

In this way, advice about discovery and discoverability includes the local collection and discovery system, but now ranges across research and learning behaviours in a rich network environment.

Discovery to fulfilment

We know that network users prize convenience and predictability. And libraries are very focused on improving the user experience so as to encourage use and satisfy demand. A major part of this is ensuring that the path from discovery to fulfilment is as efficient as possible and fragmentation or delay in the user experience is minimised. This becomes more important as more discovery and fulfilment options are stitched together. Discovery without fulfilment can be frustrating.

One outcome of this is that we will see greater convergence between discovery, resource sharing, collection development and acquisitions. We can expect to see the links between these service areas become more automated and data driven. So, in a simple example, acquisition of articles or books may be triggered at some level of demand as indicated by discovery or resource sharing patterns of use.

The links between discovery and fulfilment services are also more important. For example, libraries are interested in ensuring the connection between local discovery and a consortial discovery and requesting system works well. Consortial borrowing systems emphasise speed and predictability of delivery. Facilitating integrated access to open access materials improves delivery.

That said, the library discovery to fulfilment environment can be difficult or cumbersome to navigate. A major cause of this is precisely the fragmentation across multiple service and system boundaries. It is difficult to achieve the gravitational attraction of, say, Google Scholar, when library services are built on top of a patchwork of system boundaries. In some ways the discovery layer was a response to the fragmentation and inefficiency of approaches based on metasearch. For some libraries, there has also been some consolidation at the group level, with shared discovery environments. However, given the nature of the environment in which they work, where they are bringing together diverse services, it is inevitable that there are integration costs of systems work and user experience.

The discovery layer

The discovery layer has dominated discussions about library discovery in recent years. It is an important focus for library attention, often seen as a 'shop window'. However, we know that much discovery happens elsewhere.

It is interesting to consider the three categories of licensed, purchased and institutional materials in relation to the discovery layer. Article discovery is an evolving and fluid area, with the migration to open access creating new opportunity and uncertainty. We have seen the emergence of new network level discovery services alongside Scholar (e.g. Meta, Microsoft's Academic Search, Dimensions from Digital Science, and others), and while the long term sustainability of some of these may be unclear, they provide additional options. ResearchGate, Mendeley and other research networks are important venues. Preprint archives and other open resources continue to appear. Large publishers and others will likely have discovery offerings, but also new mining and interpretive services on top of large bodies of literature. At the same time, the range of research outputs to be discovered is growing (including research data, methods and software).

Turning to purchased materials (books, maps, etc.), these typically enter the discovery layer through the cataloguing stream. There has certainly been some move to group level for discovery of these items and this is likely to get more common as more shared approaches to managing print collections emerge.

Finally I have discussed how libraries may provide access to institutional materials (research outputs, special collections) locally, but that there is a strong interest in pushing these out to audiences outside the institution in various ways, so the discovery layer is only one place where this might happen.

At the same time, I have discussed how the scope of discovery itself has diversified, as the library addresses needs in a rich network environment. When all of these factors are taken together, the current library discovery layer addresses a part of the discovery need and the services it offers are situated in a fluid and evolving environment. It seems very much like a service category in transition.

However, few libraries have taken the step that Utrecht University Library has, in dispensing with the now conventional local library discovery layer altogether. In its place, library users now rely on several network level resources as the primary entry point: 'The university library finds that researchers and students often like to start with a wide search when looking for scientific literature, for instance by visiting Google Scholar first. That is why we offer support in major, worldwide scientific search engines' (Utrecht University, n.d.).

The library then offers a list of network level discovery resources, some openly available, some licensed (Scopus, Web of Science). Second, a search is offered in the library's collection. This is through the Dutch Union Catalogue (provided through

WorldCat) and access to the resolver for journal title searches. Interestingly, they then provide a list of services for discovery of research data.

While this model may not be widely adopted it is an illuminating response to some of the issues discussed here. It shows a particular response to the scoping, scaling and sourcing choices that face libraries as they design for changing needs. A scoping choice was made here that the discovery layer was not necessarily the best investment of library time and resources, given changing patterns of information use. The context established in the quote above is that searching behaviour starts at web scale, with a 'wide search'. This suggests that discovery often begins at network scale, rather than at library scale, but requires links back to the library. Given that, they are sourcing their solution through a mix of network level resources and library resources. They are not sourcing exclusively through a library level discovery layer.

In the discovery environment, libraries are looking at what they should do (scoping), what the relationship between library and network level external services should be (scaling), and what combination of systems and services best needs their users needs (sourcing).

Conclusion

Discovery has been core to library operations, closely coupled with a local collection for most of its history. In a network world the relationship between discovery, collections and behaviours is changing in important ways. My interest here has been to provide some background context. As the papers collected here show, there is much to explore.

References

Dahl, M. (2018) Inside-out Library Services: challenging the 'jacks of all trades but masters of none' librarian syndrome, *Advances in Library Administration and Organization*, **39**, 15–34.

Dempsey, L. (2006) The Library Catalogue in the New Discovery Environment: some thoughts, *Ariadne*, **30**, July, www.ariadne.ac.uk/issue/48/dempsey/.

Dempsey, L. (2012) Thirteen Ways of Looking at Libraries, Discovery, and the Catalog: scale, workflow, attention, *EDUCAUSE Review*, December, https://er.educause.edu/articles/2012/12/thirteen-ways-of-looking-at-libraries-discovery-and-the-catalog-scale-workflow-attention.

Fister, B. (2019) Information Literacy's Third Wave, *Inside Higher Education*, https://www.insidehighered.com/blogs/library-babel-fish/information-literacy%E2%80%99s-third-wave.

Utrecht University (n.d.) *Searching for Literature*, https://www.uu.nl/en/university-library/searching-for-literature#searchengines.

1

Introduction: technology and resource discovery

Simon McLeish

This chapter provides a background to the remaining material in the book by giving a brief overview of the current discovery landscape, looking at:

- the importance of resource discovery
- interaction of technology and the needs of library users
- how users approach discovery
- how the rest of the chapters of the book fit together.

As this chapter covers in outline a lot of material, there are many references for further reading where more in-depth treatments can be found.

The importance of resource discovery

Discovery is fundamental to almost every human intellectual activity, as two events millennia apart show.

It is considered likely that the earliest forms of writing evolved from tokens used to record quantities 'to document the affairs of an extensive bureaucratic network controlling labour, materials, and subsistence resources' (Green, 1991). This can be understood as making it possible to find out information about the assets of the community. 'Where is there grain stored?' 'How much livestock is there?' These are discovery questions, and the tokens which became writing are mediators of that discovery. They make the answers to the questions portable: you no longer need to go to the wheat stores or sheep pens to find out the answer.

Over five millennia later, a new internet search engine was launched. Google rapidly became so culturally prevalent that its name is used as a common verb synonymous with 'search'. According to the Oxford English Dictionary, the term was first used in this way on a mailing list in 1998, the same year in which Google was launched (OED, 2006). Further history of the word is discussed by Philipson (2013): within a few years, it appeared in popular TV programmes, in newspapers and books, and it is now used by virtually everybody with an internet connection. The modern online lifestyle would be impossible without discovery.

This book is concerned with discovery in an academic environment, something which has been part of the purpose of libraries and museums since they came into existence, a purpose which has gathered momentum in the electronic age. However, the book concentrates on discovery in the library; it does not discuss discovery for archives in detail.

This is essentially because the materials handled in the non-archival library collections – books, serials and so on – are amenable to being described in more easily standardised ways than one of a kind items such as many museum exhibits, manuscripts or archives. Thus, resources have often been allocated to solve the more tractable problems of describing bibliographic materials, leaving archives and museums in 2016 with large quantities of barely described or uncatalogued objects (OCLC Research, 2015). Thus libraries have had generally accepted metadata standards such as MARC (machine-readable cataloguing) for many years, while museum equivalents are still a long way behind; modern books and journal articles are even 'self-describing' (Danskin, 2014) in that the book itself will have metadata printed on the cover and/or title page. A detailed discussion of the reasons why the aspirations for the use of computers in the museum sector have to a large extent failed to materialise – why comments made almost 40 years apart look contemporary in looking ahead to the same near future, not yet realised – is given by Ross Parry in his book *Recoding the Museum* (Parry, 2007).

This does not mean that the considerations which allow for successful discovery are different in libraries and museums, however. These considerations can basically be summarised as:

- Understand your resources.
- Understand those who might wish to use these resources.

These lead to metadata descriptions in forms that enable the potential users of resources to find out which of the available resources are of relevance to their requirements, whether it is to complete an essay towards a degree, or to find out with whom it might be useful to discuss an idea for some cross-disciplinary research. In the library context, these immediately bring to mind Ranganathan's Laws.

How we got here

This book is about the present and future of discovery, but it is not possible to understand this without some idea of how it relates to its history. In place of a lengthy historical account, we give a diagrammatic, approximately chronological, concept map of the history of discovery in libraries and museums.

The briefest of summaries of this history is that it has mostly been driven by developments in collection description, with modern discovery being the meeting place between metadata and the computer science field of information retrieval. This is clearly evident in a chronologically organised concept cloud (Figure 1.1 on the next page). One important theme is that the development of standards has had a huge influence on discovery, so standards are differentiated from other concepts in the diagram.

Standards are picked out in the diagram with rectangular rather than elliptical boxes. Dotted arrows indicate links which are not truly conceptual, in one case the use of a service for discovery, in the other a use of one concept being partly inspired by perceived shortcomings in the other. References to detailed narrative accounts and interesting further reading are given in Table 1.1 on page 5.

Discovery is deeply embedded in library culture. As an example, even a cursory skimming of this book will show that several chapters directly reference Ranganathan's Laws (Ranganathan, 1931), foundational to the ethos of modern libraries, as a kind of justification for what is said.

In a modern formulation (Wikipedia, n.d.), the laws are:

1 Books are for use.
2 Every person his or her book.
3 Every book its reader.
4 Save the time of the reader.
5 The library is a growing organism.

In the context of discovery, the laws can be seen as a description of the landscape (laws 1 and 5 – where the modern library is an organism covering far more than just 'books'), and the journey taken by the reader to find the right book for them (2) through the use of appropriate technology (4); while (3) expresses an agnosticism about the items which readers need which should inform the design of the technology: every item in a library should be discoverable.

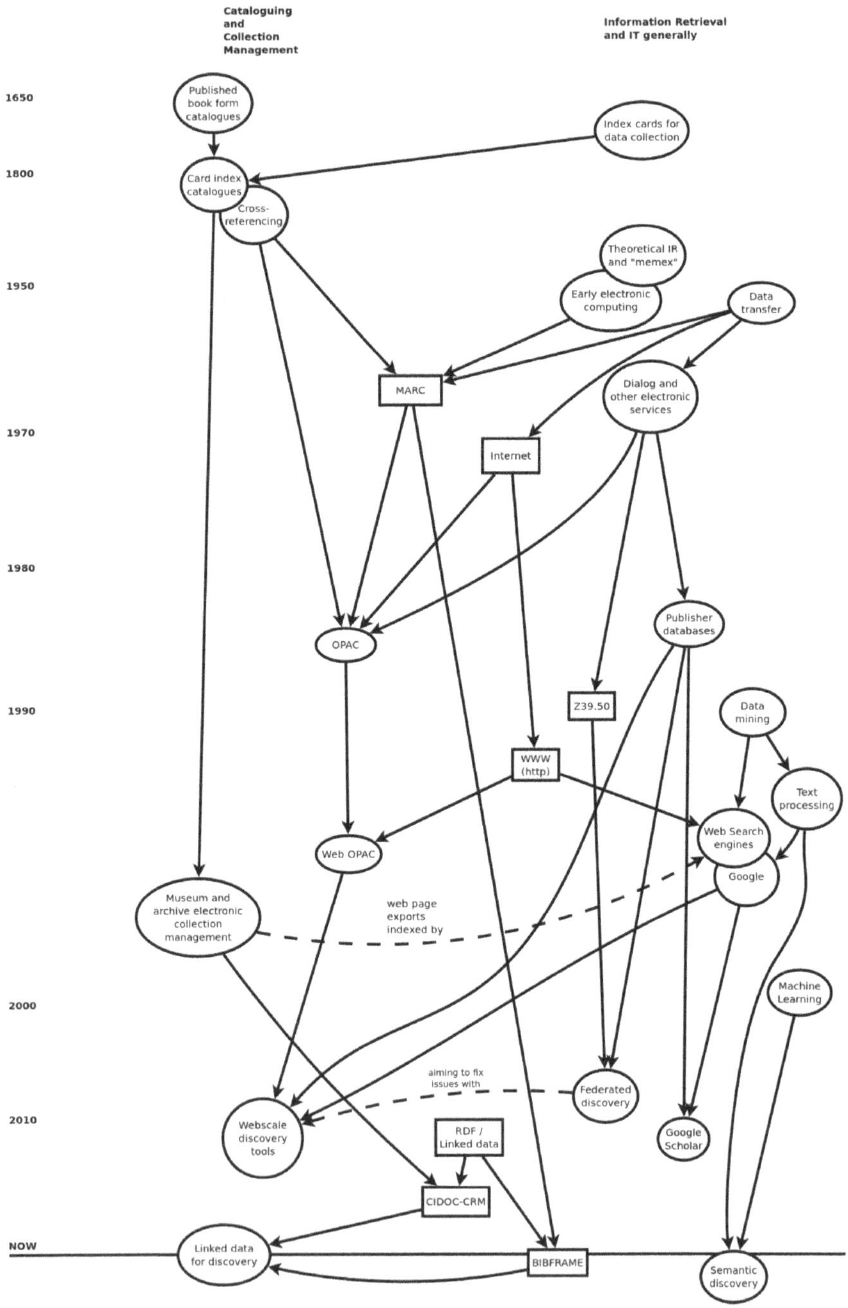

Figure 1.1 *A concept cloud for resource discovery, organised approximately chronologically*

Table 1.1 *Further reading in the history of resource discovery*

Discovery and collection management (analogue)	Early catalogues: Strout (1956) Card indexes: Charmantier and Müller-Wille (2014), Goode (1895), Hopkins (1992), Pizer (1965)
Computer systems in information management	General overview: Sanderson and Croft (2012) Visionary ideas (a 'must read' paper): Bush (1945) Early search and retrieval: Bjørner and Ardito (2003), Maron, Kuhns and Ray (1959)
MARC, OPAC, web OPAC	History and impact of MARC: Avram (1975), Seikel and Steele (2011) History of the OPAC: Borgman (1996) Federated search: Boss and Nelson (2005), Breeding (2005), Kehoe (2007)
Web search engines	Before Google: Mauldin (1997), Seymour, Frantsvog and Kumar (2011) History, design and impact of Google: Battelle (2006), Hillis, Petit and Jarrett (2013), Page et al. (1998) Googe Scholar, reasons for use and perceived drawbacks: Jacso (2005), Madsen et al. (2016)
Web-scale discovery	Common features: described in Breeding (2015) Google-like simplicity: Asher and Duke (2012), Rose-Wiles and Hofmann (2013), Vaughan (2011) Usability studies: too numerous to list individually, see Thomsett-Scott and Reese (2012) for review Criticisms: Ekström (2015), Reidsma (2016), Sherratt (2015), Shi and Levy (2015)

As Carl G. Stahmer says in Chapter 10, 'Libraries have historically engaged computing technologies to advance two primary goals: to enhance user experience, and to improve the efficiency and accuracy of library work.' This is why resource discovery, in bringing together technology and the needs of library users, is so closely connected to the laws.

Approaches to discovery: understanding users

The key issue in this field is how users approach the discovery services available to them. Studies have been carried out which have allowed the development of a taxonomy of discovery methodologies and principles.

A number of principles and strategies have been suggested to describe the ways in which people discover material, most of which have evocative names: 'principle of least effort' (Bates, 2003; Connaway, Dickey, and Radford, 2011; Law, 2010), berrypicking (Bates, 1989; Falciani-White, 2012), rational choice theory and gratification theory (Janyk, 2014) and the information search process model (Kuhlthau, 1988; Kuhlthau, Heinström and Todd, 2008; Swain, 1996). A longer discussion of these methods is included in Madsen et al. (2016).

Personal involvement in testing users in searching suggests that practical search strategies are today in the most part informed by what works for the user in contexts met before they arrive at an academic library, in particular in using Google and other web search engines. This is combined by a feeling that the contents of the collections and the way they are described is not well known to the user, so they fear they will miss items which are relevant. This leads to them using wide search terms, filtering them after the event (using facets, even though these are not available in Google), or by scrapping the current search term and trying a variation on it to see if better-looking results can be obtained.

This contrasts with a common strategy among librarians and others who are familiar with the collections (especially in some subject areas), where there is more frequent use of advanced search features such as Booleans and longer planning before starting searching, with the aim of crafting a search that will return precisely the results which are desired. This dichotomy can lead to bizarre advice, as in one paper which will not be cited here, in which user testing by librarians led to the suggestion that the reason the desired results were not found was because the subjects had an inadequate understanding of Library of Congress Subject Headings – hardly a priority part of learning for the vast majority of students. That is not to say that librarians are unable to offer good advice to readers, and an appropriate comment can produce a satisfied and grateful reader.

There are more functional ways to distinguish different resource discovery activities – methods and tactics to go with the principles and strategies in the last few paragraphs. It is common to distinguish 'known item' searches (where the user is trying to access or obtain more information about something which they already know about, such as a reference from a reading list or research article) and subject searches (where the user is looking for a broader range of items which are likely to be relevant). Some tools are more useful for one than the other – for instance online public access catalogue (OPAC) searching is in some ways better equipped to answer known item queries because there is no ranking involved and searches have to be precisely formulated; while modern 'web-scale' discovery tools often disappoint users when they discover that copying and pasting a reference into the search box frequently does not find the item, even if it is present in the indexes being searched (because too much information not present in searchable fields in the index is included in the search string).

Browsing is another common discovery activity, which has lost a lot of its importance in the digital world with its emphasis on the search box – it is not really possible to browse Amazon in the same way that customers used to browse in a bookshop.[1] For large and complex collections, browse becomes unmanageable, which is why it is not present in Google or Amazon. However, for some collections it can function at least as well as searching for discovery purposes; a good example of a well designed browse interface can be seen at Two Way Street (http://twoway.st/), using the metadata of the British Museum.

Another common discovery method is citation chaining. The reader starts from a known item (usually a journal article), and then looks at either the other items which cite the original ones, or at the items which it cites. The reader can follow a trail of related items in almost exactly the way in which this is done in Bush's memex device (Bush, 1945). This is one discovery activity which has been made far easier with the advent of digital databases, and there are specialist providers of citation information which can be used for this purpose. 'Citation chaining is ubiquitous in all areas of research across all disciplines' (Madsen et al., 2016). There are now services that aim to improve citation chaining as a discovery mechanism – after all, the simple existence of a citation does not indicate whether it is cited in approval or rebuttal, nor how influential it is to the citing work. The meaningfulness of citations is a concept used in a recently released service intended to compete with Google Scholar, Semantic Scholar (https://www.semanticscholar.org/), as described in Valenzuela, Ha and Etzioni (2014): 'Influential citations are determined using a machine-learned model analysing a number of factors including the number of citations to a paper, and the surrounding context for each citation.'

One of the concerns researchers have with citation chaining as a discovery methodology is that it can make their research feel as though it is conducted in an 'echo chamber' effect (as also mentioned in the University of Oxford report): a series of papers which cite each other and a small number of others without reference to other work in the field. In order to avoid this effect, and for other reasons, serendipity is also valued in discovery. Recommendation engines are used commercially ('people who viewed this item also viewed . . .', 'customers who bought this item also bought . . .' on Amazon, for instance) and in the academic sector (e.g. Ex Libris' bX recommender), which suggest items that may not have been expected from the original search and may prove fruitful. Browsing can also be a good source of serendipity.

A number of studies have been undertaken to analyse how the working practices of academics have evolved in the 21st century. Two recent examples based around a series of repeated surveys (both focusing more on tools than methods) are Wolff, Rod and Schonfeld (2016) (US based) and Gardner and Inger (2016) (worldwide): a total of around 50,000 responses were received in the 2015 surveys, ignoring any duplicates. The headline conclusions reached by these two most recent analyses are not identical; the former finds that the preferences researchers have for starting points for discovery are less strong than they used to be, with equal preference for general search engines and specific electronic research resources, while the second finds that abstracting and indexing services remain dominant. Library search tools are currently increasing in relevance, according to both, however. More discussion on changing working practices follows in the next section, as it is clearly closely connected to the use of social media.

People and social media

Serendipity comes into another type of discovery, that involving people. Librarians as experts have already been mentioned, but researchers value annual conferences as a way to catch up with peers and exchange ideas (though this activity has been gradually replaced by the use of contacts in social media, where they are available throughout the whole academic year). Supervisors and tutors are often used as a way to find relevant information by students. Today, people are still able to answer queries which databases cannot, because the query is too vague or requires too much background knowledge to understand (for example, there are words which have specific technical meanings in different disciplines, or even multiple meanings within the same discipline: the word 'homogeneous' meant three different things in the author's doctoral thesis, which straddled the boundary between group theory and model theory in mathematics). Finding the right person to ask is a discovery task in itself, of course.

In 2019, social media, in all its forms, is ubiquitous, and a lot of the personal interactions that are part of discovery involving people are now possible online through these tools. There is already an extensive literature on the ways in which academics and students use social media in their work. In 2011, almost 80% of the surveyed academics were using social media in their research, a proportion rising to 95% in some subject areas (Nicholas and Rowlands, 2011). There is a correlation with youth, though not as significant a one as might be expected, and a higher likelihood of use of social media by academics whose work predominantly requires cross-institutional collaboration. It is also not surprising that the different types of tool are thought to be most useful at different stages of the research lifecycle, some for identifying research opportunities or organising collaboration, others for disseminating research findings.

In *Studying and Researching with Social Media*, Poore gives a list of ten ways in which social media is used (Poore, 2014). His book should be consulted for a full length description of the use and potential of social media for teaching, learning and research. The process of discovery plays a part in at least five of them: collaboration, interactivity, sharing, creativity and distribution.

While it has been suggested that much of the role of social media in academic endeavour is to facilitate existing practice rather than creating new working methods (Priem, Piwowar and Hemminger, 2012), others disagree (including Poore), and it seems likely that research and teaching will both see the evolution of new methodology, which takes advantage of social media.

One of the most important discovery-related applications of social media is through scholarly metrics. Today's scholars can take advantage of 'altmetrics' both to measure the impact of their own work and as an aid to discover well-regarded research articles, as discussed by Priem, Piwowar and Hemminger (2012) and others. Altmetrics measure the informal citations of articles in various forms of social media, immediately giving a picture of the importance of an article which rounds out the information given by traditional citation counting (and is quicker to respond to new citations, and applicable to a wider set of academic outputs by including such resource types as research data).

Many papers discuss the idea of the 'digital native', a term introduced by Marc Prensky (2001). Digital natives have been described as 'young people [who] are said to have been immersed in technology all their lives, imbuing them with sophisticated technical skills and learning preferences for which traditional education is unprepared' (Bennett, Maton and Kervin, 2008). Many papers have been published discussing the validity of the concept, and at the least, differences seen in earlier studies between groups of researchers and their use of social media are being smoothed out as time passes (Colbron, 2015). Social media is now ubiquitous and an accepted way for researchers to work, regardless of subject area and seniority. There are many examples of this; one discussion of the usefulness and validity of blogging in a research context is Weller (2012). It should also be mentioned that it is not necessarily true that members of the digital native generation are any more proficient at discovery than older colleagues (Madsen et al., 2016).

For discovery purposes, a lot of the ways in which social media can be useful are effectively digital versions of the ways in which researchers found relevant material before it was possible to work like this online, as discussed earlier.

A trip through this book

In accordance with the theme that resource discovery is about the interaction of technology with metadata, the book begins with some case studies (Chapters 2 to 6). The oldest technology covered is that of the library catalogue, and in the hands of Roxanne Missingham of the Australian National University, it is being re-invented, with discovery driving acquisition in a 'just in need' manner, proving more successful at providing the resources needed than the previous librarian-driven processes: discovery empowering readers (Chapter 2).

This is followed in Chapter 3 by a look at the challenges presented for discovery in the multilingual environment of the National Library of Singapore (NLS), from Haliza Jailani and Chris Tang, during a project to provide a cross searching application for libraries and museums. When individuals, organisations and places mentioned in their archives may be known and discussed by different versions of their names, a way needs to be found to associate these names and make it clear to the searcher that they all refer to the same entity.

In Chapter 4 Julie Zhu of the IEEE contributes a study of how the professional association and publisher have worked to improve discoverability for the articles made available through IEEE Xplore, with the aim of promoting access to this resource. This involves work to improve processes, accompanied by significant engagement with customers who have purchased licenses for the content.

Also looking at discovery from a commercial point of view, in Chapter 5 Tamir Borensztajn, Oliver Pesch and Kate Lawrence discuss the EBSCO Discovery Service and innovations the company are making there, based on information from analytics and user testing. As they point out, one crucial element of a discovery service is the way it ranks the results which match the search; specifically, how this can make use of concept matching rather than simply literal word matching.

Resource discovery for users of collections also come to the fore in Chapter 6, in which Christine Madsen and Megan Hurst describe the theoretical background to successful testing and consultation with users, before presenting a study of a real life consultation.

Where discovery in the academic context is discussed, there is an elephant in the room: 'Why can't I just use Google?' is a question that I get asked from time to time, as I have a job title that includes the word 'discovery'. This has prompted a chapter on Google, explaining some of its strengths and limitations (Chapter 7).

Also related to search engines, in Chapter 8 my colleague Masha Garibyan and I discuss how resource description can be tailored to help with online discovery of collections and resources on the open internet. To improve the exposure of a collection effectively, it is necessary to understand its current use and internet profile before starting to optimise description and work on engagement with users.

When discovery in libraries is discussed, there is a tendency to think in terms of the offerings of the major commercial library suppliers, such as Ex Libris. However, open source technology can be used, and in Chapter 9 Christopher Awre and Richard Green describe how they implemented discovery with open source tools at the University of Hull.

The technology of linked data is frequently discussed in libraries in the early years of the 21st century. New standards such as BIBFRAME, and more established work in the museum community around CIDOC-CRM have generated significant interest on their use for resource description, and it is a frequently raised topic of interest in resource discovery. Carl G. Stahmer of the University of California looks at what might be possible if libraries start to embrace linked data for the purposes of discovery (Chapter 10).

From this point the book moves from current developments (with an eye on the future) to looking ahead (with an eye on the present). In Chapter 11 Ed Fay from the University of Bristol tries to identify the effects of technological trends on the discovery landscape of the next few years.

More speculatively, the final chapter, by Wolfram Horstmann, David De Roure and myself (from the universities of Göttingen and Oxford), presents eight science fictional scenarios, covering some ideas of future technologies, aiming to inspire thinking about the ways that new technology might revolutionise the way in which we work, research and discover information (Chapter 12).

Note

1 Browse itself can be split into two forms: that which is like looking at a bookshelf, with a simultaneous view of several items which may (or may not) be related; and browsing as in a card catalogue, using special indexes of (say) authors or subjects, organised as cross-references.

References

Asher, A. D. and Duke, L. M. (2012) Searching for Answers: student research behaviour at Illinois Wesleyan University. In Asher, A. D. and Duke, L. M. (eds), *College Libraries and Student Culture: what we now know*, American Library Association.

Avram, H. D. (1975) *MARC, its History and Implications*, Library of Congress.

Bates, M. J. (1989) The Design of Browsing and Berrypicking Techniques for the Online Search Interface, *Online Information Review*, **13** (5).

Bates, M. J. (2003) *Task Force Recommendation 2.3 Research and Design Review: improving user access to library catalog and portal information: final report (version 3)*, Library of Congress, www.loc.gov/catdir/bibcontrol/2.3BatesReport6-03.doc.pdf.

Battelle, J. (2006) *The Search: how Google and its rivals rewrote the rules of business and transformed our culture*, Nicholas Brealey.

Bennett, S., Maton, K. and Kervin, L. (2008). The 'Digital Natives' Debate: a critical review of the evidence, *British Journal of Educational Technology*, **39** (5), 775–86, http://doi.org/10.1111/j.1467-8535.2007.00793.x.

Bjørner, S. and Ardito, S. C. (2003) Online Before the Internet, Part 1: Early Pioneers Tell Their Stories, *Searcher*, www.infotoday.com/searcher/jun03/ardito_bjorner.shtml.

Borgman, C. L. (1996) Why Are Online Catalogs Still Hard to Use?, *Journal of the American Society for Information Science*, **47** (7), 493–503, http://doi.org/10.1002/(SICI)1097-4571(199607)47:7<493::AID-ASI3>3.0.CO;2-P.

Boss, S. C. and Nelson, M. L. (2005) Federated Search Tools: the next step in the quest for one-stop-shopping, *Reference Librarian*, **44**, 139–60, http://repository.uwyo.edu/cgi/viewcontent.cgi?article=1013&context=libraries_facpub.

Breeding, M. (2005) Plotting a New Course for Metasearch, *Computers in Libraries*, www.scopus.com/inward/record.url?eid=2-s2.0-13844319116&partnerID=tZOtx3y1.

Breeding, M. (2015) The Future of Library Resource Discovery, https://www.niso.org/publications/future-library-resource-discovery.

Bush, V. (1945) As We May Think, *Atlantic Monthly*, **176** (1), 101–8, www.virtualrhetoric.com/onlineclass/moodledata/12/Readings/Bush.pdf.

Charmantier, I. and Müller-Wille, S. (2014) Carl Linnaeus's Botanical Paper Slips (1767–1773), *Intellectual History Review*, **24** (2), 215–38.

Colbron, K. (2015) Surf's Up: observations from recent studies of discovery, Jisc, http://digitisation.jiscinvolve.org/wp/2015/10/06/surfs-up-observations-from-recent-studies-of-discovery/.

Connaway, L. S., Dickey, T. J. and Radford, M. L. (2011) 'If it is Too Inconvenient I'm Not Going After it': convenience as a critical factor in information-seeking behaviors, *Library & Information Science Research*, **33** (3), 179–90, http://doi.org/10.1016/j.lisr.2010.12.002.

Danskin, A. (2014) RDA and the 'Cascading Vortex of Horror': proposals for the simplification of RDA 2.7–2.10, *Catalogue and Index*, **177**, https://cdn.ymaws.com/www.cilip.org.uk/resource/collection/F71F19C3-49CF-462D-8165-B07967EE07F0/Catalogue_and_Index_issue_177,_December_2014.pdf.

Ekström, A. (2015) The Moral Bias Behind Your Search Results, TED talk, https://www.ted.com/talks/andreas_ekstrom_the_moral_bias_behind_your_search_results?language=en.

Falciani-White, N. (2012) Understanding Information Seeking Behavior of Faculty and Students: a review of the literature. In Popp, M. P. and Dallis, D. (eds), *Planning and Implementing Resource Discovery Tools in Academic Libraries*, IGI Global and Information Science Reference, http://doi.org/10.4018/978-1-4666-1821-3.ch001.

Gardner, T. and Inger, S. (2016) *How Readers Discovery Content in Scholarly Publications: trends in reader behaviour from 2005 to 2015*, www.simoningerconsulting.com/papers/How Readers Discover Content in Scholarly Publications.pdf.

Goode, G. B. (1895) The Ideal Index to Scientific Literature, *Science*, **1** (16), 433–37.

Green, M. W. (1991) Early Cuneiform. In Senner, W. M. (ed.), *The Origins of Writing*, University of Nebraska Press.

Hillis, K., Petit, M. and Jarrett, K. (2013) *Google and the Culture of Search*, Routledge, Taylor & Francis Group.

Hopkins, J. (1992) The 1791 French Cataloging Code and the Origins of the Card Catalog, *Libraries & Culture*, 378–404.

Jacso, P. (2005) Google Scholar – the pros and the cons, *Online Information Review*, **29** (2), 208–14, http://doi.org/http://dx.doi.org/10.1108/14684520510598066.

Janyk, R. (2014) Augmenting Discovery Data and Analytics to Enhance Library Services, *Insights: the UKSG Journal*, **27** (3), 262–8, http://doi.org/10.1629/2048-7754.166.

Kehoe, M. (2007) What's in a Name: federated search, www.ideaeng.com/federated-search-0404.

Kuhlthau, C. C. (1988) Perceptions of the Information Search Process in Libraries: a study of changes from high school through college, *Information Processing & Management*, **24** (4), 419–27, http://doi.org/http://dx.doi.org/10.1016/0306-4573(88)90045-3.

Kuhlthau, C. C., Heinström, J. and Todd, R. J. (2008) The 'Information Search Process' Revisited: is the model still useful?, *Information Research*, **13** (4), 45–5.

Law, D. (2010) Waiting for the Barbarians: seeking solutions or awaiting answers? In McKnight, S. (ed.), *Envisioning Future Academic Library Services: initiatives, ideas and challenges*, Facet Publishing.

Madsen, C., Hurst, M., McLeish, S., Emsley, I., Stacey, R., Garibyan, M., Abdul-Rahman, A., Khan, S. and Chen, M. (2016) *Resource Discovery @ The University of Oxford 2015*, https://www.bodleian.ox.ac.uk/__data/assets/pdf_file/0009/197118/Oxford-Resource-Discovery-Final-Report.pdf.

Maron, M. E., Kuhns, J. L. and Ray, L. C. (1959) Probabilistic Indexing: a statistical technique for document identification and retrieval, https://apps.dtic.mil/dtic/tr/fulltext/u2/272572.pdf.

Mauldin, M. I. (1997) Lycos: design choices in an Internet search service, IEEE Expert, http://doi.org/10.1109/64.577466.

Nicholas, D. and Rowlands, I. (2011) Social Media Use in the Research Workflow, www.researchgate.net/profile/David_Nicholas5/publication/262272352_Social_media_use_in_the_research_workflow/links/00b4953835750879860000000.pdf.

OCLC Research (2015) Making Archival and Special Collections More Accessible, www.oclc.org/content/dam/research/publications/2015/oclcresearch-making-special-collections-accessible-2015.pdf.

OED (2006) Google. In *Oxford English Dictionary*, 3rd edn, Oxford University Press, www.oed.com/view/Entry/261961?.

Page, L., Brin, S., Motwani, R. and Winograd, T. (1998) The PageRank Citation Ranking: bringing order to the web, *World Wide Web Internet and Web Information Systems*, **54** (1999–66), 1–17, http://doi.org/10.1.1.31.1768.

Parry, R. (2007) *Recoding the Museum: digital heritage and the technologies of change*, Routledge.

Philipson, J. (2013) The Lingua File: how Google became a verb, www.thelinguafile.com/2013/02/how-google-became-verb.html.

Pizer, I. H. (1965) Book Catalogs versus Card Catalogs, *Bulletin of the Medical Library Association*, **53** (2), 225–38, www.ncbi.nlm.nih.gov/pmc/articles/PMC198257/.

Poore, M. (2014) *Studying and Researching with Social Media*, Sage.

Prensky, M. (2001) Digital Natives, Digital Immigrants, Part 1, *On the Horizon*, **9** (5), 1–6, http://doi.org/10.1108/10748120110424816.

Priem, J., Piwowar, H. A. and Hemminger, B. M. (2012) Altmetrics in the Wild: using social media to explore scholarly impact, http://arxiv.org/html/1203.4745v1.

Ranganathan, S. R. (1931) *The Five Laws of Library Science*, The Madras Library Association.

Reidsma, M. (2016) Algorithmic Bias in Library Discovery Systems, https://matthew.reidsrow.com/?b=173.

Rose-Wiles, L. M. and Hofmann, M. A. (2013) Still Desperately Seeking Citations: undergraduate research in the age of web-scale discovery, *Journal of Library Administration*, **53** (2–3), 147–66, http://doi.org/10.1080/01930826.2013.853493.

Sanderson, M. and Croft, W. B. (2012) The History of Information Retrieval Research, *Proceedings of the IEEE*, **100** (special centennial issue), 1444–51.

Seikel, M. and Steele, T. (2011) How MARC Has Changed: the history of the format and its forthcoming relationship to RDA, *Technical Services Quarterly*, **28** (3), 322–34.

Seymour, T., Frantsvog, D. and Kumar, S. (2011) History of Search Engines, *International Journal of Management and Information Systems*, **15** (4), http://search.proquest.com/docview/900571445/fulltextPDF/D319BF91B3914550PQ/1?accountid=13042.

Sherratt, T. (2015) Seams and Edges: dreams of aggregation, access and discovery in a broken world, Discontents, http://discontents.com.au/seams-and-edges-dreams-of-aggregation-access-discovery-in-a-broken-world/.

Shi, X. and Levy, S. (2015) An Empirical Review of Library Discovery Tools, *Journal of Service Science and Management*, **8** (October), 716–25, http://doi.org/10.4236/jssm.2015.85073.

Strout, R. F. (1956) The Development of the Catalog and Cataloging Codes, *Library Quarterly: Information, Community, Policy*, **26** (4), 254–75, www.jstor.org/stable/4304573.

Swain, D. E. (1996) Information Search Process Model: how freshmen begin research, *Proceedings of the ASIS Annual Meeting*, **33**, 95–9.

Thomsett-Scott, B. and Reese, P. E. (2012) Academic Libraries and Discovery Tools: a survey of the literature, *College & Undergraduate Libraries*, **19** (2–4), 123–43, http://dx.doi.org/10.1080/10691316.2012.697009%5Cnwww.tandfonline.com.libproxy1.nus.edu.sg/doi/abs/10.1080/10691316.2012.697009#.Veew5pdjYp8%5Cnwww.tandfonline.com.libproxy1.nus.edu.sg/doi/pdf/10.1080/10691316.2012.697009.

Valenzuela, M., Ha, V. and Etzioni, O. (2014) Identifying Meaningful Citations, https://www.semanticscholar.org/paper/Identifying-Meaningful-Citations-Valenzuela-Ha/d5641d684df3a9e7c357923d109421fe4304ffa8.

Vaughan, J. (2011) Web Scale Discovery What and Why?, *Library Technology Reports*, **47** (1), 5.

Weller, M. (2012) The Virtues of Blogging as Scholarly Activity, *Chronicle of Higher Education*, http://chronicle.com/article/The-Virtues-of-Blogging-as/131666.

Wikipedia (n.d.) Five Laws of Library Science, https://en.wikipedia.org/wiki/Five_laws_of_library_science.

Wolff, C., Rod, A. B. and Schonfeld, R. C. (2016) *Ithaka S+R US Faculty Survey 2015*, 1–83, http://sr.ithaka.org?p=277685.

2

Flipping the catalogue: taking resource discovery to the next level

Roxanne Missingham

This chapter reviews the changing role of the catalogue in resource discovery, in particular for monographs. It:

- explores the changes from a customer's user experience viewpoint
- reviews the impact for libraries that move to a 'just in need' model
- discusses the benefits of opening up the catalogue to be a self-service acquisition portal
- demonstrates that reinventing the catalogue can bring a new aspect to resource discovery, with significant benefit to users; there have been challenges as well as transformations in service, leading to new expectations.

Introduction

Ranganathan proposed that 'books are for use' and we should 'save the time of the reader' (Ranganathan, 1931, 1 and 336). This sets the scene for our journey into a reinvention of the catalogue. Libraries have endured throughout our history, but today they are changing rapidly. Ranganthan's principles that books are for use and that we should save the time of the reader remain fundamental to the approach we should take in these times, and this is exemplified by recent work at the Australian National University, reinventing the library catalogue.

Libraries have collected an astounding array of resources to support knowledge seekers across a vast range of disciplines. In many ways the collections of research libraries are an investment for future and potential need, an issue that is finely balanced with current need and use, and which may relate to a fraction of the whole collection.

A major challenge has been to enable these potential users to locate and obtain access to these resources. Library and information scientists have studied information behaviour, sought to take on board technological developments and to enhance the metadata we create to open up access. The revolution of the online world has enabled us to develop more complex solutions, including new concepts such as linked data.

Over the past decades the techniques available to reveal resources have changed and improved. We are now in the era of UX, a time where our discovery services are being reviewed and renewed, see for example Curson (2016). Standing the test of time, Ranganathan's principles have been the fundamental premises for developments in resource discovery. The initiatives have sought to create a pathway between the library user and individual resources in library collections. Exploring new resource discovery solutions is now an important activity for research libraries.

While the online environment reduces the gap between users and the metadata in the catalogue, the challenge of providing metadata for collection items that is appropriate for resource discovery to an audience that may not be experts in library systems is significant. Not only is there specific library terminology, such as Library of Congress Subject Headings, but also only limited information is made accessible. This is a challenge in a world where full-text searching within documents is expected.

Saving time has been an important underlying benefit of online catalogue access. In thinking beyond the limitations of card catalogues, faculty can provide insights into the benefits of this access. The Ithaka surveys have consistently shown the importance of the online catalogue and other resource discovery tools to researchers. After approximately 20 years of availability it is perhaps surprising that the latest survey found only that 'the online library website/catalog has become increasingly important for conducting research' (Wolff, Rod and Schonfeld, 2016, 6).

In light of this the importance of the catalogue as a resource discovery tool to the academic and research community is clear. It is recognised as a major tool in research infrastructure and has the potential both to enhance research and to reveal the value of centuries of library collecting. Within this framework in the past few years university libraries have been making perhaps surprisingly radical changes to the catalogue.

This chapter explores the evolution of the catalogue through the introduction of patron-driven and demand-driven acquisition, which has reshaped it to be a 'just in need' service for access to a wealth of monographs beyond the existing library collection. The phrase 'just in need' is used to reflect the delivery of a service that provides access that matches the motivation of students to obtain information resources within their motivational framework, in addition to being accessible in a timely manner (Killi and Morrison, 2015).

In adopting these acquisition methods the academic community is able to use the catalogue as a tool for discovery and collection building, changing the very nature of these traditionally separate library functions. Ranganathan's principles are used to evaluate the impact of this new development in access to monographs.

Setting the scene

Library catalogues have been fundamental to the management of, and access to, collections. Focusing on monographs, Table 2.1 (on the next page) shows the changes through time using the model of Table 1.1 (page 5).

The great revolution in access was undeniably the world wide web and the internet. There have been many explorations of new concepts in using our catalogues. An example of this exploration by librarians is the expansion of the catalogue, with great gusto, beyond descriptions of resources which have been acquired by the library. At a conference held by the Library of Congress, Schottlaender and Thomas discussed the role of the library as a portal to the internet, taking differing views. While Thomas proposed that the catalogue take a new role as what we would now call a 'single source of truth' as a portal to the internet (Thomas, 2000), Schottlaender suggested that libraries 'have not created "a [single] mechanism". We have created several. As a consequence, not only must we *manage* several, but our clients must *navigate* several [resource discovery services]' (Schottlaender, 2000).

New developments since then have focused on single or federated search systems, combining data from the catalogue and publisher data, such as journal article and conference paper metadata. But what of the catalogue? Has it remained a wallflower waiting to be asked to dance or has it taken quiet strides in resource discovery?

To explore how the catalogue has changed with the introduction of patron-driven or demand-driven acquisition, it is useful to look at the changing pedagogy of higher education, specifically the flipped classroom model. Education, like libraries, has been reinventing delivery in light of the opening up of access through the online environment, educational research and application of learning theories. Flipped learning (Bishop and Verleger, 2013; Hemmingway, 2015) focuses the face-to-face educational experience on the interactive components of the higher education experience – tutorials, laboratory sessions, seminars, with lectures being delivered online. The pedagogy is about providing a focus for experiential learning with peer-based mentoring and other support interactions.

What would it mean if we looked at the catalogue as a flipped resource? Specifically, this study looks at what happens when the library's acquisition process follows a 'just

Table 2.1 *Further reading in the history of resource discovery for monographs*

Discovery and collection management (analogue)	Early catalogues: the Great Library of Alexandria was reputed to have been the first to have been catalogued by a tool titled Pinakes. Historians such as Bagnall (2002, 356) suggest that the level of description of the material in the collection might have been limited. Discovery was available to a component level – individual poems and elements of what we could now call monographs were recorded. Card indexes: the use of print sources of catalogue records enabled greater cataloguing of research collections. Discovery was limited to author, title and subject.
Computer systems in information management	Automation of library catalogues through the 1980s and 1990s increased the ability to enable discovery of collections, as long as users could make their way to locations that provided terminals with access to the systems. Discovery for monographs was enhanced through abstracts and summaries.
MARC, OPAC, Web OPAC	International standards such as the Anglo-American Cataloguing Rules were first published in 1967 (Spalding et al., 1967), and MARC increased the interoperability of records and established a framework that could provide for greater cataloguing productivity. Discovery for monographs remained limited to elements indexed by library staff.
Web search engines	While discussion was over whether libraries were dead and online resources and search tools would replace us, the number of records in catalogues sourced from national and international services such as OCLC and the Library of Congress continued to increase steadily. Discovery for monographs developed with the merging of full-text and bibliographic data.
Web-scale discovery	The merging of full text collections, other collections and individual library collections has fundamentally changed, with the onset of federated search services, Google Scholar and other new tools. Discovery for monographs has matured to an expectation that the merging of full-text and bibliographic data is the norm. In addition new acquisition processes are transforming the catalogue to a 'one-stop shop' rather than a single collection focused portal.

in need' model, a one-stop solution to purchasing 'on demand' monographs which are already available as e-book loans. This would flip acquisition from a 'mass' process like a lecture, with limited interactivity and a need for the lecturer or collection manager to anticipate user need, to an interactive process more like a seminar, where deep discussions can be had and the voice of the student or researcher can be heard far more clearly as an input to a far more responsive process. As a library pedagogy, uniting acquisitions and collection access provides a service that extends the concept of the collection and collection building to an open partnership model with our community.

To understand what this means in practice, the implementation of patron-driven or demand-driven acquisition at the Australian National University and some comparable research universities provides some insights into how the model can transform the catalogue into a revitalised discovery service.

Patron-driven or demand-driven acquisition

The Australian National University (ANU) is a world class research university. A founding member of the International Alliance of Research Universities, ANU has contributed to national and international research that has helped to reshape our world. The Library's collection has grown since it was established in 1947, evolving to a major research collection with more than 1.5 million items and approximately 20 kilometres of archives.

Two major factors have changed the ANU Library's acquisition of monographs in the last five years. The first is the increase in availability or rise in number of electronic books or e-books. Many suggest that the first signs that e-books would be more than a specialist fad was the publication of a mass market work online – Stephen King's *Riding the Bullet*, which was released in 2000 for the princely sum of US$2.50 (Gibbons, 2001). At the beginning of this technological development, e-books were tied to physical devices, such as the Kobo and the Kindle, which in turn supported specific formats and were not interchangeable. This has now been largely replaced with formats which can be used by any user on any device, noting that some have readers for other appliances, but some do not. The service model for libraries has moved to access through major vendors as part of standard packages without high technical or system dependencies. The extent of infiltration of e-books into library collections can be seen in the expenditure statistics. A recent Association of American Publishers publication reports that US$23 of every US$100 is now spent on e-books and the rest on print books – a massive increase from 2008 when US$1 out of every US$100 spent was on e-books (Inouye, 2016).

The second is the development of new purchase models that differ from traditional individual title selection by librarians in consultation with the academic community. The new models allow acquisition to be generated online through direct user engagement. Patron-driven and demand-driven acquisition provides the library user with access to pre-loaded data within the library catalogue that enables them to request a copy of an e-book directly. The resource is then made available without any further library staff intervention and is instantly delivered directly to the user. The role of the library in this model changes to one where an e-book supplier is selected; once this is done, works are made available to users through a profile that enables access to relevant material. Parameters such as price are set to control the number of short-term loans that must occur before the purchase of the title is triggered.

The benefits of this form of acquisition can be identified from the perspective of both the library user and the library. Users are able to access the resources they need immediately, with minimal barriers to collection building and without the complexities of interlibrary loan. For libraries the main benefit is being able to offer a range of relevant resources while minimising the staff time required to acquire e-book titles. Staff time is reduced because each title does not need to be individually selected and academic input sought to justify each individual purchase; records are loaded in bulk rather than one by one; and a single invoice is paid rather than individual invoices for each of the titles.

Evidence-based acquisition has more recently emerged as a model for acquiring e-books. With immediate access to statistical evidence of usage of the titles acquired in this manner, the model is also referred to as usage-based acquisition.

The Library implemented a pilot of e-books via patron-driven acquisition in 2015 to enable users to access resources directly and also for the Library to test the costs and benefits of the model.

The Library has been purchasing e-books for many years. At the end of 2014 the number of e-book titles available to users was 222,618. Most of the books had been purchased from major publishers such as Wiley, Elsevier, Taylor & Francis, Springer, Oxford University Press and Safari. The e-books have generally been purchased outright with bibliographic records acquired individually or included as small packages after selection by library staff with input from academic staff.

As well as the outright purchases mentioned, the Library had offered the EBSCO's e-book package (without demand-driven acquisition) to users in 2014. The service offered a large set of titles, purchased outright, and demonstrated that users were only interested in some titles, rather than whole packages. After analysis a decision was made not to continue the package on the basis that the collection duplicated titles already available and was not value for money.

Taking account of the range of experiences of other libraries (details discussed in the next section), the increasing use of electronic resources, the need for immediate access to resources by our users and the need for a value-for-money solution, ANU Library staff decided to pilot demand-driven acquisition with one supplier in 2015.

We evaluated packages according to these factors:

- the cost parameters of the purchases (considering the total cost of short-term loans and the full purchase of the books)
- the relevance of titles to the research and study undertaken at the university (scholarly content)
- the ability to select titles using a profile including factors such as date published, publishers, subject areas and costs
- overall value for money.

A number of vendor and publisher packages were considered. We decided to purchase ProQuest's e-book Library because the content met our needs well and the price demonstrated good value for money.

A profile was defined in the e-book package for ANU with 48,478 titles loaded into the catalogue. There were monthly additions and deletions to our demand-driven acquisition titles list.

The profile included the following parameters, which defined the titles included in the records obtained and included in the library catalogue:

- subject areas and disciplines
- excluded e-book Library subject categories: education, engineering: construction, geography and travel, journalism, publishing, architecture, engineering: civil, engineering: manufacturing, fiction, home economics, library science, nursing, tourism and hospitality, sport and recreation
- included Library of Congress classes: LB 2326.4–2330 (Higher Education – Institutions of Higher Education), LB 2371–2372 (Graduate Education), LB 2381–2391 (Academic Degrees), GF 1–900 (Human Ecology. Anthropogeography)
- only titles published after 2012
- publishers included in the profiles for other libraries from the Group of Eight (the leading Australian universities, similar to the Russell Group)
- titles published in the English language
- maximum cost of each item AU$250
- maximum cost of each loan AU$50.

The loan period for titles was limited to one week.

Anecdotal data has shown that undergraduates, postgraduates, researchers and academics participated in this trial. This particular vendor caters for a broad spectrum of readers and the package is not tailored to any particular group.

The profile enables the library to allow readers to review a title for a short period of time (less than 5 minutes) with no charge. If a book was requested three times it was automatically purchased by the Library.

The service was launched on 5 March 2015 and within 12 hours there were 15 short-term loans. Titles borrowed covered a wide range of disciplines, for example:

- *Dependent Archipelagos in the Law of the Sea*
- *The Extension of Coastal State Jurisdiction in Enclosed or Semi-Enclosed Seas*
- *Stories from the Skeleton: behavioral reconstruction in human osteology*
- *Understanding Postcolonialism*
- *Environmental Policy and the Economy*
- *The Sage Handbook of Public Administration*
- *Handbook of International Relations.*

The service was continued to May 2015. Unfortunately 2015 spending was affected by the fall in the Australian dollar (see Mulligan, 2015), which led to a freeze on monograph purchases in May 2015. The exchange rate significantly affected library purchasing as only 12% of the library's acquisition budget is spent in Australian dollars, 66% is in US dollars and the fall in the value of the Australian dollar against the American was approximately 10%.

The results of the demand-driven acquisition pilot were that 2,621 short-term loans occurred, at an average cost of AU$24.64 for each loan. This is significantly less than the cost of a rapid turnaround (rush) interlibrary loan of AU$33 (ALIA, 2013) (see Table 2.2).

Table 2.2 *Short-term loans at ANU Library, March to May 2015*

Short-term loan titles	2,621
Total short-term loans	3,346
Unique users	1,407
Total cost for short-term loans	AU$82,433.35
Average cost per short-term loan	AU$24.64

The breakdown of titles purchased is as follows:

- 254 titles purchased
- average use of each title (mean): 20.13
- average cost per book: AU$147.90, including the short-term loans.

Perhaps not surprisingly the titles purchased were primarily in social sciences and humanities (Figure 2.1). Since monograph publishing is primarily in these disciplines, use reflects publishing patterns.

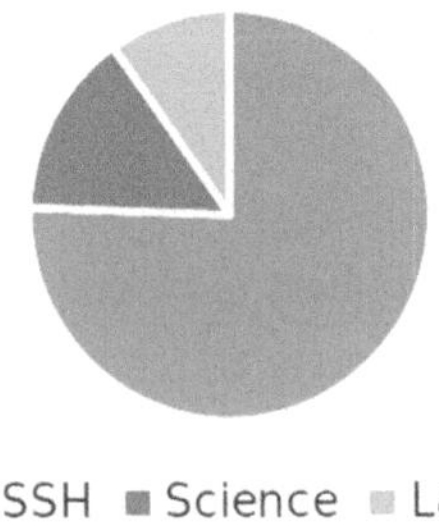

Figure 2.1 *E-book titles purchased at ANU Library by major subject, March to May 2015*

The service re-commenced in 2016 and 553 titles were acquired in the first three-quarters of the year, with a subject profile very similar to that in the 2015 pilot.

More extensive feedback has been sought from academics to evaluate not just the benefits to the academic community but also the extent to which the new service has revitalised the catalogue as a discovery service.

Feedback from users indicated that being able to access a wider range of titles immediately was of high value to academics and higher degree researchers. It was much more convenient that waiting for works to come via interlibrary loan and filling in forms to initiate that process, or to undertake the administrative work to propose a title for purchase and wait for material to be ordered and then processed and made available through the Library.

Experiences of other university libraries

A number of other Australian universities including the University of Sydney, Queensland University of Technology, Swinburne University and Western Sydney University have run similar patron-driven and demand-driven acquisition services (Borchert and Cleary, 2015; Cootes, 2016; Davis and Morgan, 2013; Dott, 2016; Li, 2016).

The findings from the evaluations of these experiences show significant benefits for libraries and for library users:

- There was a reasonable average cost per title to the library (in the case of the University of Sydney less than US$50).
- There was high use. In June–December 2015 at the University of Sydney there was a total of 18,491 downloads and 17,376 views; at Queensland University of Technology usage tripled from 2014.
- Material selected by users is highly relevant to the needs of other users – for example the University of Melbourne found that 88% of the titles bought were reused, which compares well with the reuse of titles selected by library staff, which had a reuse rate of less than 40%; while at Swinburne 'only 21% of the librarian-selected e-books recorded any use at all and autopurchased e-books

recorded much higher average use. The average number of loans across the librarian-selected e-books was 2.57 while the autopurchased e-books averaged 6.67 loans following purchase, or 9.67 loans in total if we include the three short-term loans prior to purchase' (Davis and Morgan, 2013). Western Sydney University recorded 99% reuse for titles bought using demand-driven acquisition, that had been selected by users.

Libraries have considered a number of factors in selecting suppliers to be used for demand-driven acquisition programmes, including:

- the cost parameters of the purchases (considering the total cost of short-term loans and the full purchase of the books)
- the relevance of titles to the collection (scholarly content)
- the ability to select titles using a profile including factors such as date published, publishers, subject areas and costs.

The mix of careful selection of suppliers and management of the programmes has been essential to ensuring that a range of relevant books are available and optimising the success of these programmes.

Flipped catalogue – academic views

Incorporating a service model for acquisition within the catalogue was a profound change from the perspective of the academic community. Conceptually the idea of a single service point that could provide immediate access without the barriers of traditional processes such as filling in a purchase recommendation form or requesting an interlibrary loan was very well accepted. One head of school was overwhelmed by the library's initiative and said that her life had been transformed by the flipping of the catalogue.

As with a lot of library initiatives, it appeared that many of the beneficiaries of the service believed that immediate access to required resources was essential to education and research at the university, and welcomed the opportunity to discuss how it might be extended.

A full implementation of the flipped model would result in more individualised conversations with academics on collection building. As the initiative is in its second year some of these conversations have been realised, but perhaps more significantly there has been increased engagement with academics about the resources in the collection that should be digitised to improve scholarship at the university.

Fundamentally our service model has changed permanently. The catalogue is now integrated with monographic acquisition in a way that has enhanced access, streamlined acquisition and engaged users in collection building to a degree that had not been reached before.

The catalogue is now a collection tool, rather than the metadata tool it was seen to be in the past, and it is much more integrated into the behaviour of the academic community.

Conclusion

For many centuries catalogues were the only means of access to library collections. Federated, or single search, and publisher search systems have enhanced access to resources and have gained attention as the resource discovery channels of the future. This study shows that catalogues can be transformed through reconsidering the service and business models available for acquisition, improving discovery via a different route.

Monographs will continue to be vital information resources. Traditional thinking that monographs are vital primarily for the social sciences and humanities discipline was not borne out by the behaviour of the ANU academic community. Implementing patron-driven or demand-driven acquisition revealed that monographs were used from a wide range of disciplines. Science monographs were heavily used, and a significant number of law titles were also acquired. This suggests that libraries should not just focus on a limited number of disciplines when discussing future titles with publishers.

Although the initiative at the university has only run for two years the results were clearly positive from the uptake of the users' and library's perspectives:

- Titles were immediately available to all library users (academics and students) without having to download them or create individual orders.
- Monthly updates ensured that records flowed into the catalogue for new material available currently, so it was very up to date (though this required work by library staff).
- Acquisition was much more streamlined and responsive with less manual invention (and therefore less human error) from library staff and vendors.
- Pricing for the titles acquired compared well with the purchasing cost of individual e-books.
- Academic community reaction was very positive.

The success of the initiative fits within a framework of evidence that immediate access to relevant electronic resources best meets the needs of users in the academic environment, in particular through the well respected tool of the catalogue. We need to continue to participate in global opportunities such as Knowledge Unlatched to provide rich treasures that our catalogues can reveal to users.

Update May 2019

Since the results of the implementation of patron-driven or demand-driven acquisition, ANU Library has continued to acquire e-books both through purchasing packages and by extending the funding of patron-driven or demand-driven acquisition. Feedback from our community demonstrates that there is high value in delivering content through a model that empowers users and simplifies acquisition processes. The model was extremely effective in 2018 through making monographs available as substitutes for the loss of a major part of the collection. In February 2018 a major flood affected the JB Chifley Library, which serves the colleges (faculties) of arts, social sciences, business and economics. Approximately 8% of the total collection of the Library, including over 113,000 monographs, were lost in the flood, in the Library of Congress Subject Headings range A–DU. Over the following year a donations campaign and purchasing have enabled the replacement of 3,100 monographs. Insurance claim preparation and collection relocation to accommodate the replacements has been a major task. The collection storage policy and practices have been redeveloped as flood risk has been identified for the floor that was flooded and the basement of the science library. Over $640,000 was spent on patron or demand-driven acquisition and interlibrary loan during the year, most on patron or demand-driven acquisition. In a crisis, flipping the catalogue provided a service that enabled research and education to continue effectively, despite the major collection loss.

References

ALIA (2013) *Australian Interlibrary Resource Sharing (ILRS) Code*, Australian Library and Information Association, www.alia.org.au/resources-and-information/interlibrary-lending/australian-interlibrary-resource-sharing-ilrs-code.

Bagnall, R. S. (2002) Alexandria: Library of Dreams, *Proceedings of the American Philosophical Society*, **46**, 348–62.

Bishop, J. L. and Verleger, M. A. (2013) The Flipped Classroom: a survey of the research. In Paper ID#6219. Atlanta, GA: American Society for Engineering Education, http://www.asee.org/file_server/papers/attachment/file/0003/3259/6219.pdf.

Borchert, M. and Cleary, C. (2015) An Account and Analysis of the Implementation of Various Ebook Business Models at QUT, Australia. In *Proceedings of the Charleston Conference: Issues in Book and Serial Acquisition*, Charleston, South Carolina, USA, eprints.qut.edu.au/90503/2/__qut.edu.au_Documents_StaffHome_StaffGroupB%24_ borchert_Documents_Staff%20dev_Conferences_Charleston_PRES_Borchert_Cleary_Charleston2015_sharecopy.pdf.

Cootes, S. (2016) Evidence Based Acquisition of Ebooks, presentation to ProQuest eBooks seminar held during VALA, February.

Curson, I. (2016) The Crux of User Experience, *Research Information*, September, www.researchinformation.info/news/analysis-opinion/crux-user-experience.

Davis, T. and Morgan, M. (2013) Ebooks Down Under, paper presented to the Charleston Library Conference, researchbank.swinburne.edu.au/vital/access/services/Download/swin:35843/SOURCE1.

Dott, A. (2016) University of Melbourne Experience with Evidence Based Acquisition of eBooks, presentation to ProQuest eBooks seminar held during VALA, February.

Gibbons, S. (2001) Ebooks: some concerns and surprises, *Portal: Libraries and the Academy*, **1** (1), 71–5, muse.jhu.edu/journals/portal_libraries_and_the_academy/v001/1.1gibbons.html.

Hemmingway, J. (2015) Beyond the Flipped Classroom: using problem-based learning to teach millennials at the JMP, ELI Virtual Annual Meeting of Educause, https://events.educause.edu/eli/annual-meeting/2015/proceedings/pbl-tbl-and-the-flipped-classroom.

Inouye, A. S. (2016) What's in Store for Ebooks? Looking at the digital future of libraries in 2016 and beyond, *American Libraries*, 4 January, americanlibrariesmagazine.org/2016/01/04/whats-store-ebooks/.

Killi, S. and Morrison, A. (2015) Just-in-time Teaching, Just-in-need Learning: designing towards optimized pedagogical outcomes, *Universal Journal of Educational Research*, **3** (10), 742–50, www.hrpub.org/download/20150930/UJER13-19504652.pdf.

Li, N. (2016) University of Sydney and Patron-driven and Evidence Based Acquisition of eBooks, presentation to Oxford University Press Academic Librarians Board meeting.

Mulligan, M. (2015) Australian Dollar Explainer: why is it falling?, *Sydney Morning Herald*, 8 July, www.smh.com.au/business/markets/currencies/australian-dollar-explainer-why-is-it-falling-20150708-gi7ida.html.

Ranganathan, S. R. (1931) *The Five Laws of Library Science*, The Madras Library Association.

Schottlaender, B. E. C. (2000) *The Catalog as Portal to the Internet by Sarah E. Thomas: a commentary*, Library of Congress, www.loc.gov/catdir/bibcontrol/schottlaender_paper.html.

Spalding, C. S. et al. (1967) *Anglo-American Cataloging Rules*, American Library Association.

Thomas, S. (2000) *The Catalog as Portal to the Internet*, Library of Congress, lcweb.loc.gov/catdir/bibcontrol/thomas_paper.html.

Wolff, C., Rod, A. B. and Schonfeld, R. C. (2016) *Ithaka S+R US Faculty Survey 2015*, Ithaka S+R, www.sr.ithaka.org/publications/ithaka-sr-us-faculty-survey-2015/.

3

Breaking the record: liberating data into knowledge at the National Library Board of Singapore

Haliza Jailani and Chris Tang

Introduction

Singapore is a bustling city state in South East Asia with a population of 5.6 million. It is a young nation, having become a sovereign republic only in 1965. In Singapore, the National Library, the National Archives and the Public Libraries Network are run as one united heritage organisation under the National Library Board (NLB). As stewards of the national patrimony, the NLB is implementing a digital masterplan that aims to make the joint collections of the National Library and Archives a focal point of research in Singapore for scholars, academics and our citizens.

Under the masterplan, the NLB envisioned a superior and seamless digital experience for our patrons through the achievement of key capabilities (Tang, 2015). For the purposes of this book, we focus on the NLB's metadata-driven strategies in achieving two of these capabilities, with the outcome being that our digital content would become more 'FindABLE' and 'ExpandABLE'.

'FindABLE' simply means that the NLB's digital content needs to be easily discoverable. 'ExpandABLE' goes one step further than 'FindABLE' and means that digital content that is related needs to be easily discoverable by our patrons, even if they do not know of such connections beforehand. New contextual search linkages must be created that will allow our patrons to easily discover similar content across multiple formats and languages in the NLB, and to find related content stored outside the NLB.

Essentially, we see our descriptive metadata as being 'imprisoned' or bound by the form of the conventional and somewhat old-fashioned catalogue record. In 'breaking' these catalogue records, we hope to be able to liberate the knowledge stored within the NLB's metadata by semantically linking concepts and entity relationships held in every metadata field of every catalogue record that we have. This will unleash the full potential of the data in enabling our content to be 'FindABLE' and also 'ExpandABLE'.

The first stage of the NLB's digital journey involved data harmonisation to enable a unified search platform that allowed the collections of multiple heritage organisations, including the NLB's, to be 'FindABLE'. In the second stage and beyond, data modelling and knowledge base building will be deployed to improve contextual discovery of the NLB's content by making our patrons' searches 'ExpandABLE'.

NLB data harmonisation

As with most libraries, NLB catalogues physical library resources in MARC 21 (Network Development and MARC Standards Office, 2009). Our digital collections are described using the Dublin Core Libraries Application Profile (DC-Lib; Dublin Core Metadata Initiative, 2004). The National Archives uses ISAD-G (General International Standard Archival Description; International Council on Archives, 1999) to describe its collections. When the library and archives merged in late 2012, data describing both sets of collections were harmonised so that seamless searching could occur.

To ensure that the NLB's content is easily 'FindABLE', a unified discovery platform called OneSearch was created in 2014 so that patrons would not have to search for library and archives collections separately. A year later, we added Singapore's museum collections, and in 2016 the National Gallery of Singapore's collections. OneSearch now serves as Singapore's discovery portal for its galleries, libraries, archives and museums (GLAM) collections.

The key to discovery across institutions without overwhelming the user is to organise the collections into nine containers or 'bento boxes'[1] as shown in Figure 3.1 opposite.

Internationally, not many GLAM institutions have merged their collections for searching, as materials are described and organised differently by each type of organisation. The multi-level descriptions required by archives relates objects in a hierarchy and links these to form a collection-level record, whereas libraries generally create their descriptive records at the item level. Museums and galleries, on the other hand, place emphasis on the nature and composition of an artefact, and how the artist envisions the artefact's manifestation and its relevance to the wider world, which is often described in terms of events. Singapore's museums use CDWA [Categories for

Figure 3.1 *OneSearch home page containers*

the Description of Works of Art] Lite (J. Paul Getty Trust and ARTstor, 2006) to describe its collections.

To make OneSearch possible, we used common data elements to construct mappings and crosswalked[2] these to a generic, interoperable format using the Dublin Core metadata schema. In doing this, we could not avoid losing granularity as the ability to map the different fields can only be achieved at the lowest level of description common across the records. Unfortunately, these usually end up as high level descriptions. The most difficult task was to map the subject matter, topic or collection themes and genre and relate them to the object categories for works of art. Largely, our approach is to collocate these as facets so that the different GLAM target audiences can still browse and search the collections using terms they are familiar with. The downside is that the facets displayed can appear cluttered (Figure 3.2). Nonetheless, the fundamental requirement of OneSearch in making Singapore content more 'FindABLE' was met as it provided a common search layer that can direct patrons to the respective websites.

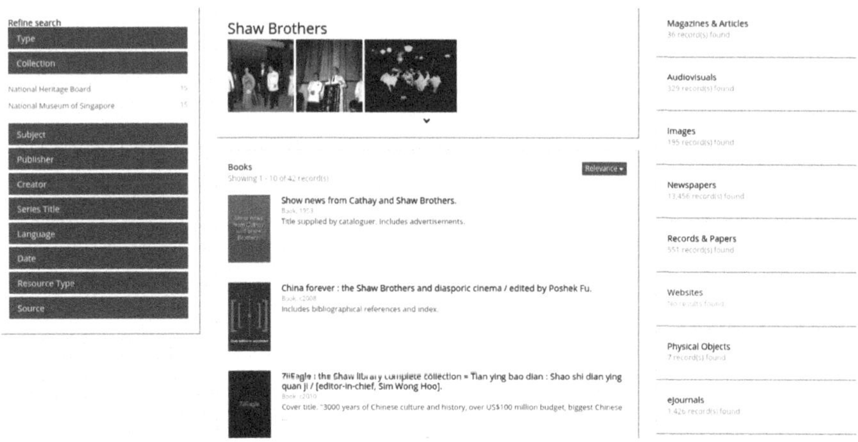

Figure 3.2 *Results display by facets and 'bento boxes'*

In the process, about 2 million library records, 800,000 archival records and 90,000 museum and gallery records were harmonised for OneSearch, and it became the first search service in Singapore that allowed users to access materials across the GLAM sector, including digitised newspapers, books, journals, photographs, three-dimensional artefacts, paintings, manuscripts, audiovisual materials, oral histories, government speeches and press releases. The launch of OneSearch contributed to increased pageviews for the heritage websites involved, including the most substantial jump for the archives which achieved nearly five times (2.1 million) its target (450,000) page views.

The knowledge organisation system

The NLB's knowledge organisation system comprises Singapore-centric terms, vocabularies and name authority records in the form of taxonomies, thesauri and controlled lists. Using the ANSI/NISO Z39.19 guidelines (National Information Standards Organization, 2005), we currently have 2 million terms including variant forms and relationships, managed by a vocabulary management tool called the Thesaurus and Taxonomy Editor (TTE). Focusing on local names and terminology, our key principles in supporting resource discovery are:

- eliminating ambiguity
- controlling synonyms
- establishing relationships among terms including linking of variant forms.

With the introduction of other vocabularies for OneSearch, we found a need to allow the use of different forms of names and terms referring to a single concept or entity. These are created as variant forms of the descriptive term. Flags, source and scope notes are used to indicate the collection and owning repository information. Properties for describing each entity were also expanded to incorporate the needs of these institutions. From a brief set of five properties like birth and death dates, these now comprise up to 15 properties per class such as nationality, affiliation and achievements for persons, and founder and group members for organisations, as well as <sameAs> links to the uniform resource identifiers (URIs) for the entity on registries such as Virtual International Authority File (https://viaf.org/) and DBpedia (http://wiki.dbpedia.org/).

When searching for entities in merged collections, results need to be retrieved according to the name a patron would enter. But a single entity usually has more than one form of name. Merging of collections without harmonisation causes search results to be fragmented. The knowledge organisation system links the different forms of names, regardless of changes throughout history, different languages used and aliases.

The NLB's knowledge organisation system faces a unique challenge as variant names for personalities can be plentiful in Singapore since our constitution recognises four official languages: English, Chinese, Malay and Tamil. Although Malay is officially the national language, English is the common language used for business and government and the medium of instruction in schools. Being a government agency, the NLB uses English as the main language of communication on its websites. Within Singapore, the Chinese (with almost three-quarters of the country's population) make up the largest ethnic group and continue to use Chinese as their mother tongue. However, with increasing westernisation, it has become common for the ethnic Chinese Singaporean to take on western or Christian names. Owing to this melting pot of cultures and languages, our knowledge organisation system needs to cater to variant English and Malay names as well as the variant names in two non-Roman alphabetic scripts (Chinese and Tamil).

In vocabulary standardisation, the knowledge organisation system team performs term-matching and analysis of matches, establishing these where applicable as variations or associations. Unmatched names or terms which are new concepts to the knowledge organisation system are created as new records. Reconciliation of differences are then carried out and an agreement reached with the submitting institution, on the authorised form to use, the non-preferred terms and the display term. The authorised name would normally follow the Resource Description and Access (RDA) standard (RDA Steering Committee, 2010), which places the person's family name first, while the most commonly recognised form of the person's name is selected as the display name if that is not the same as the authorised name.

The knowledge organisation system team also made recommendations on Art and Architecture Thesaurus terms to be adopted for the museums' object categories and material types, which were then merged into the NLB's material type list. This allowed the museum collections to be grouped by type into the nine OneSearch containers for scoped searching and faceted browsing. The standardised terms reduced ambiguity and ensured consistency and semantic correctness, thus allowing precision in searching. Regardless of format, collections from the participating gallery, archives and museum institutions are either mapped or described consistently at source for OneSearch. For the data harmonisation, about 6,000 Singapore names from the archives, a further 6,000 Singapore names from the museums and about 4,000 Singapore names from the National Gallery were processed for the NLB's knowledge organisation system.

To meet contextual discovery needs effectively, a strong knowledge base is needed to support the searching of named entities such as people, organisations, places and events. The properties used to describe an entity need to be enriched to deliver a useful entity-based discovery that can be triggered solely from our patrons' initial search for a local person, organisation, place or event. This would be the 'ExpandABLE' component of our masterplan, where such related digital content needs to be easily discoverable by our patrons even if they do not know of such connections beforehand. The manual curation of knowledge organisation system properties must be supplemented by linking to existing data on the internet using identity links such as <owl:sameAs> or <skos:exactMatch>. By using other knowledge bases, we hope to benefit from the global network of contextualised data.

Query expansion

To tap into the knowledge organisation system knowledge base, we developed a web service to allow consuming applications to query TTE, the database where knowledge organisation system terms are managed. This service queries all data elements including associations such as variant forms and properties such as 'display name'.

For example, a query 'Harry Lee' will retrieve all content indexed with the Used For (UF) forms and can be returned with the Display name 'Lee Kuan Yew'.[3] Figure 3.3 shows a TTE record displaying properties and associations for 'Lee Kuan Yew' in TTE. The query expansion service expands and increases the original search results of patrons so that relevant content is retrieved despite the different names by which an entity is known and indexed, or the different forms in which the public may enter a name, such as for:

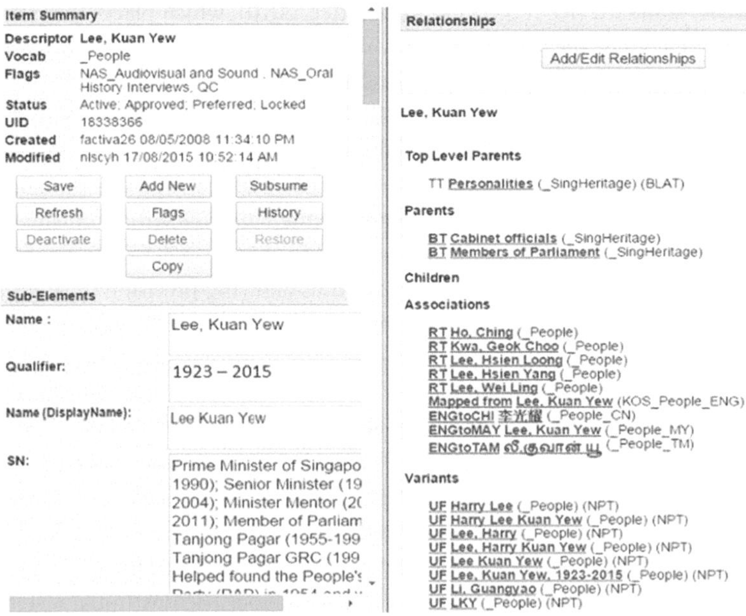

Figure 3.3 *Example of a knowledge organisation system record in TTE for Lee Kuan Yew showing properties and relationship*

- Lee Kuan Yew and his Chinese name 李光耀
- Lim Bo Seng[4] and his alias of Tan Choon Lim
- Telok Ayer Market[5] and its colloquial name of Lau Pa Sat
- SPRING Singapore[6] and its former name of Productivity and Standards Board.

The feature will also extend to a 'People also searched for . . . ' in recommending personalities and associated content linked to the original entity searched, e.g.:

- Lim Chong Pang (son) is related to Lim Nee Soon[7] (father)
- Lim Boon Keng[8] (business partner) is associated with Lim Nee Soon.

In the proof of concept test, we discovered that patrons may not wish to be inundated with contextual results that are too broad or high level, e.g. 'personalities' or 'members of parliament', when searching for 'Lee Kuan Yew'. To this end, it is important to provide the associated 'classes' and 'relationships' to the patron so that selection can be made.

NLB data model

As the library world undergoes a shift in thinking on how resources should best be described for optimum discovery on the internet, at the NLB we found ourselves replacing the long-time library cataloguing standard Anglo-American Cataloguing Rules 2nd edition (AACR2) (Joint Steering Committee for Revision of AACR and American Library Association, 2005) with the RDA standard, which is a less rigid standard more attuned to the needs of a digital world (RDA Steering Committee, 2010). Even while this change was made back in 2013, we were exploring BIBFRAME as a data model to help us break coded information out of the catalogue record so that it can be exposed for searching on the internet.

The NLB data model (NLBDM) is based on the bibliographic framework or BIBFRAME (Library of Congress, 2012), which leverages the Resource Description Framework (RDF; https://www.w3.org/RDF/) modelling practice of uniquely identifying as web resources 'all entities (resources), attributes, and relationships between entities (properties)' (RDF Working Group, 2014).

BIBFRAME vocabularies support a variety of data standards that the NLB adheres to, such as the RDA and RDF. It also supports vocabularies from Schema.org (https://schema.org/), which we are using to mark up our websites. Some of the concepts of NLBDM were also mapped to ISAD-G (General International Standard Archival Description), which defines the elements that should be in the archival finding aid (International Council on Archives, 1999), and CIDOC Conceptual Reference Model (CIDOC-CRM), which provides 'definitions and a formal structure for describing the implicit and explicit concepts and relationships used in cultural heritage documentation' (International Council of Museums, n.d.).

Use case scenarios of how patrons would access the collections were created. We used these to identify 101 classes and sub-classes and 136 properties to form our core data model. However, in developing a service to demonstrate the use of linked data for our stakeholders, we discovered gaps in the data model. For example, in the NLBDM, the class 'place' has no property for previous or historical name of a location or place in Singapore. Without this property, the service would not be able to connect to this information in its query response.

To enable this linkage, we created an extension to the NLBDM, rather than adding on to the core data model. Having a basic, core vocabulary allows scalability and easier management of data transformation to the RDF, with extensions added on when required. This extension, called the Event Service Vocabulary (ESV), was developed with a similar structure to the NLBDM but with properties required to address event-based service requirements. Hence, in the example given, 'historical name' is defined in the ESV as an additional property for the class 'place'. This approach of extending the data model would become our model for supporting services developed in future for archives, museums and galleries.

Linked data service

Linked data web feature

The main value of the NLB's linked data service is to enable serendipitous discovery for patrons in exploring content not known to the researcher, and which would probably not have been discovered at all without the use of linked data. This also ties in to the 'ExpandABLE' component of our masterplan in aiding contextual discovery of our content. At its core, linked data enables machine understanding and inference. At the same time, it was also very important for us to be able to develop a service that could display 'human-friendly' linked data. We eventually conceptualised a service that allowed multi-dimensional entry points for the exploration of entities and for contextual browsing and exploration of the linked resources.

Patrons can fully explore data regardless of source from a single interface, and retrieve content objects where available. For example, clicking on a profile image of a person may bring the user to their photograph on the Archives Online (www.nas.gov.sg/archivesonline/) or the NLB's PictureSG (http://eresources.nlb.gov.sg/pictures) website. If there are related MARC records, clicking on the link would bring patrons to the online public access catalogue (OPAC) record for books written by or about the person. Likewise, if there are written resources available about the entity, clicking on the article titles will bring patrons to the digital articles written on the person by NLB staff.

We created a backend infrastructure that functions as a URI registry and a triple store, and that enables transformation of vocabularies and metadata into the RDF. Called the Linked Data Management System (LDMS), this system also provides an interface for verification and editing of data. As a trial, over 250,000 records and named entities were transformed into the RDF based on NLBDM. Following patterns of data convergence, we incorporated a selection of the National Heritage Board's galleries and museums metadata, primarily comprising drawings and paintings, to create an initial set of triples for Singapore's library, archive and museum data. SPARQL (SPARQL Protocol and RDF Query Language) queries and web-services interact between the web feature and the LDMS in pulling triples for end-users and patrons.

Figure 3.4 shows an entity page of the web feature created on the fly from linked data.

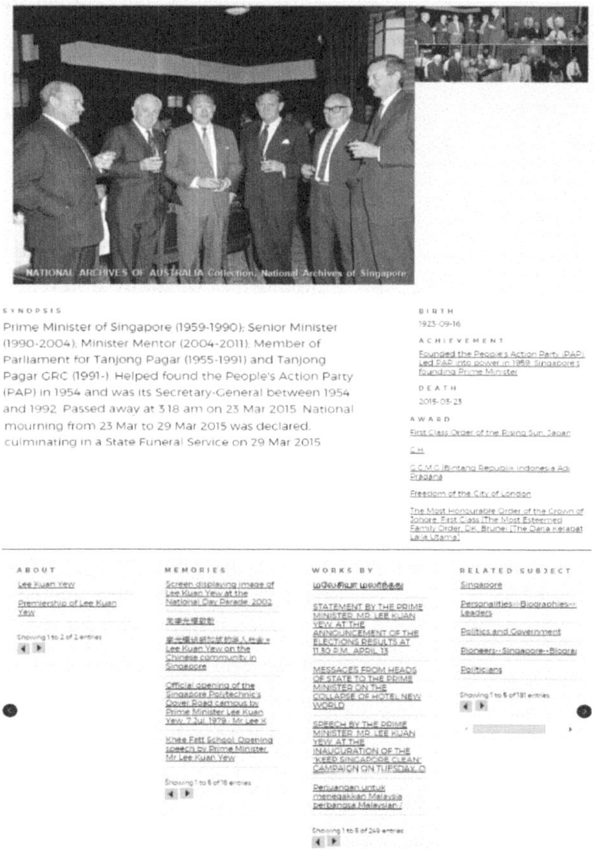

Figure 3.4 *Example of the web feature's entity page which was created on the fly from linked data*

Linked data widget

Going beyond retrieving RDF data in a 'human-friendly' way, we created a widget to allow patrons to perform contextualised searches based on entities found on any NLB content website that the widget was embedded in (Figure 3.5). This was tested as a proof of concept on an internally accessed version of the NLB's HistorySG website (http://eresources.nlb.gov.sg/history), which showcases Singaporean encyclopedic entries. Named-entity recognition and extraction from the website articles was done on the fly, to enable linking of the entities extracted from four classes (events, people, places, organisations) to information from the NLB's triple store. Named entities extracted which are new to the knowledge organisation system were disambiguated into the four classes and built into the knowledge base. The data was also analysed so that explicit relationships could be built into the extended service vocabulary.

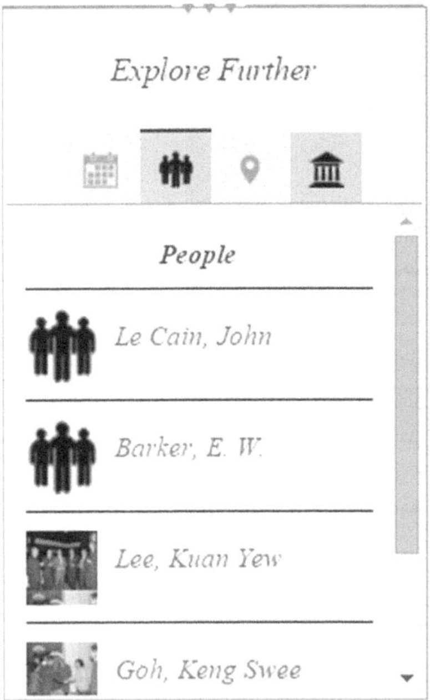

Figure 3.5 *A linked data widget*

Through using named entities as linkages, convergence points were identified in the form of subject or topic and other forms of attribution such as works creation and contribution. The results were displayed as entity attributes such as images, synopses, achievements and awards; and the content resources are contextualised into 'about', 'memories', 'works by' and related subjects (as shown in the bottom half of Figure 3.4). Spatial attributes were also used to create map-points for historical events connected to place, organisation or person entities.

With the usability of linked data established, the rest of the NLB's bibliographic and authority data have been transformed into the RDF. As an example of dynamically generated data presentation, the widget can now be embedded into any website so as to link entities on that page to resources in the NLB's knowledge graph, which is displayed using the linked data web feature.

Future plans and considerations

Moving on, we need to continue adding value to the triple store by building internal relationships that link to external references on the world wide web. As the triple store evolves from the URI connections and equivalent relationships, the triple store as a knowledge graph grows. We can develop any kind of web service that uses this knowledge graph to expose NLB resources on the web. This formulates the foundation of what search engines are doing, using structured data that are reliable. By allowing such intelligent searching of our content, we hope to enhance the findability of the NLB's content to a whole new audience.

Ultimately, the NLB plans to expose structured data on the web with the following three outcomes in mind:

- to create an organisational entity recognised by Google for delivery of resources
- to create visibility of collections with resources higher up on the results list
- to build an authoritative, canonical resource of data for Singaporean names.

These involve the creation of entity URIs for the NLB and its branch libraries and the pulling of information from the triple store and corporate pages as schema.org. Mapping was done to add schema.org vocabulary to the data model. A missing part of our infrastructure, which went unnoticed as our initial deliverable was an internally accessed web feature, was discovered as work progressed to expose the NLB's linked data on the web. Calling this a URI resolver, it is a frontend for our linked data on the web, with an additional requirement for content negotiation to resolve not only to data but to web uniform resource locators (URLs) as 'human-friendly' delivery pages.

The impact of unlimited web crawlers accessing the NLB's 2 million bibliographic records when fully exposed on the internet may also disrupt library operations at the public library branches, as these records reside on the library management system. To prevent this, a few steps can be taken such as implementing persistent URIs to prevent sequencing approach and setting up a content distribution network environment. The NLB will likely create a shadow website or an OPAC 'visibility' page for accesses on the web. This is not the preferred approach as there are additional clicks before patrons can reach the delivery page, whether to download a file or to place a hold on the item. Even one click too far from the ultimate delivery screen may turn potential patrons away. It is best to embed the payload into the actual web page. Until then, our challenge is not to introduce too many clicks before patrons are directed to the availability information of a book or some other actionable page.

The NLB's RDF has been published on data.gov.sg, the Singapore government's portal to publicly available datasets from its public agencies. Our intent in the coming years is to enable the whole of government to use our knowledge base, starting with the local names database that is maintained in the knowledge organisation system. Whether the other agencies use their own name terms and are subsequently linked by the NLB's entity URIs for standardisation, or they choose to use the preferred or non-preferred labels from the NLB's knowledge organisation system records, the option will be there for information from the knowledge organisation system to facilitate better discovery and linking of related resources. In order to keep the knowledge organisation system database as up to date as possible, the team that manages it provides real time updates as far as possible, so the NLB's knowledge base building will be tied to active environmental scanning of Singaporean information sources and the team's Singaporean entity-curatorial skillsets. For example, it will:

- update changes of titles of government ministers from a Cabinet reshuffle
- update death and career highlights, or organisation name changes reported in the media
- add new Singaporean personalities, organisations or places that can be linked to content found on OneSearch.

In the meantime, the National Library and National Archives of Singapore will continue to serve the needs of the nation by providing resources and materials on Singapore. Both have traditionally been more research based and somewhat passive in making our collections accessible. However, with the push to use our NLB data to facilitate ever more intelligent, contextual and semantic searches, it is envisioned that our consolidated resources will become more easily discoverable online. NLB staff view this as an unprecedented opportunity to provide new ways for Singaporeans and Singapore researchers to access and engage meaningfully with the content. From being demand-driven in serving researchers' needs, the liberation of data to knowledge will signal the NLB's supply-driven effort to inspire Singaporeans to explore, discover and engage more actively with our collections.

It is our cherished hope that the newfound ease of finding, experiencing and using the NLB digital collections will in turn help to ensure a future where every Singaporean has easy access to Singapore's past, is inspired by it, and is stimulated to contribute actively in weaving the fabric of the nation.

Notes

1 'Bento' is a single portion takeaway meal common in Japanese cuisine, usually served in a box-shaped container.

2 'Crosswalking' is the process of identifying equivalent elements in metadata schemes in order to facilitate interoperability.

3 Lee Kuan Yew (b. 16 September 1923, Singapore; d. 23 March 2015, Singapore) was the first prime minister of Singapore and held this post from 1959 to 1990.

4 Major-General Lim Bo Seng (b. 27 April 1909, Nan Ann, Fujian, China; d. 29 June 1944, Perak, Malaya) was a prominent Hokkien businessman who undertook active leadership

in anti-Japanese activities during the Second World War and is recognised as a local war hero in Singapore.

5 The former Telok Ayer Market (now known as Lau Pa Sat, meaning 'old market') at Raffles Quay was completed in 1894. It was gazetted as a national monument on 28 June 1973 and converted into a food and entertainment complex in 1989.

6 SPRING Singapore, a statutory board under the Ministry of Trade and Industry, aims to raise productivity to enhance Singapore's competitiveness and economic growth. SPRING stands for Standards, Productivity and Innovation for Growth. It was renamed SPRING Singapore in April 2002 from the former name Productivity and Standards Board.

7 Lim Nee Soon (b. 12 November 1879, Singapore; d. 20 March 1936, Shanghai, China), planter and general merchant, was one of the pioneers of rubber planting with Dr Lim Boon Keng (1869–1957). He was a generous charitable benefactor with a keen interest in social and community matters. A respected community leader and one of the most influential businessmen of the day, he was made a Justice of the Peace in 1925.

8 Lim Boon Keng (b. 18 October 1869, Singapore; d. 1 January 1957, Singapore) was a pioneer Straits Chinese who sought to improve the status of the Chinese in Malaya through education and social activism. He held top positions in the Legislative Council and liaised actively with the Manchu government.

Bibliography

Chan, S. S. and Jailani, H. (2015) Data Harmonisation between National Library Board, National Archives and National Heritage Board of Singapore. In *[Proceedings of the] International Conference on Dublin Core and Metadata Applications, DC-2015*, 1–4 September 2015, São Paulo, Brazil, https://dl.acm.org/doi/abs/10.5555/2907896.2907934.

Dublin Core Metadata Initiative (2004) Library Application Profile, https://www.dublincore.org/specifications/dublin-core/library-application-profile/2004-09-10/.

Hussein, H. (2015) *Linked Data @ NLB, Singapore Journal of Library and Information Management*, **44**, 20–34, www.las.org.sg/wp/wp-content/uploads/SJLIM2015-Hussein-2.pdf.

International Council of Museums (n.d.) *The CIDOC Conceptual Reference Model*, http://cidoc-crm.org/.

International Council on Archives (1999) *ISAD(G): general international standard archival description*, 2nd edn, www.ica.org/en/isadg-general-international-standard-archival-description-second-edition.

J. Paul Getty Trust and ARTstor (2006) *CDWA Lite: specification for an XML schema for contributing records via the OAI harvesting protocol*, www.getty.edu/research/publications/electronic_publications/cdwa/cdwalite.pdf.

Jailani, H. (2015) Building Knowledge Bases Using Named-Entity Recognition, Query Expansion and Linked Data, to Support Enhanced Discovery. In *[Proceedings of the] Innovations In Knowledge Organisation Conference 2015*, 8–9 June, www.greenchameleon.com/uploads/CSC2_10_Haliza.pdf.

Joint Steering Committee for Revision of AACR and American Library Association (2005) *Anglo-American Cataloguing Rules*, ALA, CLA, CILIP.

Library of Congress (2012) *Bibliographic Framework as a Web of Data: linked data model and supporting services*, www.loc.gov/bibframe/pdf/marcld-report-11-21-2012.pdf.

National Information Standards Organization (2005) *Guidelines for the Construction, Format and Management of Monolingual Controlled Vocabularies*, https://ils.unc.edu/courses/2015_fall/inls151_002/Readings/NISO.pdf.

Network Development and MARC Standards Office (2009) Introduction: MARC 21 authority, Library of Congress, www.loc.gov/marc/authority/adintro.html.

RDA Steering Committee (2010) *About RDA*, www.rda-rsc.org/content/about-rda.

RDF Working Group (2014) *RDF*, from www.w3.org/RDF/.

Tang, C. (2015) Achieving the Ables: reimagining the digital discovery services at the National Library of Singapore, paper presented at IFLA WLIC 2015, session 147, Asia and Oceania 16–20 August, Cape Town, South Africa, http://library.ifla.org/1156/1/147-tang-en.pdf.

4

Case study: clearing library discovery-to-access pathways for IEEE content

Julie Zhu

Introduction

The Institute of Electrical and Electronics Engineers (IEEE) is the world's largest technical membership association with over 422,000 members in more than 160 countries. It publishes approximately 200 IEEE transactions, journals and magazines in the fields of electrical engineering and computing, over 25,000 volumes of conference proceedings with papers presented at over 4,000 IEEE conferences globally, including over 1,400 annual conferences, over 5,000 technical standards, and over 400 educational courses. IEEE hosts its publications and content from several publisher partners in its IEEE Xplore platform, containing 4-5 million full-text records.

End-users of IEEE content come to the IEEE Xplore platform through multiple channels of discovery, such as direct visits to the platform, general search engines (e.g. Baidu, Bing, Google), academic search engines (e.g. Baidu Xueshu, Google Scholar, Microsoft Academic), library discovery services (e.g. EBSCO Discovery Service, Encore, Primo, Summon, WorldCat Local, WorldCat Discovery), abstract and indexing databases (e.g. Inspec, Scopus, Web of Science), subject repositories (e.g. arXiv, Medline), institutional repositories, e-mail alerts, social media, professional networks and more.

For several years IEEE received inquiries from end-users and library customers regarding content discovery and access from library discovery services. The issues can be broken down into five major categories:

- Discoverability: users cannot find in library discovery services certain IEEE content to which their libraries subscribe.
- Visibility: IEEE content sometimes does not show up in the first few pages of the search results.
- Linking: for some IEEE content, full-text links are missing, break or do not resolve to the correct articles.
- Access: off-campus users sometimes experience authentication problems when they go from library discovery services, abstracting and indexing databases or other search engines to access full-text content in the IEEE Xplore platform.
- Analytics: libraries are not sure how many visits and usages can be attributed to library discovery services and abstracting and indexing databases and whether these investments provide sufficient return on investment.

IEEE strategies for content discovery and access

To facilitate users coming from multiple discovery-to-access pathways, IEEE has developed several strategies:

- Make IEEE Xplore the only platform for accessing IEEE full-text content.
- Collaborate with search engines and abstracting and indexing database partners to disseminate metadata.
- Focus on clearing library discovery services' discovery-to-access pathways.
- Appoint a discovery service relations manager.
- Form a discovery service working group.

Investment in developing browsing, searching, alerting, personalisation and other functions and features will attract direct visits and aid the user experience. IEEE's Client Service Team visits universities, corporations and government agencies, all over the world, to train researchers on using the IEEE Xplore platform.

IEEE continues to collaborate with major web search engines, academic search engines, and dozens of abstracting and indexing databases. It provides content for deep indexing, evaluates the performance of IEEE content in these services, and works with partners for troubleshooting discovery and access issues and linking search results to the full text hosted in the IEEE Xplore platform.

Most importantly, IEEE focuses on clearing the discovery-to-access pathways from library discovery services to IEEE Xplore. Figure 4.1 opposite highlights this pathway, in which users enter search terms into the search boxes, retrieve results from the indices, choose among the available linking options, go through authentication (internet protocol access, username or password access, single sign on, etc.) and proxy

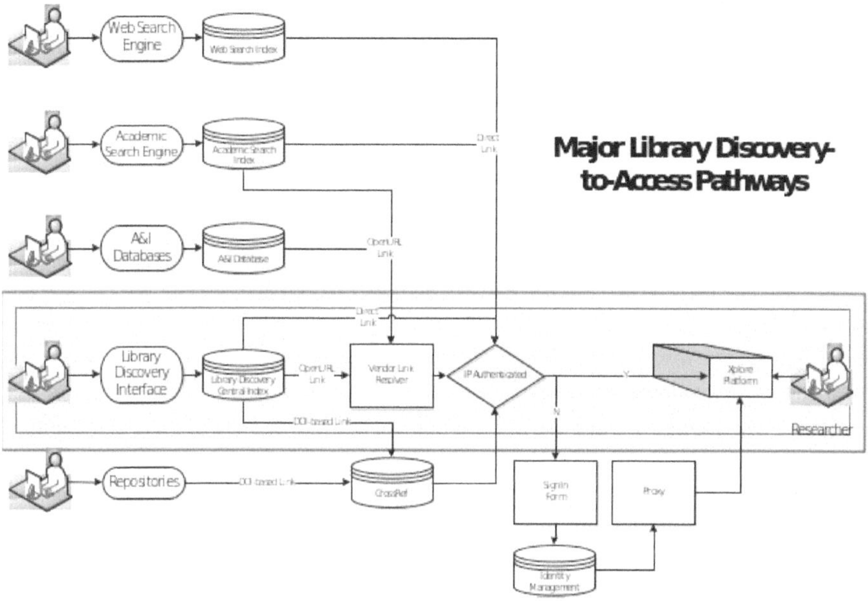

Figure 4.1 *Major discovery-to-access pathways to the IEEE Xplore platform*

(EzProxy, Wam Proxy), and finally access the full text on IEEE Xplore. There are three main types of linking in discovery services: direct linking uses publisher-provided proprietary article IDs to provide seamless linking to articles on hosting platforms; DOI-based linking resolves DOIs (digital object identifiers) via Crossref; and open URL (uniform resource locator) linking uses article metadata gathered from various content providers to form open URL links.

Even though visits starting from library discovery service tools do not form a large portion of the overall traffic, IEEE decided to look closely into this set of pathways, for several reasons:

- More libraries all over the world are installing library discovery service tools (Breeding, 2015).
- Library discovery service tools are becoming more important not only for undergraduate students but for researchers as well (Gardner and Inger, 2016).
- Working closely with vendors and helping libraries troubleshoot their discovery and access configurations will improve usage, develop goodwill and help with sales efforts.

- Improving this set of pathways, including the three major linking options also used by other discovery channels, will help users not only starting from library discovery service interfaces but also starting from other discovery channels as well.

To implement the strategy of clearing library discovery-to-access pathways, IEEE developed an organisational support system. In 2013 IEEE assembled a three-person team to look for the problems in discovery services, start working with vendors and create configuring guides for libraries. In June 2014 IEEE hired a dedicated discovery service relations manager, to conduct deeper research and analysis of the problems regarding library discovery services, create roadmaps for overall improvement, and co-ordinate internal and external resources for improvements.

In 2015, with support from the IEEE management, a nine-person discovery service working group was formed, including members from business (content operations, product development, platform design, web metrics, marketing, client services) as well as technical units (covering database operations, content engineering, software development). The team meets regularly to discuss detected issues, ongoing projects, and ways to collaborate with vendors and library customers (Figure 4.2).

Figure 4.2 *Functions of the IEEE discovery service task force*

Assessing the library discovery service landscape

One of the initial tasks for the discovery service working group was to map out the data flows of discovery services and the tasks performed by key stakeholders along the data supply chain (Figure 4.3 opposite).[1]

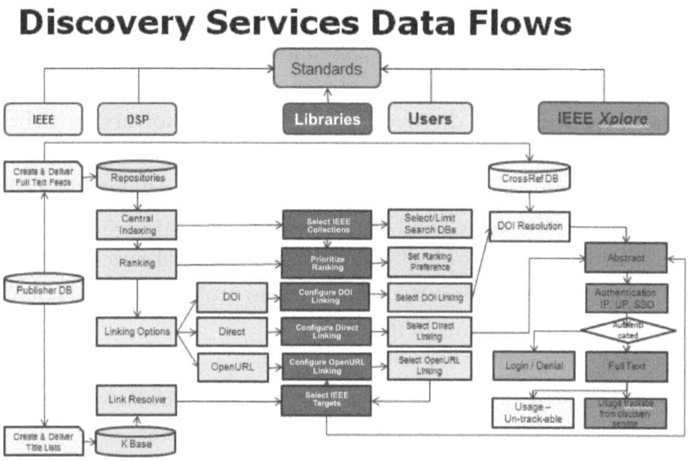

Figure 4.3 *Discovery service data flows*

First, IEEE, as a content provider, needs to perform four major tasks: to create content full text and metadata, to provide metadata and/or full-text syndications to discovery service vendors for indexing, to provide subscription package title lists to link resolver vendors for setting up linking targets, and to deposit DOIs to Crossref for article-level linking.

Second, library service vendors, for discovery service and link resolutions, form the second part of the data chain. The discovery service provider has three major tasks: to index the content delivered from content providers, to create search and ranking algorithms, and to programme linking options. OpenURL links need not only article-level but also publication-level metadata for correct linking. Link resolvers are built for this specific purpose. Link resolver vendors should create subscription package linking targets from title lists provided by content providers.

Third, library staff need to make a number of configurations. In the discovery index, they need to select the correct subscribed collections, rank collections based on library needs, and select and configure linking options. In the link resolver knowledge base, they need to enable the correct targets for subscribed packages. They also need to configure their authentication and proxy systems correctly to ensure end-users can access subscribed content on and off campus.

Data and configuration problems can occur at each stage of the data supply chain, and cause content discovery, linking and access problems.

To help troubleshoot discovery and access problems for IEEE content in library discovery service tools, IEEE also needed to understand customers' library discovery ecosystems. In May 2015 IEEE sent out a survey to library customers about their experience with discovery tools. According to the survey, over 35% of the respondents in libraries received assistance from vendors in implementing their discovery and link resolver tools, on site or online. Only 5% of respondents were aware of and consulted IEEE's guides for configuring discovery tools and link resolvers for IEEE content. About 3% of the libraries received assistance from other channels (Figure 4.4). Close to 25% of the libraries did not receive any type of assistance. When asked whether the libraries had selected all the relevant IEEE collections in their discovery indexes, 64% of respondents believed that they had selected all, 22% partial selection, 7% none, and 7% not sure (Figure 4.5 opposite). The configuration problems turned out to be much worse than reported by librarians in the survey.

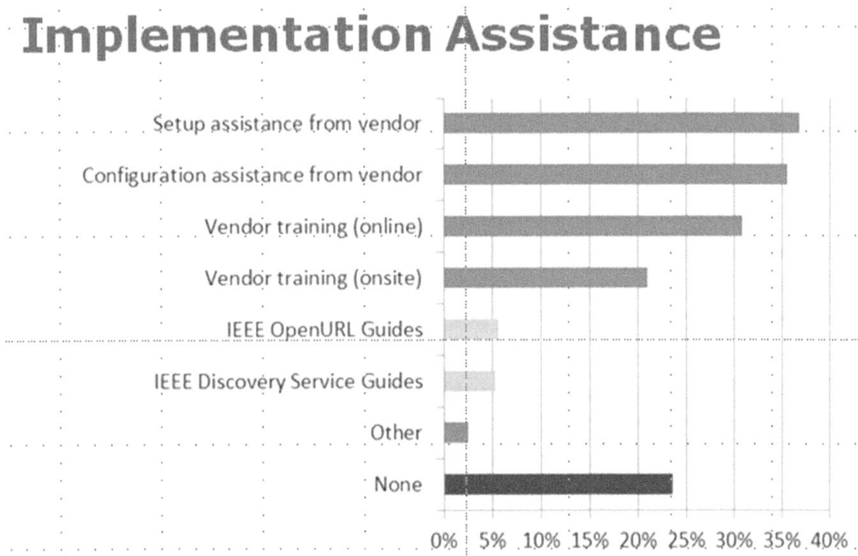

Figure 4.4 *Implementation assistance received by libraries in configuring discovery services, IEEE survey on users' experience of using discovery tools, May 2015*

Since a large percentage of IEEE customers use discovery tools and link resolvers, we needed to know more about which customers are using which tools before we could provide targeted help. We started building technology profiles for our customer accounts in Salesforce. We found that 33% of all customers currently have at least one discovery service tool, including 47% in the academic sector, 12% in the government sector and 5% in the corporate sector (Figure 4.6 opposite). The discovery service penetration rates in the academic sector are high in many countries, especially in North America and Europe. The numbers of discovery service instalments are increasing year by year in Asia, South America and Africa as well (Figure 4.7 on page 52).

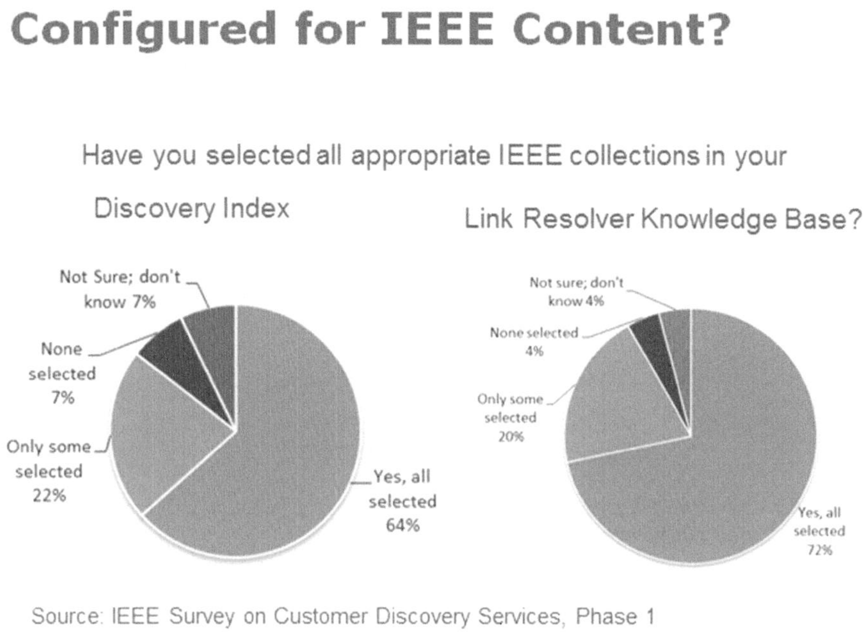

Figure 4.5 *Librarian reporting of configurations for IEEE content in discovery services and link resolvers, IEEE survey on users' experience of using discovery tools, May 2015*

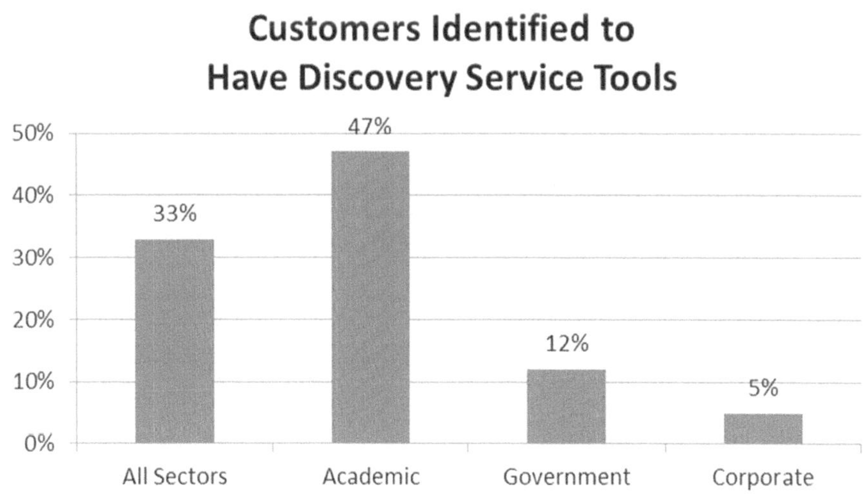

Figure 4.6 *The proportion of customers with discovery service tools, by sector, IEEE survey on users' experience on using discovery tools, May 2015*

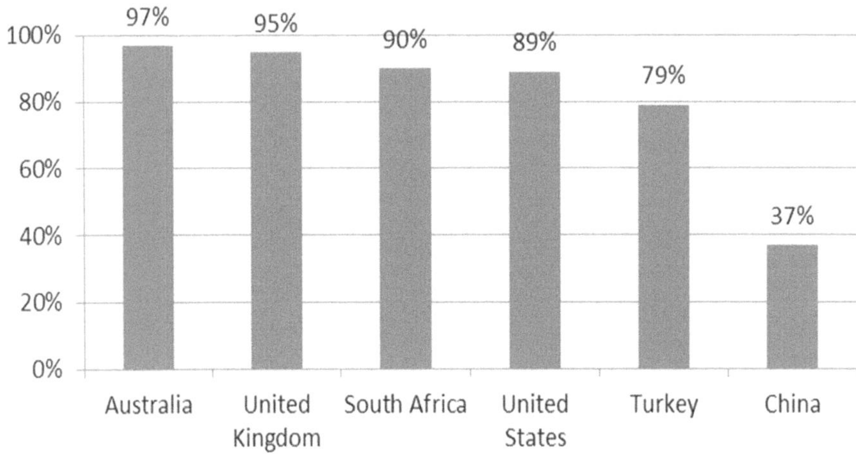

Figure 4.7 *Use of the discovery service in the academic sector, by country, IEEE survey on users' experience of using discovery tools, May 2015*

In the middle of 2015 IEEE conducted a study to assess the gaps in IEEE content in various discovery service tools and the library customers' discovery interfaces. The study sampled data from four major sources (Table 4.1). It found a small gap between the IEEE content on the IEEE Xplore platform and the content fed to the discovery service vendors. There are significant content gaps between the content delivered to the vendors and the content indexed by the vendors, some small and some large. Furthermore, content gaps can be further widened by libraries that fail to correctly configure their discovery service indices and link resolver targets for the IEEE content

Table 4.1 *Gaps of IEEE content in various discovery service tools, IEEE survey, 2015*

IEEE records	Full text records	Conference papers	Journal papers	Standards
IEEE Xplore	X	X	X	X
IEEE Syndication to Discovery service providers	X	X	X	X
Discovery Base Index as reported by Discovery service providers	X	X	X	X
6 libraries using service provider A	X	X	X	X
6 libraries using service provider B	X	X	X	X
6 libraries using service provider C	X	X	X	X
6 libraries using service provider D	X	X	X	X

(Figure 4.8). The detailed results and analysis were published in the December 2016 issue of *Science & Technology Libraries* (Zhu and Kelley, 2015).

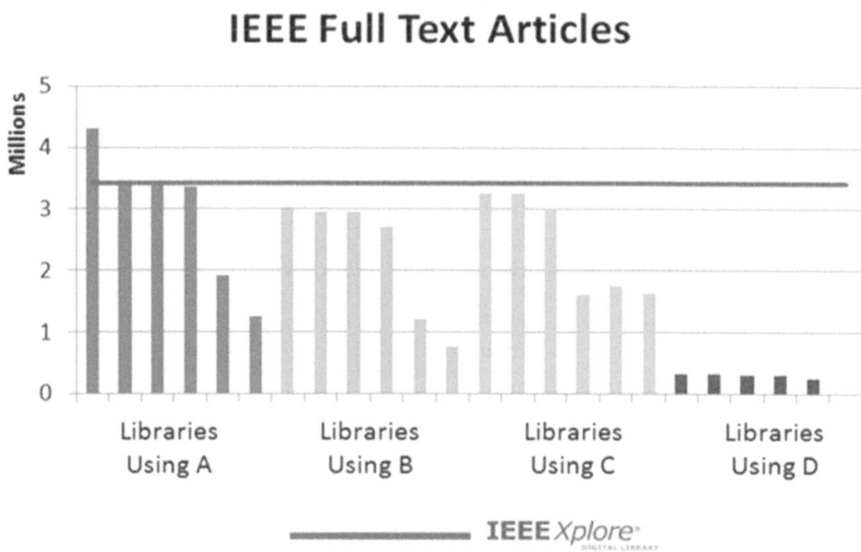

Figure 4.8 *Gaps of IEEE content in full-text articles on library discovery interfaces, IEEE survey, 2015*

Initiatives to improve discovery and access of IEEE content

Armed with more knowledge about discovery service data flows and customers' library discovery ecosystems, the IEEE Discovery Service Working Group started composing a plan to further investigate and troubleshoot problems from three major areas: IEEE's data quality and workflows, vendors' indexing and linking of IEEE content, and libraries' configurations for IEEE content. In each area we do as much auditing as possible, record problems uncovered, initiate projects to remediate them, and track the status of remediation projects.

Improve internal data quality and workflows

We carefully audited IEEE's data quality and workflows, identified problems in several areas that affect content discoverability and linking, and started several projects to address them. Table 4.2 on the next page is a summary of the auditing, results, remediation and status as of October 2017.

Table 4.2 *IEEE data quality and workflow checklist, October 2017*

Area	Auditing	Results	Remediation	Status
Content discoverability	Is the content delivered complete?	Early access, updated and deleted articles and some proceedings without copyrights were not included in the feeds	Project to re-deliver content archive and deliver additional content	Completed
	Are there problems in the content delivery process?	Some vendors reported File Transfer Protocol (FTP) access problems	Project to improve and track content transfer	Completed
	Is IEEE ready to conform with the Open Discovery Initiative (ODI) (NISO, 2014)?	Yes	Project to publish the statement	Completed
Content access	Are there consolidated title lists for all subscription products?	There were no consolidated lists across content type nor title lists for dozens of products	Project to create KBART II compliant title lists for all products	Completed
	Are all the linking related elements complete in the title lists?	There were significant problems for international standard serial and book numbers (ISSNs and ISBNs) for journals, proceedings and standards	Project to correct and fill in missing ISSNs and ISBNs	Completed

Through our self-auditing, we found that not all the vendors downloaded and processed IEEE content feeds from the FTP site in a timely way so that some deliveries were missed and some content was not indexed. After discussions with all four major discovery service vendors, we re-delivered the complete archive of 3.4 million records in USB drives in 2015. All the four vendors received the complete archive and used it as a base to either fill in the missing content or re-index the IEEE content. To strive for completeness of IEEE content in discovery service indices, we also added more content to the feeds, for instance early access, and updated and deleted articles. We have developed reports to track which vendors download which feeds at which time, so that we can spot which content feed could be missed by vendors. Then we send reminder e-mails to vendors if they do not download content within a certain period of time.

IEEE also strives to conform to industry standards and recommendations. In March 2015, IEEE was the first publisher to publish the ODI content provider conformance checklist (NISO, 2017) (Table 4.3), showing that it could respond 'yes' to each recommendation for conformance, from the choice Y ('yes'), N ('no'), or P ('partially').

Table 4.3 *IEEE ODI content provider conformance checklist*

Y/N/P	Recommendation	Paragraph	Comment
Y	Content provider makes available to discovery service providers core metadata and underlying full-text or original content for complete offerings	3.2.1.1 (1) (15)	
Y	Content provider makes available to discovery service providers the core set of metadata elements (see 3.2.1.2) for each item submitted for indexing	3.2.1.1 (2) (15)	
Y	Content provider provides the content item and additional descriptive content for as much of their content as possible	3.2.1.1 (3) (15)	
Y	Content provider provides libraries, on request, with a statement of participation in the discovery services, including disclosure of coverage depth and content depth	3.2.2 (22)	
Y	Content provider's agreements with discovery service providers do not include non-disclosure agreements	3.2.3 (22)	
Y	The transfer of content provider's data to discovery service providers makes use of existing standards where applicable and uses one of the metadata encoding schemes listed in 3.3.3	3.2.4 (22)	

IEEE wished to comply with the standard KBART (knowledge base and related tools), a project intended to improve the efficiency of OpenURL resolution. KBART is a two-phase project, KBART I up to 2014 and KBART II subsequently. In 2014 IEEE had a limited number of KBART I compliant title lists, for periodicals only, and there were no consolidated lists for IEEE and IET (Institute of Engineering and Technology) Electronic Library, IEEE's main subscription product, which includes serials (journals) and monographs (conference proceedings and standards). This lack of consolidated lists created problems for link resolver vendors, which had to download and merge title lists from multiple online public access catalogue (OPAC) lists, and resulted in missing a large number of IEEE publication titles in the linking targets.

In 2015 IEEE started the project to create KBART II compliant title lists for all subscription packages. We managed to merge titles of different content types, and also filled in title histories for serials and parent–child relationships between conference serials and conference proceedings. By the end of 2015, we created an IEEE KBART portal and published over 80 KBART II compliant title lists. In March 2016, IEEE became the first publisher to receive KBART II endorsement from the National Information Standards Organization (NISO).

Libraries often use publication ISSNs and ISBNs for managing entitlements, surfacing content and linking to full-text records, so correcting and filling in missing ISSNs and ISBNs in publication title lists is very important. The IEEE Discovery Service Working Group initiated several projects to correct and add ISSNs and ISBNs for journals, conference proceedings and standards. The improvements are made in several areas:

- Sort out and correct the ISSNs and ISBNs of different media types
- Streamline the processes of applying for ISSNs for journals and conference serials through the US ISSN Center, and ISBNs for conference proceedings and standards through Bowker, for both new and legacy content
- Synchronise ISSN and ISBN data in multiple databases, and display them correctly and completely in title lists.

The projects are complex but are making good progress.

Work with vendors to improve content discoverability and accessibility

IEEE is developing close collaborations with all four major discovery service and link resolver providers. We visited three of them in 2015 and 2016. We continue to audit IEEE content in the discovery service indices and link resolver knowledge bases, identify content gaps and problems, conduct joint remediation projects, and hold regular meetings with business and technical staff from both the publisher and the vendor sides to discuss status of these joint projects (Table 4.4 opposite).

During the auditing process, we found that some discovery service vendors did not index all the IEEE content received, because of prioritisation, oversight, or other

Table 4.4 *IEEE discovery service and link resolver vendor checklist*

Category	Auditing	Results	Remediation	Status
Discoverability	What published content is missing in the discovery base index?	Some content was missing in all four major discovery indices	Re-deliver the IEEE content archive to all four major vendors	Completed
	Has the vendor downloaded and indexed all the content received?	Some vendors did not download content in a timely way and did not index all the content received	Improve content delivery and tracking mechanisms	Ongoing
	How well does the vendor do in filling missing content, matching or merging records or re-indexing content?	There are record matching problems for all vendors, some more serious than others	Work with vendors to analyse, match and (re-)index records	In progress
Accessibility	Are targets for the publisher packages complete, accurate, and up to date in the link resolver knowledge base?	All knowledge bases were missing some targets. Some vendors had multiple targets for IEL (IEEE/IET Electronic Library) and IEEE Enterprise	Work with vendors to set up, consolidate and update targets in link resolver knowledge bases	Ongoing
	Are direct links, custom links and OpenURL links available and working?	Some vendors are missing direct links; OpenURL links do not work correctly for some link resolvers	Work with vendors to set up and monitor all linking options	In progress

business or technical reasons. Some indexed the IEEE content from dozens of third-party abstracting and indexing databases, with incomplete or inaccurate metadata, and were not able to match or merge the records from multiple sources. Some vendors indexed the IEEE content into one single IEEE database collection, while others separated the IEEE content into three or four separate collections or databases. Some clearly labelled the IEEE content as an independent database, but one embedded it along with all the other publisher-provided full text, so it became confusing to IEEE library customers.

IEEE collaborates with discovery service vendors to remediate the detected problems. It has been working closely with them to assess the content gaps, fill in the missing content, match records and re-index the content. These activities help not only the discoverability of the IEEE content, but also the visibility, linking and usage tracking. Figure 4.9 shows the numbers of IEEE full-text records available for search in four discovery tool interfaces, showing changes between 2014 and 2015. There were significant increases.[2] IEEE is continuing to work with vendors to match and de-duplicate the records, re-index the content, and develop discovery content coverage analysis tools to better identify the content gaps.

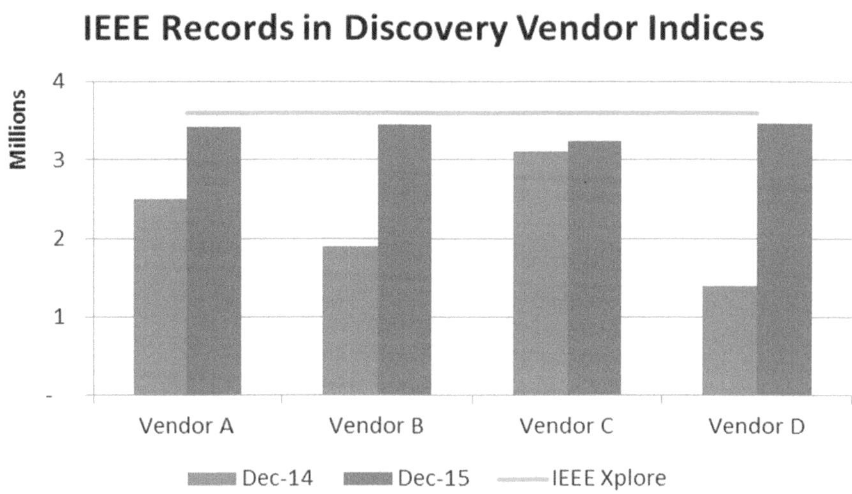

Figure 4.9 *IEEE records in discovery vendor indices, December 2014 and 2015*

We also found major problems in vendor link resolver knowledge bases. All of the knowledge bases were missing some IEEE Xplore targets, some more and some less. There were problems with the targets for IEEE/IET Digital Library (IEL) and IEEE Enterprise, two leading subscription products that include content of multiple types (journals, conference proceedings and standards) and from multiple publishers (IEEE and several publishing partners). Two of the knowledge bases separated the IEL content into four or five separate targets, divided by content type and publisher source.

One knowledge base had only six IEEE targets, with no target for IEL. After we published over 80 consolidated title lists to the IEEE KBART portal, we worked closely with each of the link resolver vendors to set up new IEEE Xplore targets and consolidate the IEL and IEEE Enterprise targets. Figure 4.10 shows the numbers of IEEE Xplore targets available in each link resolver knowledge base before and after the projects.

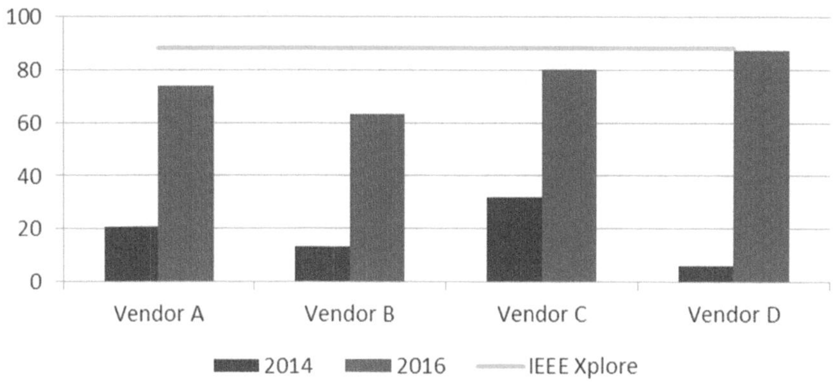

Figure 4.10 *IEEE Xplore targets in link resolver knowledge bases, 2014 and 2016*

We found that all four major discovery service tools provided OpenURL linking for IEEE content, but there were linking syntax problems for some content types. We continue to work with each of the vendors to correct and improve the linking syntax. We are also working with the vendors to set up direct links, which have higher linking success rates. In 2014 only one of the four discovery service vendors was providing direct linking for IEEE content. Since then, we have worked with all the other vendors and added the direct linking for IEEE content.

Work with libraries to improve content discoverability and accessibility

IEEE recognises the importance of working with libraries directly to make their subscribed IEEE content more discoverable and accessible from their discovery service systems. For several years IEEE was carrying out more reactive troubleshooting of content discovery and access problems reported from individual users, library customers and sales staff. Now we are auditing our customers' discovery and link resolver configurations more proactively and systematically (Table 4.5 on the next page). We are trying to automate the steps as much as possible. Moreover, we are

Table 4.5 *Library discovery and linking configuration checklist*

Category	Auditing	Results	Remediation	Status
Discoverability	Has the library selected all the relevant publisher collections in the discovery index?	Several libraries did not select all the subscribed IEEE collections	Work with customers and vendors to select all the relevant (subscribed and open) collections in discovery index	Ongoing
Accessibility	Has the customer activated all the linking options and selected all the relevant targets in the link resolver knowledge base?	Possibly half of the libraries did not select all the relevant IEEE targets in link resolver knowledge bases	Work with customers and vendors to select all relevant targets in the link resolver knowledge base	Ongoing

training the client service team and sales staff so that more people will be able to conduct some basic auditing. We record the results in an electronic system so that more staff can have access to them. We encourage all customer-facing staff to report discovery-related problems so that we can not only help troubleshoot problems individually but also find patterns that can be dealt with on a larger scale. Through auditing, we have found that at least half the libraries have significant problems in their configurations of their discovery and link resolver tools for the subscribed IEEE content.

We have experimented with ways to reach out to libraries and help them improve configurations. In late 2015 and early 2016, IEEE conducted several discovery service auditing and configuration improvement workshops.[3] Dozens of librarians, including engineering subject librarians, electronic resource librarians, collection development librarians, systems librarians and usage statistics librarians, participated in the workshops. Afterwards we made usage comparisons of libraries that improved the configurations and those that did not. We found a significant increase in overall usage of IEEE content in libraries that improved their discovery and link resolver configurations, compared with those that did not change their problematic configurations.

After undertaking more systematic auditing by discovery service product and by country or region, the IEEE client service team, along with other customer-facing staff, reached out to libraries to share results of auditing and tips on configuration improvements. Librarians gave the outreach campaigns very positive feedback. The client service and sales staff are able to use these outreach campaigns to connect with librarians, including those who have been out of reach for a few years. They use these opportunities to enhance relationships with library customers and establish stronger business relationships. Meanwhile more libraries turn to IEEE for help in troubleshooting the problems for discovering and accessing IEEE content, and take into consideration IEEE's willingness to work with vendors and librarians in the library discovery ecosystem as an important factor in their handling of business deals with IEEE.

Conclusion

IEEE understands that there are still many things unknown in the complex library discovery ecosystem. We are actively engaged in industry activities and contributing towards industry standard activities that make the discovery-to-access more seamless. IEEE currently serves on several NISO standing committees and working groups, such as the Discovery to Delivery Topic Committee (D2D), ODI Standing Committee, KBART Standing Committee, Tracking Link Origins Working Group and KBART Automation Working Group. IEEE is also active in other related industry initiatives to improve identifiers (such as ISSNs and ISBNs), authentication and access.

IEEE is watching out for the ever-changing library resource discovery landscape and adjusting its discovery strategies. It collaborates more with major search engines, like Google, Microsoft Bing and Baidu, and academic search engines such as Google Scholar, Microsoft Academic Search and Baidu Xueshu. It works with abstracting and indexing databases to help them improve linking syntax and set up direct links to IEEE Xplore. Moreover, it is strengthening its relationships with library service providers and library customers to continue to tackle content discovery, visibility, linking, authentication, access, usage trackability and other challenging issues. Whatever the discovery channels are, IEEE is open to collaborate to make its content more discoverable and accessible.

Notes

1 This chart was first published in the December 2015 issue of Against the Grain, in Donald T. Hawkins' summary of The Future of Discovery: a NISO forum, held in October 2015, where I gave a presentation on IEEE's work on library discovery services (Hawkins, 2016).

2 The numbers could be inflated, though, as they may include duplicated copies of the same records that have not been successfully matched or merged.

3 I thank Content Online, IEEE's sales agent in UK and Ireland, who initiated and organised these workshops.

References

Breeding, M. (2015) The Future of Library Resource Discovery: a white paper commissioned by the NISO Discovery to Delivery (D2D) Topic Committee, National Information Standards Organization, https://www.niso.org/publications/future-library-resource-discovery.

Gardner, T. and Inger, S. (2016) How Readers Discover Content in Scholarly Publications, *Renew Training*, www.simoningerconsulting.com/nar/how_readers_discover.html.

Hawkins, D. T. (2016) Don's Conference Notes: the future of discovery: a NISO forum, *Against the Grain*, **27** (6), 67–9, www.against-the-grain.com/wp-content/uploads/2016/01/dons_conf_notes_v27-6.pdf.

NISO (2014) *Open Discovery Initiative: promoting transparency in discovery*, NISO RP-19-2014, National Information Standards Organization, www.niso.org/publications/rp/rp-19-2014.

Zhu, J. and Kelley, J. (2015) Collaborating to Reduce Content Gaps in Discovery: what publishers, discovery service providers, and libraries can do to close the gaps, *Science & Technology Libraries*, **34** (4), 1–14, http://dx.doi.org/10.1080/0194262X.2015.1102677.

5

Case study: putting discovery at the heart of the library experience

Tamir Borensztajn, Oliver Pesch and Kate Lawrence

Introduction

Ensuring the best possible end-user experience and optimal collection usage lies at the foundation of the library's mission to support research and provide access to information. A library's success stands or falls by the ease with which its users can swiftly find the information they need. Today's users expect a discovery solution that enables them to search and retrieve rapidly the most relevant information from any device, anywhere and anytime.

This chapter explores what today's users expect in a discovery solution. The chapter looks at the emergence of discovery, the fundamental technologies and approaches that underlie a modern discovery solution, and what we may expect as discovery further evolves to meet emerging user needs.

Background

With the rise of the internet, the online public access catalogue (OPAC) emerged: an online interface for end-users to find items in a library's catalogue. The OPAC was tightly coupled with the integrated library system and functioned in effect as a portal. Library users searched for items in the OPAC and performed a variety of functions, such as placing holds, renewing items and paying fines. Additionally, the library services platform arose, seeking to enable the management of print and electronic materials in a single environment. Building on these evolving notions of library service, around the year 2010 a new model for library discovery appeared: discovery.

Google had set the standard for 'search': a single search box providing immediate access to all resources became the norm. In the library space, discovery became the means to provide access to all of the library's resources, thereby defining the library end-user's experience, and becoming the essence of library success. As well as providing access to resources from a single search box, discovery solved the 'where to start' challenges posed by the proliferation of databases, e-books and e-journal platforms. Discovery depends on several factors:

- the ability to customise the service to meet institutional and user needs
- the inclusion of all content types from many content providers
- the technological approach to search and relevance ranking
- the interoperability of the solution with third-party applications such as the library services platform (or its previous iteration, the integrated library system).

Certainly, discovery resides within a complex technology ecosystem where applications must work together to ensure success for users. When applications are open and interoperable, libraries can support workflow efficiencies and end-user services that meet their institution's strategic objectives. Library staff must be able to select the resource management platform, knowledge base and discovery service of choice to readily manage holdings and support discoverability of print and electronic resources. A February 2015 NISO white paper noted that 'many libraries need the ability to set discovery and management strategies independently and expect these systems to have mutual interoperability' (Breeding, 2015). It is in this evolving notion of discovery that we witness divergent approaches among services as well as opportunity for innovation.

This chapter discusses new and evolving innovations in search; how usability research informs the delivery of content on all devices; options for customisation to support institutional needs; access to a robust knowledge base of electronic resources; and workflow integration, analytics and application programming interfaces (APIs) for management functions.

Search innovation

A critical aspect for any discovery service is the type of search results that are returned to users. The user queries seen in EBSCO Discovery Service (EDS) are mostly through the primary search form (not the advanced search form), represent basic search terms, and have a word count average of 1.72 words.[1] The top search terms for EDS include a combination of broad concept searches ('social media', 'autism', 'black lives matter') and more targeted, known item searches ('Harvard Business Review', 'PubMed', 'Beloved', 'Harry Potter'). Known item searches comprise on average 10% of the top search terms. Usage metrics indicate that users conduct between two and three searches per session, consistent with observed and anecdotal behaviour, paralleling the way that users use open web sources. Metrics further show that users are asking for more detailed information for approximately 2+ items per session.

Relevance ranking

Apart from the content, delivering the most relevant results for a search first is the most important aspect of a discovery service. So, how does a discovery service determine what is relevant?

Consider the range and volume of content in a library's collection: an ocean of resources from in-depth academic journal articles to long e-books to short news items to local catalogues and institutional repositories and everything in between. Books, magazines, videos, dissertations, trade publications, conference proceedings, audiobooks, government reports, poems, maps, musical scores, reviews and more from tens of thousands of publishers all need to be accessed for their value to be realised and ranked by relevance for all matching records on a given search. A good discovery service starts with bibliographic metadata: content is king and metadata is queen. Vendors can partner with content providers that provide the highest quality subject indexing and abstracting and the highest quality content. A successful vendor will invest heavily in subject indexing the content in its own databases.

There is no simple formula to determine relevance: it blends many factors to deliver the best results. But among the approaches, there are 'better' ways of doing it.

Relevance ranking should start with field weighting. Some fields (subject, title) are more important than others (abstract, author, full text). Search terms found in more important fields contribute more to the relevance score. Exact matches – all words from the query in the exact order – in certain fields receive a boost. For instance, exact matches on book titles in library catalogues should ideally receive a relevance-ranking boost.

Concept-based searching

Concepts matter, too. When a search term matches a known concept in a subject-indexing-controlled vocabulary from a content provider partner, such as the American Psychological Association (APA), PubMed, Modern Language Association (MLA), Atla, EconLit or GeoRef, the search should be expanded to include the exact terms for that concept in mapped vocabularies. Records that match the concept would receive a relevance-ranking boost. For example, a search for 'workplace injury' would map to the concept 'work-related injuries'. This matches the PubMed term 'occupational injuries' and the APA term is 'industrial accidents'. The search is expanded to find highly relevant records by searching the PubMed preferred term (occupational injuries) in PubMed records, along with the original search. For PsycINFO, the search is expanded using the APA preferred term (industrial accidents), along with the original search term. In each case, records that have the preferred term, from the mapped vocabulary, in the subject field would get a boost in relevance ranking.

The discovery service vendor needs close partnerships with leading subject-index providers, allowing it to tap into their subject-indexed content. Second, the concepts in the various taxonomies should be mapped in a unified subject index. Third, the unified subject index must be incorporated into real time search by rewriting queries to include the concepts in each of the taxonomies. Fourth, the relevance-ranking algorithm should be flexible, incorporating a scoring boost for each record with the matching concept. Fifth, the solution must be scalable, to incorporate additional mappings from new partners and from mined search logs to ensure continuing usefulness. The result is advanced search functionality that complements ordinary, unstructured, imprecise keyword search with structured, precise, concept search, thereby increasing search precision and improving relevance ranking. Table 5.1 opposite shows some problems and solutions when carrying out a concept search.

Metadata attributes such as publication date, publication type, whether peer-reviewed and document length can also contribute to relevance, following user preferences. Newer articles should get more points than older articles and generally rank higher. Reviews would be weighted lower than other content types. If sought, they can easily be retrieved through a facet for content type.

As most users get news items from the web, these items should be considered less relevant in a discovery service. Peer-reviewed status can influence scores up or down depending on the context; peer-review status is more important in the academic market than for public and school libraries.

Document length is an important consideration for both long and short items. A half-page article should be ranked lower than a five-page article. Very long articles such as e-books, government reports, etc. could easily overwhelm relevance ranking with multiplied hits in the full text. A discovery service should balance the contribution of full-text hits based on the document length.

Discovery vendors must continually evolve and improve relevance ranking, aiming to give users the results they want for every search in every context. This leads to better application of search intelligence to user queries to understand user intent and search context.

Table 5.1 *Problems, solutions and examples of carrying out a concept search*

Problem	Solution	Example
Users generally do not know the specific vocabulary terms used by different publishers to index content	When a user's search term matches a known concept, the search is expanded to include the exact terms for that concept in mapped vocabularies	User searches: 'workplace injury'; the search term maps to the concept 'work-related injuries'
Users often enter popular terms when searching, or they enter terms used by one publisher for subject indexing but not another publisher to index similar content	Records that match the concept (contain mapped vocabulary terms in the subject field) receive a relevance-ranking boost	The concept 'work-related injuries' maps to the following subject-indexed concepts in different vocabularies used on different databases: • occupational injuries • occupational-related injuries • work-related injuries
Entering popular terms can lead to search results that don't include relevant records and to poor relevance ranking on some high-quality records whose subject-indexed terms for the concept searched don't exactly match the user's search terms	High-quality records that match the concept searched by the user appear at the top of the search results list	The original search ('workplace injury') is expanded to include the three concepts above targeted at the specific databases that have records subject-indexed with those concepts Records in databases subject-indexed with these concepts get a boost in relevance ranking

Features such as autocomplete, 'did you mean' and autocorrect, when based on data mined from search logs, anticipate and clarify query intent. Search intelligence also includes known item features such as recognition of citation queries, or standard identifiers. A bibliographic citation pasted into the search box should be recognised at search time and processed to deliver the matching record. Searches for DOIs, ISBNs and ISSNs are rewritten to enforce exact matching on them. Phrase recognition is used to decipher intent and increase precision by rewriting such queries into proximity searches or by favouring implied phrases based on word adjacency. By searching phrases rather than only individual words, search results are greatly improved. For example, the search query 'childhood obesity primary care physician' contains two phrases (childhood obesity) and (primary care physician). By taking account of this information and searching for phrases, in addition to individual words, documents are returned that match the query intent of the user more closely.

Search intelligence and machine learning take discovery to a new level in personalised search. Discovery ultimately needs to provide a personal experience presenting relevant results based on knowledge of individual users. Knowledge about academic discipline, focus, search history and goals will find answers intelligently, precisely and rapidly. The user's market, institution, language, location and session history can guide the search engine. Ultimately the goal is to provide the right results and answers to every search for every user in every context, while ensuring that any privacy concerns are adequately addressed.

User experience

Today's students start research not at the library website but on the open web – specifically, Google. This isn't as much a choice as a natural, unconscious habit. Humans enjoy the ability to shift into autopilot and complete tasks without making conscious choices, says Charles Duhigg, author of a book about why humans make the choices they do (Duhigg, 2012). Searching in Google, then following the (often) first result to Wikipedia for an overview, demonstrates what Duhigg refers to as the 'powerful psychological pattern' of a habit. Students are rewarded with the confidence to scale the second part of the research journey: the library website.

Emotional baggage, expectations from the pre-search phase, accompanies users moving to the library website (Head, 2013). On arrival, they are met with a new, potentially intimidating language – the language of research – or, as one participant in an EBSCO study called it, 'library-ese' (Lawrence, 2015). Working out which resources to search and then understanding and interpreting complex results make this new territory indeed. The volume of options can be overwhelming after the apparent simplicity of the open web.

A discovery tool aims to bring the familiar experience of open web searching to scholarly research, and so reduces the spike in anxiety that students feel when using the library website. Creating a single search of the breadth and depth of a library's resources to provide a familiar, highly usable path to scholarly sources is a major benefit of modern discovery. Content modules and overviews that can be provided for basic search topics help users acclimatise to the new language by giving them background at the top of the results page.

Some discovery services mimic the familiar 'Google-style' search result listing. Libraries may want to experiment with differently organised results, but consistency is key. More complex designs than the usual result listing can be polarising. The bento box design, as first brought to the library field by North Carolina State University, presents a results page that 'boxes' results in categories laid out like the Japanese-style lunch boxes. While tempting because it can fit more into a single results page, the bento box design was shown by EBSCO's user research to require too high a cognitive load: 'It's like having ten search results at once. It's too much' was one representative's comment during user testing.

How students navigate the library site search result

The traditional linear navigation model from search to results to detailed record has served as a consistent standard. But with the recent changes in Google's search results – the addition of the Knowledge Graph in the right panel in 2012 – students now expect more from the results page, and won't settle for just a page of links. What was once a pass-through en route to detailed information about a resource has become the most important page.

Here users are answering the question: 'Is this the tool for me?' Several cues help answer it – the language used (the right level?), the number of results shown (better quality results rather than many results) and how easy it is to skim and scan the page (because deep reading is not possible).

Students are likely to check for their search terms repeated in the title of the items, as an indication that the result is relevant, according to studies from the EBSCO User Research Group. This contrasts with librarians, who judged the quality of a search by the representation, diversity, depth and scope of library resources available in the first page of results.

Processing a results page is about skimming and scanning, not deep reading. This makes the relevancy algorithm even more important. Since most users do not venture beyond page 1 of the results, it is critical to feature the best and most relevant items early.

From ethnography to usability: research on discovery

Satisfying user experience for scholarly search requires a deep understanding of the needs and pain points in this process. While usage metrics may reveal a user's clicks, the story behind them risks remaining untold. Structured usability testing proves useful in identifying areas for improvement, but gathering user pain points is not always sanctioned. A multi-pronged research approach can capture and understand the behaviours powering the fast-moving, binary decision-making reflexes of the search process, informing decisions about how discovery tools are customised for a particular institution's users. Usability testing can be conducted by libraries in its in-person live form, or modernised by leveraging new virtual testing technologies such as UserTesting.com or other similar tools.

Further, ethnography, particularly lean ethnography, is emerging as a popular research method within the library community because it meets the need to understand authentic user behaviour. Users do not employ a single tool or search strategy when looking for scholarly sources. Therefore, a single usability test would not adequately investigate the discovery process. Ethnography studies the entire digital ecosystem, in a way that is natural and organic to the user. It starts from the user's vantage point, analysing his or her typical searches, without the influence of manufactured scenarios. Ethnography is an essential method in any research toolkit focused on discovery, for its value in deriving insights that are unique to each individual user, not influenced or filtered by a special product lens.

User interface customisations (apps)

With the user experience more fully understood, it follows that the next generation of discovery would offer a dedicated, open, custom approach to working directly with libraries to create and implement extra apps and extensions. These are the most popular areas for extensions:

- *Anticipating user intent, intelligent suggestions*: for searches like 'library hours', 'web of science', 'nature', etc., systems should be intelligent enough and tuned to the library's end-users' intended goal, not just render articles and books. Autocompletion, autocorrection, 'did you mean', language selection, using specialised search boxes, browsing authority lists of subjects, etc., device type and mobile apps used, subject guides and library websites, and many other search entry points can also be a basis for understanding user intent.
- *Content highlighting*: no discovery service contains 100% of the world's published content.
- *Content not meant for keyword searching*, e.g. medical references, auto-repair manuals, statistical datasets: for this material, libraries can offer contextual navigation and linking: related info for a book record; a dynamic widget on a result list; suggestions based on the number or quality of results; links to popular open web and social media sources such as YouTube, Twitter, Slideshare, Flickr.
- *Specialist groups*: if a library caters for a highly specialist group, the discovery service can provide tightly integrated access to thesauri and authorities.
- Even when searchable, expensive encyclopedias and reference materials might not receive optimal relevance-ranking placement. An app can promote these items, along with special journal collections or institutional repositories.
- *Library interaction:* as remote access increases, libraries need to be available wherever their patrons are. Many choose to embed instant messaging ask-a-librarian apps in the discovery interface. An app can also promote branded tutorials and helpsheets and can even deduce if a student is stuck. A feed of the

library's latest news and events can be integrated into the user experience, or promote surveys to obtain feedback.

Open web search engines are great search tools: simple, habitual, and a 'go to' for most students, as documented in many studies. Library discovery services try to emulate the best-in-class relevance ranking of open web search engines, but librarians know that academic users require and deserve more than open web search engines offer. Libraries should expect a high level of customisation to their content collections, integration with chosen internal systems, alignment with the library or institution's mission and their end-users' specialties and uniqueness, and support for sustainable open source.

Mobile

Students still primarily rely on their laptops to conduct research. The 2015 Educause Center for Analysis and Research study of undergraduates reported that students were very interested in using their mobile devices for academic activities but the adoption still remained low (Dahlstrom et al., 2015). Laptops are used for taking notes in class, researching for class projects and completing assignments. Mobile devices, typically a phone and not a tablet, are for social activities: texting and social media. EBSCO's user research team has found that iPad and tablet usage skyrockets in middle schools and then tapers off in high schools when Chromebooks become popular.

While the use of mobile phones for academic purposes remains low, students still expect websites to work via phones or tablets – this includes their library's discovery platform. Sites should be responsive, automatically resizing to fit the screen size. They expect a similar but optimised experience on both devices. Progressive disclosure is a key way to limit the amount of information displayed on a small screen. With this, users only see the information that is relevant to their current activity. Additional functionality is displayed as users request it or as they dig deeper into the site. In library search, students accessing from a smartphone won't want to see all the available filters on search results, just the most important two or three options; with others, like subjects, geography or publisher, hidden until requested. Similarly, mobile devices lend themselves to certain operations and thus mobile user experience needs to be designed to enable these tasks.

Mobile researchers may not sit in a library; they may access devices while waiting in line or moving between classes. Students who are researching via their mobile devices aren't keeping the content they select on that device (Walsh, 2012). Content is quickly located and evaluated on the phone, then transferred elsewhere, through e-mail, Google Drive or Dropbox. Mobile phones are just part of students' network of devices, all connected and offering a similar experience, and the library's discovery platform should fit into this established model.

Holdings management, knowledge databases and workflow integration

The importance of the knowledge base

Discovery services, once an add-on to an OPAC, are an increasingly integral part of a library's collection strategy and a key component of the library workflow. Figure 5.1 shows the scholarly information lifecycle as experienced by most librarians. Resources are selected, acquired, described (catalogued) and managed, then marketed to users so they are used, made available for discovery so they can be accessed, and finally their impact is assessed to determine whether they should be renewed or retained.

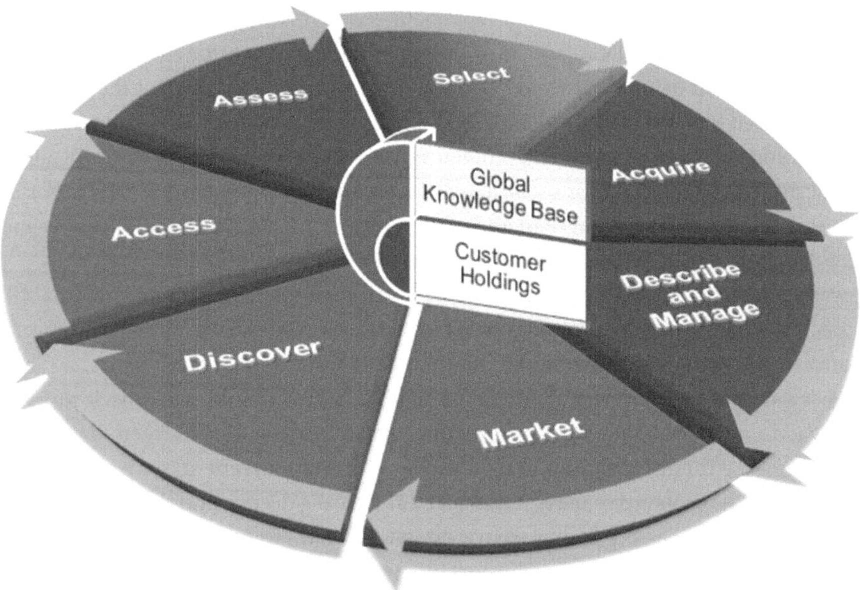

Figure 5.1 *The scholarly information lifecycle*

A global knowledge base and an accurate record of a customer's holdings is central to the lifecycle. Applications at each stage interact with the knowledge base and holdings to provide continuity and integration. For example, a faculty member could be using the discovery system and find a resource that would be valuable for a course she is teaching. With the resource identified within the global knowledge base, she can easily alert library staff who can then tag the resource in the selection system. Once approved, the acquisitions system simply references the same resource in the knowledge base for purchase details. Then, the resource is activated in the customer holdings through a simple status change. The discovery system automatically recognises the new resource as part of the library collection and facilitates access. Over the course of the year COUNTER (Counting Online Usage of Networked Electronic Resources) statistics are retrieved and connected to the same resource in the knowledge base, allowing for assessment.

While many libraries do not yet have a single global knowledge base for holdings, the knowledge base is the central authority for collection resources and connects resources across all the modules and applications that drive the lifecycle.

Workflow integration benefits discovery

A comprehensive knowledge base, including an accurate listing of customer holdings, and effective search technology and relevance-ranking techniques are critical for researchers. It is equally important to identify which items are subscribed to by the library and provide direct links. It is extremely difficult to manage holdings of electronic resources licensed or purchased from publishers. Most libraries have literally thousands of titles to track – and each may have unique coverage entitlements, change publisher or move between packages. Keeping holdings accurate and up to date manually can be a monumental task but is key to accurate discovery of what is available at the time of searching.

Workflow integration is the solution to the holdings management challenge. When ordering systems leverage the same knowledge base as the discovery system and its holdings management features, the task of managing holdings can be automated:

- Subscription management systems can automatically manage an institution's entitlement to access titles included with a purchased subscription or licence.
- Hosted e-books can be automatically activated on acquisition and reflect changes in holdings triggered from demand-driven acquisition or patron-driven acquisition programmes.
- Intermediaries that share the same knowledge base can manage an institution's e-book holdings for multiple hosts. When the intermediary is used to manage demand-driven acquisition or patron-driven acquisition programmes, the titles involved can be reflected in holdings as well.
- Full-text and abstracting and indexing databases acquired from the same vendor should also be managed automatically in the library's holdings.

A library shouldn't need to purchase all resources and services from the same vendor; however, when the various services share the same knowledge base the holdings management system workflows can be optimised, leading to more accurate holdings and a better discovery experience, all while requiring much less effort to manage.

Analytics and assessment

When a common knowledge base is central to discovery, holdings management and ordering applications present other opportunities for workflow optimisation. Support for publisher-provided COUNTER statistics (automated via SUSHI) and tracking cost details (through automated imports) generates analytics and collection analysis. A vendor-hosted knowledge base presents further opportunities for peer comparisons and trend analysis. All of these combine to help improve the discovery experience by assisting librarians in providing researchers with the right materials to discover.

Extending the reach of the knowledge base through application programming interfaces

Beyond workflow automation, the rich data captured in the knowledge base and holdings management system can be valuable to other applications related to the scholarly information lifecycle. When customer holdings and COUNTER statistics are exposed via an API, subscription management systems, e-book management tools, acquisitions modules and other applications can greatly increase their value by integrating decision data, such as holdings, usage and cost-per-use right in the applications where librarians do their work, thus assisting them in delivering the right collection to their users.

Other applications can also embed holdings management features like knowledge base look-up, holdings look-up, holding selection and customisation. Imagine using a simple open source e-resource management system like CORAL to look-up a resource in a commercial knowledge base and automatically add it to your holdings account. APIs provide the opportunity to extend and combine applications with minimal technological skill or training.

Providing researchers with an exceptional discovery tool is paramount to achieving successful research outcomes. The chances for success increase when the discovery system is tied to a comprehensive knowledge base and when the related holdings management services are integrated into the librarian's workflow.

One might ask how improving the librarian workflow helps discovery; when holdings are maintained automatically, the discovery experience is better, because up-to-date holdings means more accurate limits to library holdings and more accurate linking to content. When decision data is available in the workflow, better collection decisions can be made, and when systems combine to provide rich analytical and assessment data, librarians can curate a better collection for their researchers and their budget improving discovery by presenting the right materials to researchers.

The future of discovery

Future trends for discovery are not really driven by libraries, but by evolving user behaviours and emerging technologies outside the sector. It is already evident that discovery of citable scholarly research is needed beyond the confines of the library, for example within the learning management system. Discovery will become increasingly contextual, allowing research within different environments.

Another likely focus is to employ user information to deliver a more personalised discovery experience. Anonymisation protects privacy but even anonymised data (such as academic status or departmental affiliation) can allow a search system to provide more precise and relevant results. Moreover, the discovery experience must be tailored to a specific library's reader community, its focus areas and interests.

Even going beyond the ability to leverage user information, machine learning will help to connect the dots further. Cognitive computing and artificial intelligence will combine the endless sources of data available in the library and throughout an institution, with information collected about users, and allow libraries to make the necessary connections between thousands of users and millions of items of content.

Note

1 Data in this section was obtained from analysis of the EDS logs from 2016.

References

Breeding, M. (2015) The Future of Library Resource Discovery, white paper commissioned by the NISO Discovery to Delivery (D2D) Topic Committee, National Information Standards Organization, https://www.niso.org/publications/future-library-resource-discovery.

Dahlstrom, E., Brooks, D., Grajek, S. and Reeves, J. (2015) ECAR Study of Students and Information Technology, Educause Center for Analysis and Research, https://library.educause.edu/resources/2015/8/~/media/24ddc1aa35a5490389baf28b6ddb3693.ashx.

Duhigg, C. (2012) The Power of Habit: why we do what we do and how to change, William Heinemann.

Head, A. (2013) *Learning the Ropes: how freshmen conduct course research once they enter college*, Project Information Literacy Passage Studies Research Report, www.projectinfolit.org/uploads/2/7/5/4/27541717/pil_2013_freshmenstudy_fullreportv2.pdf.

Lawrence, K. (2015) Do Your Students Speak Library-ese?, EBSCO blog post, https://www.ebsco.com/blog/article/do-your-students-speak-library-ese.

Walsh, A. (2012) Mobile Information Literacy: a preliminary outline of information behaviour in a mobile environment, *Journal of Information Literacy*, **6** (2), 56–69.

6

Investigating resource discovery needs at the University of Oxford

Christine Madsen and Megan Hurst

Aims and objectives of the University of Oxford's resource discovery project

The University of Oxford aims to lead the world in research and education (University of Oxford, 2013). This aim is driven by its consumption and production of priceless intellectual assets including publications and data, teaching resources, library resources, archives and museum collections. However, though some collections, resources and expertise are catalogued and listed in great detail, they can be hard to find, take diverse forms and are often not suited to discovery by potential users. And the catalogued collections only represent a part of the overall holdings of the University's museums and libraries. Therefore Oxford researchers and students are not benefiting as fully as they should from the wealth of knowledge that has been collected, created, purchased or licensed on their behalf. Thus the University's riches are hidden from view, underexposed and underused, in a time in which, increasingly, information that cannot be easily found on the internet is assumed not to exist. Even for more persevering hunters, the process takes longer than it could, the risk of missing a piece of vital information is high, and the tools do not adapt well to individual users' requirements.

The aim of the Oxford resource discovery project was to understand the current state of resource discovery, users' behaviours and needs in the resource-finding process, and to scope new approaches to finding information and collections of relevance to research and teaching at Oxford. It explored new tools and approaches to enable students and researchers at Oxford and abroad to understand the scope of collections held by the University and to find them quickly and efficiently. It examined recent developments in the semantic web, linked data and data visualisation; considered the application of domain-specific tools in other disciplines; and investigated commercial enterprise search solutions to understand the benefits and costs these could bring. In short, the project sought world-leading solutions for connecting students and researchers at Oxford (and abroad) with the collections that are available to them. Good resource discovery tools, though, are not simply about making research easier and faster, but about facilitating the creation, preservation and discovery of knowledge by enabling new modes of research – especially across disciplines (University of Oxford Digital Strategy: https://web.archive.org/web/20181118210315/http://www.ox.ac.uk/about/organisation/strategic-plan-2013-18). At the heart of this project was a set of user needs research that afforded the opportunity to understand how best to enhance the resource discovery capabilities available to staff, students and alumni of the University of Oxford, as well as to external researchers admitted to the libraries and museums, so that they can carry out their work more effectively.

Scope

The project took a wide ranging view of the meaning of the term 'resource discovery'. Here it is defined as any activity which makes it possible for an individual to locate information which she or he needs. Such material and such activities may be digital or analogue in nature.

In scope

Alongside digital discovery facilities, the scope of this project included investigation of strategies which do not currently use IT (e.g. printed catalogues and personal discussions) or which may be digital in nature but do not use University of Oxford services (e.g. social media).

Similarly, the scope of relevant stakeholders was defined widely, including members of the University of Oxford (students, faculty, staff and researchers), external researchers, and any members of the public who visit the University museums or access the University's virtual estate for the purposes of teaching, learning and research. While these users are considered the primary stakeholders, a secondary group of stakeholders are the myriad departments and individuals tasked with building and managing the current and future resource discovery tools at Oxford. For them, this project aimed to provide a unified vision (although not necessarily a single, unified solution) that will facilitate their work within the context of the broader University.

Out of scope

While it is clear that underlying metadata quality is of vital importance to successful resource discovery (which is well supported in the data collected), the scoping study did not include cataloguing enhancements within its recommendations. The recommendations have taken the approach that resource discovery needs to start from the current situation, and not require many years of cataloguing work to be completed before improvements can be made.

Similar remarks apply to fulfilment – the actual access to the information the discoverer wants (e.g. downloading an article after it has been located). The results of this project show that work is needed to improve fulfilment mechanisms, particularly around authentication, but that work is tangential to that proposed here. Again, resource discovery needs to start from the current situation, and not depend on enhancements elsewhere to provide improvements. Essentially, the position adopted by the analysis is that resource discovery is the process that comes between data or metadata creation and fulfilment.

The shape of the project

In order to create innovative approaches to the discovery of resources across the University of Oxford, the project comprehensively assessed the landscape of resource discovery.

The project staff conducted 113 interviews, 18 site visits and 3 literature reviews in order to:

- discover the requirements of users of University services (including non-members of the University of Oxford) for resource discovery
- audit the major local resources which need to be discoverable by these users and their current resource discovery provision
- investigate the responses of other academic institutions and commercial organisations in the UK and globally with similar requirements
- evaluate the currently available commercial solutions.

This chapter focuses on the outputs of the first point listed above, but it is important to understand that this work took place in the context of a more comprehensive analysis of not just users' needs, but also their environments. Users do not operate in a vacuum, so those carrying out user needs analysis should understand the wider context of the user.

Therefore, the work to understand the current state of resource discovery at the University of Oxford took place in five areas of activity, of which user consultation was only one part:

- User consultation: speaking to those in the University and outside to find out what their discovery needs are and how they want them to be provided for.
- Oxford collection providers consultation: speaking to those who professionally guide users to discover the resources they need.
- Peer institutions consultation: recognising that Oxford is not alone in having resource discovery problems, and seeking to learn from ideas and work elsewhere.
- Vendor and publisher consultation: speaking to providers of software and services which include resource discovery, including search engines, publisher websites and databases, union catalogues and portals, etc.
- Literature search and innovation consultation: looking at possible sources for innovative ideas which may not be originally intended for resource discovery, as well as the now fairly extensive resource discovery literature.

The teams and groups overseeing this work were similarly comprehensive. While the work was led by the Bodleian Libraries, it drew on expertise around and outside the University of Oxford, the steering committee, project team and stakeholder group.

Project staff conducted:

- 45 interviews with users of collections around Oxford
- 30 interviews with collection 'providers' (representing all of the collections at Oxford and their users)
- 22 consultations with external institutions (11 of which were site visits)
- 16 interviews with vendors or suppliers
- 7 visits to Oxford libraries and museums to observe researchers
- 3 literature reviews.

User consultation activities

Interviews were conducted with 45 known users of library and museum resources. Members of the faculty were identified using existing personal and professional networks, while students were identified primarily through a list of volunteers gathered at the 2015 fair for incoming students. Efforts were made to recruit interviewees from all four divisions of the University (Humanities; Mathematical, Physical and Life Sciences (MPLS); Medical Sciences; and Social Sciences; www.ox.ac.uk/about/

divisions-and-departments) and to represent as much diversity in academic and research practice as possible. Medical science interviewees were the most difficult to recruit, possibly owing to their greater schedule constraints. The intended diversity involved not just representing these departments but ensuring the selection of interviewees who use a wide variety of research materials. Interviewed users mentioned looking for printed books and journals, modern papers and archives, manuscripts, museum collections that included text (including coins, tablets and plaques), visual works (objects and works on paper), e-books and e-journals, data sets, open access materials, preprints and computer code. The final dispersal of respondents among the divisions is shown in Figure 6.1.

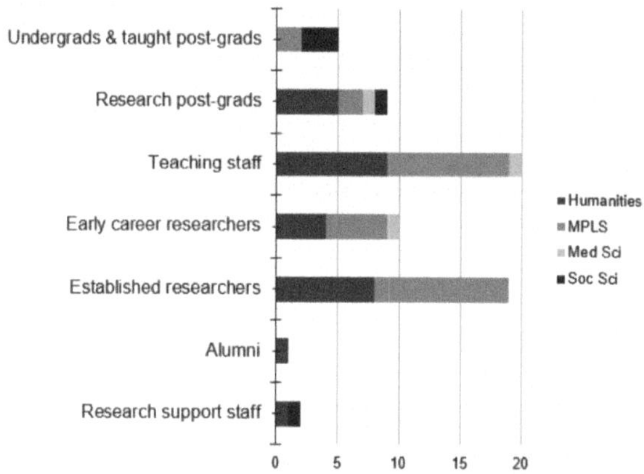

Figure 6.1 *Distribution of user consultations during the University of Oxford's resource discovery project, by division and user type*

Efforts were also made to select participants at all levels of their research activities and careers. This resulted in participants across seven different researcher 'types': undergraduates and taught postgraduates; research postgraduates; teaching staff, including lecturers and tutors; early career researchers; established researchers; alumni; and research support staff (Figure 6.2 on the next page). Interviewees often fell into more than one category within this matrix – someone could, for example, be both an alumnus and a senior researcher. Therefore, in the analysis of the data, respondents were assigned both a primary and a secondary 'type' category. Figure 6.3 on the next page shows the breakdown of respondents by age and gender.

All interviewers employed semi-structured and person-centred interview techniques. Interviewers began with a structured set of questions (see Figure 6.4 on page 83), but allowed for significant personalisation in responses. Each interview was approximately 60 minutes in length and was recorded in full in order to enhance and substantiate written notes. The interviews were not transcribed in full, but the

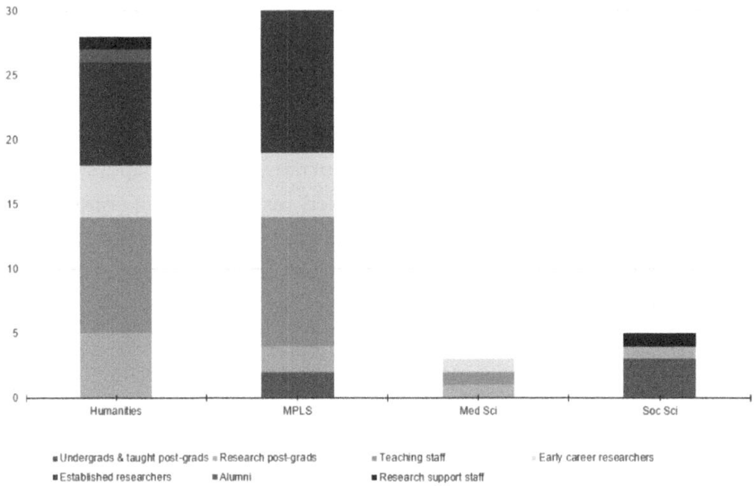

Figure 6.2 *User interviews during the University of Oxford's resource discovery project, by division and researcher type*

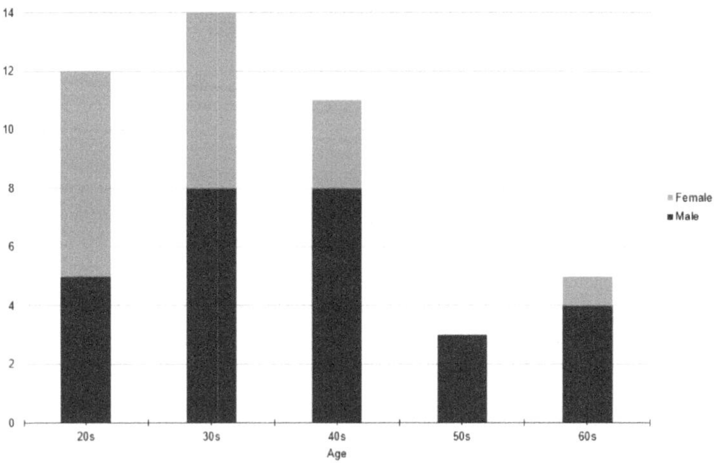

Figure 6.3 *User interviews during the University of Oxford's resource discovery project, by age range and gender*

recordings were revisited when clarification was required. The data was analysed by creating a table of responses to each interview question. As patterns emerged from the responses, the table was broken into more and more columns to accommodate more granular analysis.

In order to find the 45 interview respondents, the project team approached over 92 people, mostly via e-mail. As the interviewees were volunteers, the team recognised

User interview questions

1 Can you briefly describe your area of research or course of study or teaching area?
2 Can you describe a typical research task?
   a What kinds of materials are you generally looking for?
   b How do you know where to start?
3 What are your 3–5 most heavily used resources for finding materials?
   a (If they answer with all electronic discovery tools, then which is their favourite and least favourite and why?)
4 How do you keep up with the work in your field?
   a How do you find out about new publications?
5 On what type of device do you usually do this work?
6 Where do you do your research? From home, office, library?
7 Did you ever have any training – either here or at another institution – in how to find resources?
   a How was it? Useful?
   b How did you learn to become a researcher?
8 Can you show us a typical 'research task' that you have done recently? Talk us through the decisions you are making.
9 Do you see anything on the horizon that may change how you do your work or find things?

Additional questions for teaching faculty

10 How do you instruct your students to find things in their area of study?
   a Do you send them to specific resources?
   b Do you give them 'instructions' on how to search?
11 Do you provide any training for your students?
   a Or do you recommend certain training for your students?
12 How do you share resources with your students? (e.g. printed lists, online reading lists, websites, etc.)

Figure 6.4 *User interview questions for the University of Oxford's resource discovery project*

that they were a self-selecting group, who were already likely to be users or supporters of the libraries and museums. When asked for an interview, several people responded that they 'didn't use the library or museums at all' and therefore could not be of use to the project. Such respondents were actually sought after as they provided valuable data about non-use of existing discovery tools and perceptions of University resources. The number of interview respondents who did not use existing university discovery tools was therefore far below the suspected ratio.[1] Thus the interview data is skewed towards users of existing library and museum discovery tools and this has been taken into consideration in the analysis of the data by weighting the responses from the 'non-users' more heavily.

Consulting Oxford collection providers

For the consultation with the Oxford collection providers, researchers interviewed those from around the University who already have a role in the provision of resource discovery, principally those who:

- answer user queries about discovering resources
- provide training to users
- oversee work which produces resources with a discovery element.

While not typically considered end-users, this group represents those who rely on the University's resource discovery tools for their daily work. This group also comprises those 'front-line' staff who have the most frequent contact with end-users who are searching for collections. Their needs are therefore significant in two ways – as users of resource discovery tools and as representatives and observers of end-users.

This aspect of discovery was first investigated by executing a set of exercises designed to look at the types of queries that experts receive and how they are resolved. Four departments (the Radcliffe Science Library, Bodleian Special Collections, and two departments from the Ashmolean Museum) were selected to participate and an ethnographic approach was employed. The technique was a combination of shadowing and discussion with the providers of typical queries (using real examples) – the latter because it would not be possible to guarantee that enough interesting queries were received during a few hours on a help desk. The purpose of this was partly to orient the investigators as to the sorts of questions answered, in order to prepare for the later parts of the work.

The second stage – five weeks of interviews – engaged with archivists, curators, managers and librarians from the Bodleian Libraries, colleges, museums and other academic related departments. We held 25 interviews with 29 interviewees, all of which (except one) were recorded for note-taking purposes. They can be broken down by role and affiliation (so each is listed twice) as follows:

- librarians (13)
- curatorial staff (5)
- holders of IT and digital content related posts (9)
- archivists (2)
- employees of Bodleian Libraries (13)
- employees of university museums (9)
- employees of colleges (5)
- employees elsewhere (2).

Interviews were held in summer 2015. They were semi-structured in form, allowing concentration on areas of special interest or relevance from the work of each consultee. Additional, supporting information was also gathered from SOLO Live Help[2] session logs and from query statistics.

Peer institutions, vendor or publisher consultations and literature reviews

As mentioned above, the goal of the resource discovery project was not only to understand the needs and behaviour of end-users, but to paint a picture of the state of resource discovery both at the University and beyond. To that end, the user needs analysis was accompanied by three other strands of work: an analysis of the current state of resource discovery at peer institutions, research about the future of resource discovery as understood by vendors and publishers, and a general literature review. All of this work aimed to understand the broader context in which users operate and contributed to the recommendations by providing a sense of where the University stands relative to its peers, and looking into the near and distant potential futures of resource discovery. These components of the project are not discussed in detail here, but more information can be found in the final project report (Madsen et al., 2016).

Data analysis and findings

Interview data analysis

Two project staff conducted end-user interviews, taking elaborate notes. Recordings were made of all interviews and used for clarification or elaboration, when needed. Notes from the interviews were put into a spreadsheet for analysis. Every interview respondent was distinguished in a row on the spreadsheet, and the first set of columns contained the answers to each interview question. This enabled the researchers to read down each column and identify patterns and themes in the answers.

Findings

The interviews with current teaching faculty, research staff, students and alumni uncovered a far more nuanced understanding of search behaviour than is often portrayed in the literature on resource discovery. This project found a number of important patterns, which provide the background for the recommendations. A full report on the findings from users can be found in Appendix 1 of the report (Madsen et al., 2016); here we present a brief summary of the findings that had the greatest impact on the recommendations.

First, *resource discovery at Oxford is very discipline-specific*. While quite a few researchers start their search using Google, others start at the Bodleian Libraries' SOLO catalogue (http://solo.bodleian.ox.ac.uk/primo-explore/search?vid=SOLO&lang=en_US&sortby=rank). Within certain disciplines, though, searchers jump straight to the top resources in their field (ArXiv for physics, PubMed for medicine, WestLaw or similarly specialised tools for law). These findings are consistent with the well-documented understanding of the differences between 'known item' and subject searching,[3] and demonstrate that while both types of search are made in all disciplines, in the sciences end-users more often undertake known item searching. One notable exception to this is evidence-based medicine, where researchers are often engaged in very thorough subject-based searching.

There is continued evidence that *students need to learn how to search*. As one professor said, 'It's clear that reasonably diligent students are strikingly not sophisticated in their searching. Students search in one place, and if they don't find anything on the first try, they think it doesn't exist.'

Nonetheless, *discovery is not as simple as 'novice' vs 'expert'*. Experts in their fields may use some of the same discovery tools and techniques as incoming students in certain circumstances. For example, a professor in one discipline may use Wikipedia or basic Google searches to familiarise herself with a new topic just as a new student might.

At Oxford, *resource discovery is still a very 'analogue' process for many collections and within many disciplines*. Searchers rely heavily on printed catalogues and 'hand lists' in many different areas, as these are the only forms of descriptions about certain catalogues.

Nearly every interviewee said that they rely on asking someone (colleague, supervisor, curator, librarian or known specialist) for information at some point in their search process. This was as true of 'expert' researchers as of 'novice' ones. *Asking people, and knowing who to ask, seems to make the difference between simply finding what you need to complete an assignment and becoming an expert researcher.* A senior researcher in chemistry told us, 'At Oxford, information is power, so nobody shares information online. That's why people are so important to finding information.'

Despite the discussion in the literature around the use of social media for resource discovery (see Appendix 5 of the report), none of the respondents in this project said that they used open or public social media platforms for asking resource discovery questions. Two said that they have used social media to ask a question, but rarely. Those who do use social media, use it as a way to monitor interest groups, people, conferences and blogs in their field, or as a mechanism to promote their own projects or work. Ten used Twitter and seven used Facebook for 'keeping up' with developments, including publications, in their field. Ten used Academia.edu for this purpose, and four interviewees explicitly mentioned using ResearchGate. Students used closed e-mail lists, WhatsApp or Snapchat groups to share articles and news items, but this was very much an extension of simply speaking to their colleagues in person.

Perhaps most importantly, this project found that *many searchers believed the discovery process was as much about becoming expert in their field as it was about finding individual items in their collections*. Multiple interviewees cited 'trial and error' as key to their evolution as researchers. In other words, the more people search and successfully find, the more expert they become in their field. This is in part because they learn the boundaries and the tips and tricks for finding the most credible sources and the less well-known parts of the collections.

Expertise in a domain requires an understanding of two things: the parameters of your domain and the available and relevant resources in those areas. The 'expert' researchers interviewed had varying levels of confidence about their mastery of these domains, but all seem to have a clear sense of its 'borders'. One senior researcher in the humanities used a cartographical metaphor for this: 'If I get dropped into the middle of the landscape, I can deduce where I am and navigate my way out, whereas my students will latch on to the first tree that looks interesting.'

Recommendations

The following recommendations were made to the University in late 2015. They were based on a combination of all of the data and literature consulted over the course of this project. The recommendations were intended to improve the resource discovery situation at the University of Oxford without replacing existing useful tools or attempting to implement a single, monolithic solution.

The recommendations below are based on the general and well-known understanding of the difference between 'known item' searching (searching for something specific and known to the searcher) and other forms of searching, which are less well understood. While recommending solutions to improve both types of searching, this project has greatly increased understanding of the latter forms and has uncovered a far more nuanced understanding of how and why people search for resources.

Areas for investment, part 1: Map the landscape of things

The journey from novice information seeker to experienced researcher is not only about gaining skills for searching and finding but about gaining expertise in a particular domain. As mentioned above in the section 'Data analysis and findings', this expertise requires two things: an understanding of the parameters of one's domain and an understanding of the available and relevant resources in those areas. 'Experts' have varying levels of confidence about their mastery of these domains, but all seem to have a clear sense of its 'borders'. Therefore, resource discovery should, at least in part, be about helping people to identify and define these borders. Figure 6.5 shows the levels of discoverability for different types of material when searching a library catalogue.

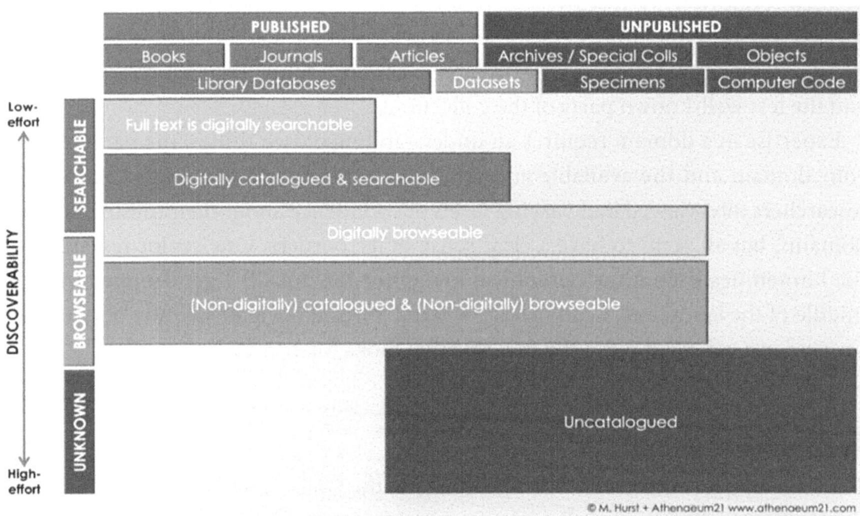

Figure 6.5 *The levels of discoverability for different types of material when searching a library catalogue*

DPhil students are particularly sensitive to the problem of novelty and domain mapping as they are tasked with finding and creating something original, possibly for the first time in their academic careers. They have to have a firm grasp of what has already been done or discovered in their field (see Figures 6.6 and 6.7 opposite).

These recommendations are intended to help searchers of all levels understand their domains and the information or collections environment at Oxford. They are about orienting users to the corpora of collections (digital and non-digital) at Oxford, and they include projects on visualising the scope of the collections at Oxford and cross collection search.

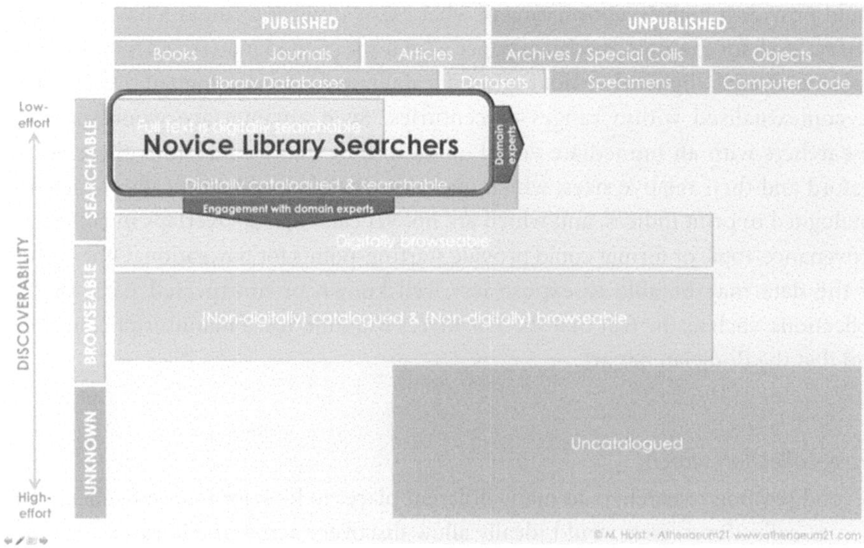

Figure 6.6 *Novice library searchers' discovery of library materials*

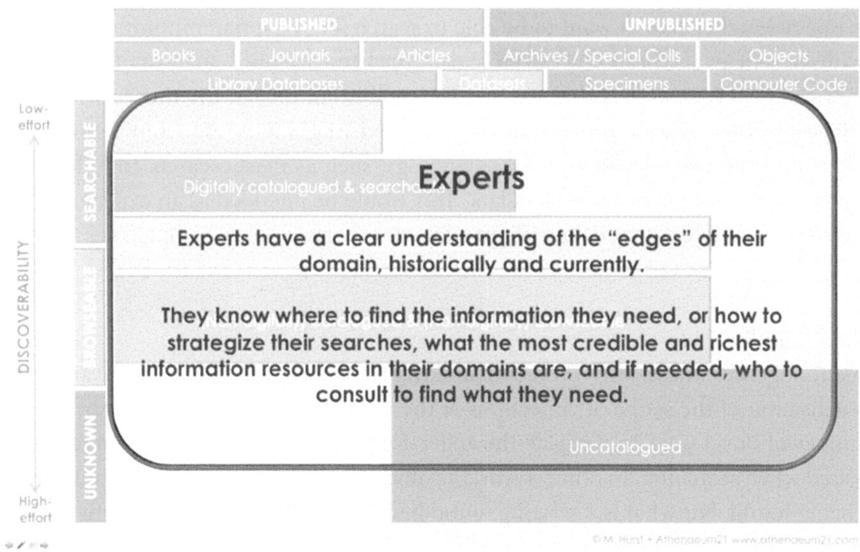

Figure 6.7 *Expert library searchers' discovery of library materials*

Visualise the scope of the collections at Oxford

It is possible to use collection-level metadata to provide an interactive diagram that represents the range of collections at Oxford. Interactive Venn diagrams (for example) could provide a high-level overview of what exists in what form, at a basic, or even binary, level; for example, works on paper vs objects; printed material vs manuscripts; visual vs textual; digitised vs not digitised; catalogued vs uncatalogued. Dates could be contextualised within ranges of centuries. Such an interface would provide researchers with an immediate visual guide to how many collections there are at Oxford and their relative sizes; which ones are searchable electronically; which are catalogued in print indices; and which are not yet catalogued. Overlaps in collection provenance, topic or format could provide starting-points for navigation. Other views of the data may be able to expose less well-known or unexpected parts of the collections, such as the fact that the Pitt Rivers Museum has a manuscript collection and that the Bodleian has art.

Cross-collection search

Beyond sending researchers to many different places to look for relevant collections, a cross-collection search would ideally allow discovery across the libraries, gardens and museums, while still allowing users to narrow their search to one or more collections (and allowing the individual collections to brand their own home pages). As one researcher said, 'I want to be able to search for "Egyptian mummies" and get results of articles and books by Egyptologists, the latest scientific analysis of mummies from chemistry, as well as find where the actual mummies in the museums are.' A cross-collection search project would take existing metadata from across the collections and use a Lucene-based technology, such as Elasticsearch, to index and expose the existing item-level metadata. This would be intended as an experiment to make the most of existing data without expecting 'perfection' or completeness.

Taken together

Taken together these two projects (looking at cross-collection search and the visualisation of the scope of collections at the University) would provide not only a number of novel ways to navigate the collections, but a clear sense of what is being missed when searching. In other words, the object would be to visualise not only what is being found, but what is *not* being found because of a lack of item-level metadata. As previously mentioned, a professor in the humanities observed, 'It's clear that reasonably diligent students are strikingly not sophisticated in their searching. Students search in one place, and if they don't find anything on the first try, they think it doesn't exist.' These projects are aimed squarely at addressing that problem.

The data gathered in this project suggests that the expected users of these potential tools would be both 'novice' and 'expert' researchers. For incoming students or faculty at all levels, the tools would provide an immediate visual representation of what is available to them and in what format. This would provide the opportunity for seasoned researchers and teachers to explore what they may not have known exists – even after working many years at Oxford.

Areas for investment, part 2: Map the landscape of people

A second series of recommendations are about connecting people. The research conducted indicates that searchers at all levels rely on people – librarians, colleagues, supervisors, mentors or experts in their field – to find resources when other search methods have failed[4] and also when they have not. Asking people, and knowing who to ask, seems to make the difference between finding what one needs to complete an assignment and becoming a skilled researcher or an expert in one's field. Therefore, these recommendations are intended to help with navigating the landscape of human expertise at Oxford.

Create a directory of expertise at Oxford

The current research collaboration tool project, which initially began as the Business Research and Innovation Initiative (BRII) project in the Bodleian in 2009, and then became the Blue Pages project, aims to provide a directory of research and expertise. Ideally, this project should be built with an open and flexible framework in order to identify the network of experts and research.

Visualise the network of experts and research

A graph of the professional networks at Oxford would facilitate discovery and navigation within and between fields. It should be noted, however, that a number of institutions have attempted this in the past, with varying degrees of success. Care should therefore be taken to learn lessons from others' successes and failures. There is some evidence from the user interviews that discipline-specific resources were more heavily used than general ones by those participating in our project. Academia.edu is heavily used by the interviewees, but mainly as a source of new publications and not necessarily as a means of locating relevant people.

Connect people, resources and events

Several interviewees cited Oxford lectures and talks as being of high value but difficult to find or know about. If there was a reliable source giving information about upcoming talks by division or subject area, it would be heavily used and well received. It would contribute to researchers' impact and promote knowledge exchange. Such a system could also be designed to highlight resources relevant to the topics being presented and to Oxford experts (faculty, research groups, etc.)

The expected users of this tool would all be researchers and university staff. All the interviewees for this project had sometimes asked people (colleagues, librarians, curators) for help in locating resources. Tools to assist with finding someone to ask for help were requested by a number of interviewees in the sciences, and it is likely they would be used for a number of different reasons by a wide variety of users inside and outside Oxford. As previously mentioned, a research chemist said during an interview, 'At Oxford, information is power, so nobody shares information online. That's why people are so important to finding information.'

Areas for investment, part 3: Support researchers' established practices

The question of whether it should be possible for end users to undertake research more quickly or more conveniently is a controversial topic. The benefits of serendipity and finding the unexpected are well documented in the literature and fully supported within this research. Many (across the disciplines) believe the process of research is as important as the outcome. Nonetheless, there are clear things that can be done to make the work of end users easier, particularly students on taught courses and experienced researchers looking for a particular citation. These investments will facilitate what is largely called 'known item' searching.

Get existing metadata out to the places where many researchers work

Exposing metadata for indexing by Google and Google Scholar would undoubtedly assist those who start their searches on the open web. Working with subject-specific repositories like arXiv and PubMed, and publishers like JSTOR, would further assist users in connecting with specific Oxford resources, particularly those who say, 'I always start with Google.'[5]

A number of interviewees were frustrated at finding an electronic resource and not being able to access it, though, so exposure of metadata on the open web should go hand in hand with *making improvements to authentication systems*. Some users expressed frustration at finding resources through Google and not being able to access them, and at the variation in search results when working from different locations. A DPhil student in medicine told us, 'I wish someone had told me when I started my degree why I should use the VPN [virtual private network] connection. I get totally different search results.' Most interviewees realised that they got different search results in Google and in some other databases from different locations, but didn't understand why. An improved authentication experience and education around the differences between authentication options would support users – particularly in their use of Google.

Facilitate citation chaining

Citation chaining is ubiquitous in all areas of research across all disciplines. A social sciences postgraduate researcher told us, 'I find one or two articles and then I just go from there.' Crossref and other individual tools and databases have gone some of the way towards making this easier, but citation chaining is still not simple. Searchers in all disciplines use cited references as authoritative points of departure for finding more resources on a topic.[6]

Expected users

In contrast (and complementary to) the tools for mapping landscapes, the work suggested in this section would facilitate precise 'known item' searching by anyone looking for a specific work or citation. Making metadata available to those who start their searches on the open web also facilitates engagement by those outside Oxford.

Laying the foundations

Undergirding all of these recommendations is a set of general principles, as a means of moving forward and for best practice.

Moving forward

Shared discovery necessitates shared infrastructure of systems, people and policy. This should be supported by *establishing an interdisciplinary research group* to take forward the recommendations. Participants should include the museums, libraries, and the relevant research centres and institutes from the University. The group would need an executive to ensure momentum and delivery.

Embedding this work in research will support *investment in the analytics and data infrastructure to support evidence-based decision making across the collections*. The findings from the project demonstrate that collection managers have very little data about how their tools and collections are being used, yet this data is essential for assessing the impact of current and future innovations. The University should also investigate the creation of a single 'Collections @ Oxford' portal that would provide access to:

- cross-collection search
- 'navigate the collections'
- a platform for digitised content throughout the University
- new scholarship @ Oxford, linking to the Oxford University Research Archive (ORA) and OUP (Oxford University Press).

A number of existing and proposed projects will help move the University towards executing the recommendations, including implementing:

- a researcher collaboration tool project
- the Oxford Linked Open Data (OXLOD) project
- a platform for digitised content throughout the University.

Best practice

Collaboration

Collaboration within the University and with partner institutions around the world is essential to providing innovative solutions for discovery. Collaborators should be sought with similar academic institutions but also in private industry and the 'bleeding edge' of information design.

Digital is not always faster, so it needs to add value

Digital is not always faster. A Bodleian archives researcher observed, 'I used the digitised card catalogue, which is just pictures of the cards. It was so imprecise. You had to flip through it. It took forever. I would have rather physically handled the cards, and it would have been faster. Digital is not always faster.' Physical card catalogues are faster than browsing images of cards online. There are many reasons for digitising collections, and digitisation projects should be based on a firm understanding of desired outcomes and the added benefit brought by the digital.

Complete collection metadata

Collections cannot be discovered using electronic search tools unless they have some sort of representative electronic description. High-quality description is key to discovery, and funding should be made available to improve metadata and prioritise the creation of good metadata in workflows around such tasks as ingest and digitisation.

Thorough and relevant training and education around discovery

Users who participated in museum or library inductions or specialised training services were unanimous in finding them valuable, in helping them find what they needed, and in improving their information skills.[7] Negative comments were largely about conflicts in scheduling and availability. One participant recommended that these sessions be rebranded in order to increase attendance: instead of describing them as being about 'how to find things in the collections' promote the idea that they were about 'how to become an expert in your field'. Partnering with the open access and online research repository teams to train researchers (for example in how to write an abstract that will make one's research findable) in the entire scholarship or research lifecycle may further enhance participation.

Benefits to the University of implementing the recommendations

In trying to encourage the University authorities to implement the recommendations set out above, the project team set out the potential benefits of doing so by referring to the University's strategic plan (University of Oxford, 2013).

Facilitate knowledge exchange

Benefit teaching, research and public engagement by facilitating knowledge exchange around collections. This is in direct support of the University's Priority 1, 'Global reach', and helps to realise the importance of public engagement (Point 10 of the University's strategic plan).

Support interdisciplinary research

Support interdisciplinary research by showing the overlaps in collections and expertise at Oxford. This supports the University's Priority 2, 'Networking, communication, and interdisciplinarity', in recognition of Point 13, 'Many of today's research questions cut across traditional subject boundaries.' This will further support the University's digital strategy Aim 1, to 'Enable new modes of research, especially across disciplines'.

Support students, staff and external researchers in not having to understand how the University is organised

Support students, staff and external researchers in not having to understand how the University is organised to find what they are looking for. This supports Commitment 6, 'To ensure that the unique richness of the collegiate University's academic environment is both retained and refreshed.' Providing an IT infrastructure that allows a more seamless experience across University resources will enable a better student experience, as outlined in the University strategic plan, Enabling Strategy 4, points 72 and 75.

Make the most of what we have by using existing metadata

Making efficient use of the resources at hand and partnering to fulfil some of the identified needs should free up resources for other areas. See Enabling Strategy 1.

Stimulate new research

The recommendation to stimulate new research is addressed in Commitment 1, 'To maintain originality, significance and rigour in research within a framework of the highest standards of infrastructure, training, and integrity.'

Aid the discovery of collections that are not yet digitally catalogued

This supports the University's strategic plan, Point 40: 'Strengthening Oxford's global and digital online presence, as signalled in our new priorities, will ensure students studying at Oxford have improved access to materials.'

Enable innovation across the collections by exposing metadata for use by machines as well as people

This supports Point 9, 'An enhanced online presence' and 'Promote new ways of generating, curating, and engaging with data (e.g. visualisation, data analytics, digital collections, augmented datasets, health)' from the digital strategy.

Allow the libraries and museums (and colleges) to provide mutual technical and policy support for one another

This supports Enabling Strategy 4, 'To invest in information technologies that enhance the capacity of Oxford's academic communities to collaborate with each other and with global partners, and that support the student experience.'

Enable new modes of research and collaboration

Enable new modes of research and collaboration by making prominent some of the overlaps in collections and expertise supports Point 16, 'Sharing resources, advanced facilities, and collections is a useful way of developing research interdisciplinarity through bringing individuals together who have common interests', and Point 15, 'Oxford has long pioneered multidisciplinary degrees. New thematic research collaborations will lead to new study opportunities for undergraduates and postgraduates.'

Combat the problem of end users believing that 'if it isn't digital, it doesn't exist' by demonstrating the gaps in digital metadata

This supports Point 20: 'The maintenance of a sustaining research environment is crucial to the University's research standing. We will enhance the infrastructure which supports research at the highest level, including libraries, laboratories, museums, and information systems.'

Conclusion

This set of recommendations is an evidence-based roadmap for increasing the effectiveness and rate of research and knowledge production at the University of Oxford, and beyond. Connecting with real users' current behaviours and explicit and implicit needs, and connecting them to the University's strategic plan and digital strategy, these recommendations provide an ambitious yet pragmatic path forward to enable researchers of all types to find what they are looking for, and to discover what perhaps they didn't know to look for. The University of Oxford's work in pursuing these recommendations commenced in 2017, and continues at the time of this publication.

Notes

1 To take one example, it is suspected that 20% of students and faculty at the University of Oxford use SOLO (Search Oxford Libraries Online), the Bodleian Library's primary discovery tool.

2 On the homepage of SOLO (http://solo.bodleian.ox.ac.uk/primo_library/libweb/action/search.do?) is a chat box, which allows users to interact in real-time chat format with a member of library staff. This is known as SOLO Live Help.

3 For a brief description of known-item searching and a short bibliography see Lee, Renear and Smith (2006). Recent discussions about known-item searching have largely been within the context of library discovery services and whether they are meeting the needs of known-item searching. See, for example, Tay (2014) and Singley (2014).

4 Researchers deem their search to have failed at different points depending on their experience and practice. According to their teachers, students often try one or two keyword searches and then give up. More experienced researchers have a more sophisticated understanding of when they should be finding resources but just aren't.

5 The University should also be aware of the tradeoffs of exposing its metadata to search engines in this fashion. The metadata will be used and re-used by commercial companies; this may be a fine tradeoff for achieving enhanced findability, but any agreement with commercial repositories should be entered into knowingly.

6 Much as with 'saving time', citation chaining is quite controversial. It can create an echo-chamber effect where the same few sources are cited over and over. This appears to be the case with both published materials and archival collections.

7 The researchers admit there is a likely bias in the data collected as the interview respondents were likely to be library and museum enthusiasts and/or supporters (by virtue of their willingness to be interviewed).

References

Lee, H. J., Renear, A. and Smith, L. C. (2006) Known-Item Search: variations on a concept, http://eprints.rclis.org/8748/1/Lee_Known-Item.pdf.

Madsen, C., Hurst, M., McLeish, S., Emsley, I., Stacey, R., Garibyan, M., Abdul-Rahman, A., Khan, S. and Chen, M. (2016) *Resource Discovery @ The University of Oxford 2015*, https://www.bodleian.ox.ac.uk/__data/assets/pdf_file/0009/197118/Oxford-Resource-Discovery-Final-Report.pdf.

Singley, E. (2014) Discovery Systems: testing known item searching, blog, Usable Libraries, 18 March, http://emilysingley.net/discovery-systems-testing-known-item-searching/.

Tay, A. (2014) Is Known Item Searching 'Really' an Issue for Web Scale Discovery?, blog, 23 March, http://musingsaboutlibrarianship.blogspot.com/2014/03/is-known-item-searching-really-issue.html.

University of Oxford (2013) Strategic Plan 2013–18, https://web.archive.org/web/20181126043816/http://www.ox.ac.uk/sites/files/oxford/field/field_document/Strategic%20Plan%202013-18.pdf.

7

'Why can't you just use Google?'

Simon McLeish

Introduction

The title of this chapter is a question I am sometimes asked as someone whose job title includes the words 'resource discovery'.

Google is the ubiquitous technological tool which comes to mind whenever discovery online is thought about. As mentioned in this book's introduction, it took root so rapidly that within a few months of its launch, the name was being used as a synonym for searching, usage which has continued to the present day. In libraries, modern web-scale discovery tools such as Ex Libris' Primo and its rivals are often discussed as being 'like Google' – there is a clear aim to promote these as similar to the web search behemoth.

In this chapter, 'Google' is used to refer to both the company and the web search tool, as is common usage. Clarification is given whenever it is not obvious which is meant.

In the chapter, we look at:

- what Google is and why it is so successful
- what is covered by Google – and what is not
- how Google approaches resources which are not web pages
- how Google has changed over the 20 years of its existence (and where it has not)
- whether there is any reason to use other web search engines and technologies
- the role of Google in the library sector and the future of Google.

What Google is and why it is so successful

Google was not the first discovery service for the internet. In the early days of the world wide web, there were sites listing other websites (notably one hosted at the European Organization for Nuclear Research, known as CERN, then later the Yahoo! Directory), and also search engines (Lycos and AltaVista being the best known), which sent out 'spiders' or 'web crawlers' (today probably better known as 'robots') to harvest the text within pages so it could be added to the search indexes. But when Google appeared, it revolutionised the business of finding web pages.

The reason for this is twofold. First, the simple and iconic design, which has changed very little over the two decades of Google's life, at least when compared with other major websites. The design is confident, distinctive, and yet simple and uncluttered. The search box takes centre stage, and everything suggests to the user that this is going to be an easy experience.

Even more important, especially in the early days, was the ranking algorithm, PageRank (Page et al., 1998). This used a revolutionary new idea. Instead of just using the contents of a web page to determine its relevance to a search (as the earlier algorithms used by the earlier search engines had done), PageRank used the property which marked out hypertext as different from other information stores: the links between pages. Pages were no longer considered as self-contained entities; they were part of the web of information; pages describe other pages, or link to pages which are similar; important and useful pages are linked to by many other pages.

These two features were enough to wipe out the competition effectively for a while, and bring a new word into being. It was not long, however, before people started 'gaming' the PageRank algorithm – making a page seem important by creating many other pages which link to it (this process, especially in the more benign version where there is just a legitimate desire to be found, is known as search engine optimisation). The history of Google's development of its search since then has been an arms race between those who wish to exploit the ranking algorithm for their own ends (advertisers and, more maliciously, spammers and tricksters) and the corporate survival of Google, which needs people to use and trust the search engine in order to maintain its position commercially. The oblivion to which Lycos and AltaVista were consigned when a better discovery service came along is a lesson which Google has taken very much to heart.

Incidentally, the use of the ranking algorithm is still misunderstood by many. The 2018 interview of Google's Sundar Pichai by the US Congress included a discussion why searching for 'idiot' returned a suggested search for 'Donald Trump'. The questioning assumed that millions of search queries entered in Google daily, producing search results over the billions of web pages on the internet, the most complex repository of information in history, are susceptible to detailed human intervention; for more detail see (Griffin, 2018).

What is covered by Google – and what is not

The immense achievement which is Google web search is not without limitations. The major limitation on Google's search is in what is accessible to its web crawlers. While there are tens of billions of publicly available web pages,[1] there are perhaps many more which are hidden away from access to the Google web crawlers. Estimates vary wildly, suggesting that Google may cover between 0.03% and 20% of the potential pages in existence, as quoted in Gamer (2015).

What reasons are there that items might be inaccessible in this way? There is talk about the 'dark web' or 'deep web' in the media, which is usually understood to mean those sites that operate outside the normal workings of the open web, hiding themselves away with tools to prevent discovery by law enforcers. While such sites would be known to their clients and/or victims, they would not want to appear in Google, nor would they be welcome there. They use technologies such as The Onion Router (Tor) to remain hidden, and this is likely to defeat search engine robots. Goodman (2015) provides an overview of the dark web for non-IT professionals.

But the vast amount of hidden material is not dominated by such illegalities. It is estimated that far more is hidden behind corporate firewalls and in private websites which are perfectly legitimate. Few organisations, other than the very smallest, would operate today without material on the internet accessible to employees or members but not to the general public. Wikis, document stores, e-mail attachments and so on are a huge but hidden collection of data sets. Generally, these are hidden from web search engines and unwanted visitors simply by the existence of internet protocol (IP) range limitations or password-protected website configuration.

Web administrators of individual websites can also choose for their website not to be crawled by search engine robots, or to limit what is crawled. Some possible reasons include:

- data not being in a form which would lend itself to indexing (e.g. many small, fragmented items)
- a high proportion of data being duplicated elsewhere or of limited usefulness (e.g. bibliographic records – do searchers in Google want to find a record for a copy of *Jane Eyre* in a library they are unable to use?)
- rapidly changing dynamic data
- the effect of the robots on sensitive or elderly infrastructure (they can take up lots of precious bandwidth, and may even knock vulnerable servers offline).

Two main methods of controlling the activity of robots are used: robots.txt and sitemap descriptions. The robots.txt file tells a robot whether it is allowed to access the site, and the sitemap provides information about which pages on a site can be indexed by a search engine.

None of these types of hidden material are of immediate relevance to the library world, though individual researchers can be interested in them, and sometimes there are archival interests and deliberate releases of data (for example, UK government material de-classified under the 30 year rule), or less legitimate whistle-blowing leaks (such as the material published by Wikileaks).

There is another category of hidden material, which is far more closely aligned to library interests. This consists of items that are partially available – where there is metadata but not full text, at least from the point of view of data freely accessible to a web search engine. This category includes both paper books which have not been digitised (but have been catalogued) and journal articles which are kept behind a paywall, most of which have freely searchable metadata, though some publishers do not make this available to shared metadata indexes. Initiatives aimed at making more of this data available include two Google projects, Google Books and Google Scholar, and, working in a rather different way, the open access movement. (There are less legitimate players as well, such as Sci-Hub.) The first two of these are discussed in the next section of this chapter; for the others, see Wikipedia (n.d.) for open access and Russell and Sanchez (2016) for Sci-Hub.

New discovery mechanisms are also being developed which take advantage of full text, such as Yewno and Semantic Scholar. It is perhaps worth mentioning that work on machine generation of abstracts for journal articles has exposed a perhaps surprising level of inaccuracy of the abstracts created by the authors (Pitkin et al, 1999).

How Google approaches resources which are not web pages

Images and video

Even today, the ranking algorithm relies heavily on the structure of the world wide web, and it is not surprising that at least some of the subsidiary searches which have developed use it for determining the relevance of items of other kinds than web pages (such as images and videos). Other searches have moved in different directions, searching metadata (Google Scholar) or large bodies of minimally linked text (Google Books). These are all kept away from the Google front page, even today, in order not to bring confusion to the simplicity of the design.

There are interesting features to image and video searching. The ultimate goal in both instances is to be able to search using an idea of the media content – what is portrayed in the image, or the spoken words in audio or video. To do so without laborious human description or transcription is currently beyond our technology, but clearly it is only a matter of time.

To give an idea of the difficulty, I was speaking in 2017 to a company working on machine transcription of a video of political speeches. Having trained their software to a fair level of accuracy on an archive of one speaker with a particular regional American accent, they had found that it was hopeless at understanding speeches by a speaker with a different, but still American, accent, something which most human beings have little difficulty with. Google image search, however, already offers a service where it is possible to upload an image and make a search for similar images. I tried this myself with a photo of a wooden pergola in my garden; although it was mis-identified as an iron gate, the images which were offered as 'similar' did indeed look quite like the pergola (and in fact were iron gates).

Enhancing searching of such resources through machine intelligence is clearly going to be an important part of resource discovery in the near future, so it is not at all surprising that Google as a company is working in this area.

Books

One part of Google's operations which is directly of interest to libraries is the Google Books project. Starting in 1996[2] with the initial idea of finding out how long it would take to digitise every book in the world, by 2004 the Google Print service was available with digitised works from many libraries, before being renamed Google Books a year later. By the end of 2015, 25 million books had been scanned (Heyman, 2015) – and Google had seen its way to the end of complex legal challenges to the project, which are summarised in Rosenberg (2017). Today, Google Book search is integrated into the family of search options seen at the top of the results page, and digitisation continues, though at a slower pace than before. Books are available to read, as long as they are definitely out of copyright, with previews for those which are potentially still protected. Even though many of the scanned books cannot be read, data from the whole corpus can be made available for computational analysis without specific texts being visible to researchers.

Journal articles and Google Scholar

Google Scholar was launched in 2004, to improve access to scholarly knowledge. In many of its features, it is very similar to web-scale search tools familiar to today's librarians (and on the design of which it had an obvious influence). Unlike those tools, however, it explicitly takes citations into account, using the full text of each document, where it was published, and who it was written by, as well as how often and how recently it has been cited in other scholarly literature[3] to rank search results. Citations are very important in Google Scholar, with prominent indications in the brief results of the number of citations. Citation chaining, as mentioned in Chapter 1, is an important discovery method for researchers, and the number of citations is frequently used as a method to determine which papers should be prioritised.

Google Scholar has been criticised by researchers over the years, and some of the criticisms are also a measure of the success of the service. Studies over the years, including the recent Rovira et al. (2017), have consistently shown that citation counts are a major part of the ranking algorithm. This has two effects: highly cited articles tend to appear at the top of the search results and are therefore read and cited more frequently, reinforcing their position at the expense of new or unorthodox publications; and articles which appear at the top of the search results tend to be cited for that reason, to lend credence to a paper, rather than because they are actually needed for the argument (the feeling is that readers, and especially journal editors and reviewers, expect to see these articles in the references, and so cite them just so they are there). Even partial knowledge of the ranking algorithm has led to a certain amount of search engine optimisation specifically targeted at Google Scholar, in exactly the same way as happens with the main Google web search. The same information has been used to create 'spam' on Google Scholar (Beel and Gipp, 2010), though the conclusion reached is that doing this is considerably more difficult than the equivalent for web pages, and provides less obvious returns for the spammer.

Google does not publish a list of journals or sources for Google Scholar, so it is on the surface unclear how comprehensive it is. In general, the advice given by and to researchers has been that to ensure comprehensive results it is necessary to supplement any Google Scholar search with subject database queries (or just use the latter). One recent study (Gehanno et al., 2013) suggests that this is no longer necessary in medical sciences, backing up Beckmann and Wehrden (2012), which compared Google Scholar and Web of Science for vegetation science searches. It is likely that the coverage will continue to improve. Google Scholar is quick to obtain new material and has older literature too: searches for 'moon' and 'Mannheim' returned results from 1700 (the cut-off date) through to 2019. While in coverage it now appears to match subject-themed databases and commercial cross-subject discovery tools such as Summon, it perhaps lacks some of the more advanced features which can be very useful for academic searching.

How Google has changed over the 20 years of its existence (and where it has not)

While Google web search has always had a strong leaning towards simplification of the search experience, when it started, it included a fair number of advanced search features which were readily accessible. The available features have changed over the years, and become less visible. Indeed, significant changes happened in the first few months of Google's existence.[4] By about 2000, a large number of features were available, through special operators in the search string rather than by using an advanced search form. Bloggers have catalogued changes to the operation of these operators since then, including Karen Blakeman[5] and Phil Bradley.[6] By 2001, the operators were encapsulated in an advanced search form, with prominent links from just to the right of the search box. Today, the form still exists, but is hidden away in the settings menu at the bottom right of the screen. Features are fewer, or deprecated, and it is clear from user behaviour studies that most users only look at the initial few results, very rarely clicking to see a second page – see for instance Barry and Lardner (2010) – and this behaviour with Google has also been referenced by subjects in user testing for the discovery service I run for the University of Oxford.

While the search page in Google has become even more stark and simple, the results page is now more complex. In order down the page, the searcher now sees links to other searches (news, images, video, etc.) and sometimes featured results from those searches, quick links to Wikipedia entries and relevant Twitter feeds (if they exist), and sponsored links (advertising), before the main results start with an estimate of the number of pages containing matching text. For prominent individuals, organisations and so on, the searcher also sees a knowledge panel as a right-hand column. For author Charles Dickens, this includes images, information about him and his family (from Wikipedia), quotes, books and related searches, followed by a sponsored item advertising the Charles Dickens Museum in London. The amount and type of information seen differs by the subject of the search, and how much information is in the sources which are curated into the panel – it roughly correlates to the reported number of matching pages. Clearly, the purpose of the knowledge panel is to give a quick overview of the subject; it is not designed to be scholarly, and information given there is not always entirely correct.

Another area in which Google has made many developments is personalising the results to the searcher. Work in this area started fairly soon after Google web search was launched, and today Google uses a lot of information about a user's activity on the internet (especially if they have and are logged into a Google account) to try to give relevant results. For instance, this makes it possible to search for 'the nearest restaurant to me' and get meaningful results. This analysis raises privacy concerns, and yet there are relatively few people who do not welcome the convenience over the potential issues.

Faceting, the availability of filters alongside the results, is familiar from many search tools, including popular shopping sites, where searchers can select price ranges, manufacturers, minimum ratings and so on. It is also present in many discovery interfaces in the library world, including web-scale search tools. However, it is completely absent from Google web search, and from other large-scale search engines, including Bing and Yahoo!.

The obvious difference between the two kinds of data sources is that the ones which provide facet filters are based on structured metadata, while the web search engines use the much less structured full text of web pages – even if web pages can contain metadata, only a small minority do so. Modern text analysis tools have the potential to be able to provide such data from unstructured sources, but doing so would have a cost in search processing time and further complicate an already quite busy results page, with what must seem to the managers of the search engines to be a dubious benefit (how many casual web searchers would actually use facets, if there?). Where Google does provide facets, in Google Scholar, they remain minimal and are very functional – the one thing that it might be nice to have in Google web search is the limit to recently updated items, and that is available in the advanced search if wanted; it is possible there to limit results to within 24 hours, a week, a month or a year.

Other web search engines and technologies – is there any point in using them?

In some ways, Google really doesn't have any rivals. According to Statcounter Global Stats,[7] Google's lowest market share among web search engines in 2018 was 90.14%, in May; this makes any of its competitors trivial in comparison. The nearest rival was Microsoft's Bing, with a 3.24 % peak, also in May – and that's despite having the advantage on Windows of being the default search engine. There is little reason to use another web search engine: the functionality and interface of the main rivals are quite close to Google. One reason to choose a search engine is convenience, which is clearly the reason Bing is second. In fact, checking the chart for different platforms, Google does best in mobile, where their Android operating system is dominant and on which their search engine is the default.

There are parts of the world in which Google is not dominant, however. China has the largest number of internet users of any country on earth,[8] and search there is dominated by Baidu, which has over 70% of the market. While the language barriers may have played a part in this, Google has also had issues with official censorship (Waddell, 2016) and a project to return to the market in 2018 has led to staff resignations and criticism (Poulson, 2018). However, even a quick look at Baidu shows that its design has been heavily influenced by Google's user experience, so in a way Google's web search user experience is dominant even in China.

Geography and culture are not the only factors which prompt people to use search engines other than Google. The search engine Everyclick (https://www.everyclick.com/), for example, allows its users to earn money for the charity of their choice whenever it is used, funded by advertising revenue. It also provides curated links to online retailers, which pre-select giving a percentage of the money spent to charity. Powered by the Russian search engine company Yandex, it is less accurate and less comprehensive than Google, though this is improving. Its users are clearly willing to put up with a little inconvenience in order to benefit their chosen good cause.

Another niche search engine is DuckDuckGo (https://duckduckgo.com/). This started out in 2008 as a specialist tool for IT specialists, and it recognises thousands of 'bangs' – short codes which can be prefixed by a '!' or bang, as the character is sometimes known, which make the search only return results of a particular type or from a specific site. For instance, the search '!w library' will take you directly to the Wikipedia page on the topic of libraries. In more recent years, however, bangs have been sidelined somewhat – they're no longer obvious on the home page, and users would either have to know the ones they want to use or go through a menu under settings to discover them. Instead, the main focus of DuckDuckGo is now on privacy. This is a tool which does not track searches, unlike the majority of commercial search engines, including Google.

Modern web-scale library search tools, and other widely used tools in the academic and library world such as publisher databases, are effectively also examples of niche search engines, if not web search engines. They pick up resources which are not available through web searching, as well as ones which are; they allow filtering to the resources which are available to a specific institution through their e-resource subscriptions; they make heavy use of metadata, and as a result have the ability to use facets for filtering and to have complex advanced search interfaces for those who wish to use them.

The role of Google in the library sector

Like it or not, the company Google is not going to go away, at least in the short to medium term. The existence of such a dominant force in the online world has a huge effect on the lives of many of the human beings alive today, including librarians and library users. Today's library users will come to the door – in real life or virtually – with much experience of searching the web, with strategies and expectations formed by their online life. In addition to these expectations, which are not always met in the more complex user experience of library discovery, there is direct pressure from Google Scholar, which is for many academics the first choice of discovery tool over those purchased for their use by their university or college. While web search and Google Scholar can be portrayed in this way as competitors with libraries, the Google Books project may seem to be a collaboration with libraries.

The project set out to change the world of the library. In the end, Google 'wasn't ultimately able to resolve a persistent cultural challenge: how to balance copyright and fair use and keep everybody – authors, publishers, scholars, librarians – satisfied' (Howard, 2017). Perhaps more significantly than any of the research based on the largely unreadable collection of scans, it is a project which has been an important part of the way that libraries have moved away from being limited to the physical collections inside their buildings; the project has perhaps changed perception in this more than other initiatives such as global journal article indexes.

Librarians in the early 21st century look at Google and are worried. This is partly because of the feeling that the commercial sector does not have the same priorities as the largely idealistic library sector, partly because there is a fear of the effect that Google's monopoly of discovery can have on the world, and partly because the services it offers are not just competing with services libraries would like to offer, but being chosen first by many library users. There are librarians who find it difficult to suggest Google products as solutions to users' needs, or to offer help to those who have difficulties finding what they want with Google other than guiding them instead to web-scale discovery tools or publisher databases which those users do not wish to use. With the risk this brings of alienating library users, this is not a viable response to Google. The question librarians need to ask themselves is, what is? It's worth reading Little (2011) for a constructive view on this topic.

At the same time, Google is facing a world which is increasingly making unwelcome demands on it. In recent years, it has faced political attacks, such as the one mentioned at the beginning of this chapter; it has had to cope with legal challenges, such as those imposed by the European Union's 'right to be forgotten' and privacy legislation restricting the company's use of personal data, and it is under financial pressure over issues such as tax payments to governments around the world. Rival search engines are constantly working to both mimic Google's success and develop new features which will bring them closer to overturning Google's dominance. (An instance of this is Microsoft Academic, a clear attempt to rival Google Scholar.) Google is no longer just a search provider; many projects including the Android operating system have diversified away from the original focus of the company – see for example Kennedy (2018) reporting on Google news from the I/O 2018 conference. Perhaps its most recent search-related innovation is Google Assistant, which gains a lot of its power from its ability to search the internet in order to respond to queries and commands.

More specifically, Google's plans for search in the near future were outlined at its event 'Future of Search' in September 2018, the 20th anniversary of the launch of the web search. As reported on the TechCrunch blog (Chapman, 2018), there is a focus on mobile devices, along with a still more intense analysis of the context of a search – considering previous queries from the same person, and allowing results to be saved in 'Collections', which are then included in the analysis of the most relevant results. The aim is clearly to save the time of the searcher, at the cost of them being less able to choose what they think are the most relevant results. While the presentations at the event covered only fairly short-term developments, it is clear that Google is moving towards serving up more and more personalised results across multiple devices. How well this will continue to serve the library and academic sectors is debatable.

Notes

1 Between 50 and 60 billion according to https://www.worldwidewebsize.com/, which estimates the size of web search engine indexes from the result counts for searches for words with known frequency from a large sample of web pages.
2 Dates taken from the project page at https://books.google.com/googlebooks/about/history.html.
3 From https://scholar.google.com/intl/en/scholar/about.html.
4 See the snapshots – over half a million of them at https://web.archive.org/web/19981202230410/http://www.google.com:80/.
5 www.rba.co.uk/wordpress/.
6 https://philbradley.typepad.com/phil_bradleys_weblog/google_specific/.
7 http://gs.statcounter.com/search-engine-market-share. All the statistics about search engine use in this chapter come from Statcounter Global Stats.
8 https://www.worldatlas.com/articles/the-20-countries-with-the-most-internet-users.html (updated 2018-02-14).

References

Barry, C. and Lardner, M. (2010) A Study of First Click Behaviour and User Interaction on the Google SERP. In 19th International Conference on Information Systems Development (ISD 2010), Prague, Czech Republic, August 25–27, 2010.

Beckmann, M. and Wehrden, H. (2012) Where You Search Is What You Get: Literature Mining: Google Scholar versus Web of Science using a dataset from a literature search in vegetation science, *Journal of Vegetation Science*, **23** (6), 1197–99.

Beel, J. and Gipp, B. (2010) Academic Search Engine Spam and Google Scholar's Resilience Against It, *Journal of Electronic Publishing*, **13** (3), (December 1), https://doi.org/10.3998/3336451.0013.305.

Chapman, G. (2018) Here's Everything Google Announced Today at its 'Future of Search' Event, *TechCrunch blog*, 24 September, http://social.techcrunch.com/2018/09/24/heres-everything-google-announced-today-at-its-future-of-search-event/.

Gamer, N. (2015) What Lies Beneath: the deep web and future crimes, blog, 29 April, https://blog.trendmicro.com/what-lies-beneath-the-deep-web-and-future-crimes/.

Gehanno, J.-F. et al. (2013) Is the Coverage of Google Scholar Enough to be Used Alone for Systematic Reviews?, *BMC Medical Informatics and Decision Making*, **13** (7), 9 January.

Goodman, M. (2015) *Future Crimes: everything is connected, everyone is vulnerable and what we can do about it*, Bantam Press.

Griffin, A. (2018) Google's Boss Just Explained Exactly How Search Results Work, *Independent*, 11 December, https://www.independent.co.uk/life-style/gadgets-and-tech/news/google-algorithm-explained-search-results-how-work-ceo-sundar-pichai-donald-trump-a8678466.html.

Heyman, S. (2015) Google Books: a complex and controversial experiment, *The New York Times*, 25 October, https://www.nytimes.com/2015/10/29/arts/international/google-books-a-complex-and-controversial-experiment.html.

Howard, J. (2017) What Happened to Google's Effort to Scan Millions of University Library Books?, *EdSurge News*, 10 August, https://www.edsurge.com/news/2017-08-10-what-happened-to-google-s-effort-to-scan-millions-of-university-library-books.

Kennedy, J. (2018) The AI Future Is Now: 5 ways Google wowed at I/O 2018, *Silicon Republic*, 9 May, https://www.siliconrepublic.com/machines/ai-google-io-2018.

Little, G. (2011) How I Learned to Stop Worrying and Love Google, *Journal of Academic Librarianship*, **37** (5), 1 September, 443–4.

Page, L., Brin, S., Motwani, R. and Winograd, T. (1998) The PageRank Citation Ranking: bringing order to the web, *World Wide Web Internet and Web Information Systems*, **54** (1999–66), 1–17.

Pitkin, R. M., Branagan, M. A. and Burmeister, L. F. (1999) Accuracy of Data in Abstracts of Published Research Articles, *JAMA*, 1999, **281** (12), 1110–1111, doi:10.1001/jama.281.12.1110.

Poulson, J. (2018) I Quit Google over its Censored Chinese Search Engine: the company needs to clarify its position on human rights, *The Intercept*, blog, 1 December, https://theintercept.com/2018/12/01/google-china-censorship-human-rights/.

Rosenberg, S. (2017) How Google Book Search Got Lost: backchannel, *Wired*, 11 April, https://www.wired.com/2017/04/how-google-book-search-got-lost/.

Rovira, C. et al. (2018) Las citas recibidas como principal factor de posicionamiento SEO en la ordenación de resultados de Google Scholar, *Received Citations as a Main SEO Factor of Google Scholar Results Ranking*, **27** (3), 559–69.

Sanchez, E. and Russell, C. (2016) Sci-Hub Unmasked: piracy, information policy, and your library, *College & Research Libraries News*, **77** (3) (March), 122–5, https://epublications.marquette.edu/cgi/viewcontent.cgi?article=1086&context=lib_fac.

Waddell, K. (2016) Why Google Quit China – and Why It's Heading Back, *The Atlantic*, 19 January, https://www.theatlantic.com/technology/archive/2016/01/why-google-quit-china-and-why-its-heading-back/424482/.

Wikipedia (n.d.) https://en.wikipedia.org/wiki/History_of_open_access (accessed 4 November 2019).

8

Exposing collections and resources effectively

Masha Garibyan and Simon McLeish

Introduction: why should you care?

It is almost traditional to quote Ranganathan's Laws in any discussion of libraries, but his summaries of the purpose of libraries remain incredibly relevant. He suggested that 'books are for use' (Ranganathan, 1931), but more generally, *collections* are for use, whatever their contents and whether they are held by libraries or museums. For collections to be useful, it is necessary to enable discovery of both the collections themselves and the contents within the collections. While the organisation of archives into collections is well understood by their curators and managers, it can be extremely opaque to potential users, because collections are frequently organised in ways which are connected to their acquisition (and may, therefore, be labelled with the name of the donor, rather than an informative title), and the researchers who have an interest in the collection generally do not care about acquisition but content and relevance to their work. This immediately suggests that libraries and museums need to do more than just list research collections by name.

While library holdings of books and journals (electronic or paper) are catalogued to well known standards, and can be found in library catalogues, discovery tools, publisher databases or Google Scholar without much difficulty, unique archival collections are harder to find, for a number of reasons:

- lack of cataloguing standards historically and a heterogeneous range of material types with different descriptive needs (a Neolithic stone axe in a museum does not have a title, for instance): library discovery services are generally designed for bibliographic materials, so can work poorly when item descriptions do not easily fit into relevant standards, such as MARC

- the need for individually crafted descriptions for unique items (as opposed to books and journals, where identical copies may already have been catalogued elsewhere to provide descriptions which can be copied, or where publishers also provide descriptive metadata)
- incomplete descriptions, both per item and on a collection level (major archival collections may have kilometres of uncatalogued boxes of material): there is no hope of finding uncatalogued material except by asking the right person, and incomplete records lessen the chance of discovery through most if not all tools
- limited knowledge of what is available where (even researchers in early 19th century history may not know which libraries in Europe hold letters written by combatants in the Napoleonic wars): there may not be comprehensive, accurate and accessible collection-level descriptions to guide searches
- limited exposure of the available descriptions in locations which are visible to researchers who may be interested in the collections.

The last of these is the topic of this chapter. The one place that anyone with a potential interest in a collection has access to is the open internet, and that is where they are likely to start finding information. Today's internet culture has basically two major types of resource which are used to find information: search engines and social media. While it is true that every library and museum in the world is making some effort to expose information about their collections, many find it difficult to do this in an effective way (and there is a discussion below about what effectiveness means). The aim of this chapter is to help curators to think about how they should expose information about their collections in a way that enables the researchers who have an interest in them to find them.

Finally, note that exposure online of discovery information is not always appropriate. Information may be exposed at the wrong level: searchers often do not really want to find results which lead back to metadata records rather than the actual object (allowing search engines to index the metadata records in a library discovery system is probably not a good idea). It can similarly be a problem wherever the items are not unique: if you are searching for Harry Potter or *The Lord of the Rings* online, you probably don't want to see the results page dominated by listings of records at all the libraries in the world which have copies of the books and/or films. So anyone developing a project to work out how to make descriptions findable online needs to consider not just how to do it but also whether it is appropriate for each collection.

Understanding search engines

Search engines are a natural way of finding information in an environment like the web, where metadata is sparse but where there is a significant amount of full-text data available. The hyperlink made it possible to gather this information from public websites around the world; software tools known as spiders or robots follow hyperlinks to find new information (exactly what information is gathered and stored depends on a number of factors, which can differ between the various search engine products). This is added to an index searchable from a simple form – there is little need for complex search design screens when there is no structured metadata – and matches obtained are ranked by a (usually secret) algorithm to display as search results.

Alongside Yahoo!, the earliest web search engine of note was Lycos, established in 1994 as a spin-off from a research project at Carnegie-Mellon University; it became one of the most popular websites in the world in a few years (CNN, 1999). Its success was based on storing more information from the web pages crawled (Mauldin, 1997), enabling more accurate results to be obtained than earlier rivals such as WebCrawler. A newcomer, AltaVista, was the next dominant search engine. This offered users the exciting new option of natural language querying, as well as being faster than the rivals (Seymour, Frantsvog and Kumar, 2011).

Google appeared on the scene in 1998, and almost immediately became the dominant web search engine, a position which it has retained until today, as can be seen clearly at Statcounter (n.d.) (as well as from the use of the word 'google' to mean 'search'). The rapidity of its rise to ubiquity was due to a number of factors, including ease of use and the perceived accuracy of its ranking algorithm, called PageRank (Page et al., 1999), whereby a Google search was able to present good, relevant pages at the very top of its search results. The revolutionary idea was to include ranking factors which are not solely determined by the content of the page itself: the number of links to a page, and the relevance of the pages that the links come from. The way that Google ranks pages in search results now includes other factors, such as the user's search history. This reliance on what could be termed 'social factors' is what differentiated Google from the purely page by page processing methods used by its competitors, and gave the search engine an immediate primacy, which it still enjoys today.

The importance of search engines was quickly realised by commercial sites, which depended on being found for revenue, and so was invented the concept of 'search engine optimisation', where content (and other factors) are used to improve the chances that a page will be given a higher ranking for particular search terms than other relevant pages. This has been a popular activity ever since, with ranking algorithms constantly changing to prevent the latest attempt to promote a site higher in the results than it perhaps deserves. This 'gaming' of the ranking algorithms and its links to dishonest commercialisation may have made academic institutions less keen than they might have been in the past to use search engine optimisation, but relying on search engines randomly picking up information about library and museum collections without any planning from the institutions is a sure way to ensure that their target audiences do not easily find the collections. In recent years, search engine optimisation often also includes social media campaigns as a way to get information out to the world directly, and to make the collection more attractive to search engines. Social media campaigns are covered in more detail later in this chapter (see 'Using engagement and social media to expose collections').

Search engines cannot (so far) understand the intention behind the data they index. Nor will they fill in gaps where data thought by the curator to be common knowledge is omitted. Data which is missing cannot be invented or inferred. Therefore the data exposed to a search engine must clearly carry the message which is most relevant to the intended users of the data, whether it is 'this is a good site to buy fashionable clothing', 'this site has up-to-date news stories written by professional journalists' or 'this is a description of an archive of medieval French coins, of interest to numismatists'.

As well as understanding the ways in which search engines work, it is also important when planning to expose data to understand something about how people use search engines.

First, there are two major modes for discovery: known item searching and general subject searching. Known item searching corresponds to a desire to recover a specific item of information or to locate a specific item. Examples include retrieval of a journal article based on a citation in another article, or a web search to find the opening hours of a local shop before a proposed visit. General subject searching corresponds to a desire to gain understanding of a field, where it does not matter which items are discovered, provided they follow a theme. Examples include looking for an introductory guide to the philosophy of Kant, or a general web search to find a new pair of jeans where you don't care which shop they come from, as long as they are right for you. Both types of search are used by academics interested in archives: they may want to find high resolution images of Mughal vases from India, such as www.nationalmuseumindia.gov.in/prodCollections.asp?pid=3&id=6&lk=dp6, or to discover what archives contain medieval manuscripts from Hungary. To plan exposing data, the curator needs to think about what kind of queries of both types they are expecting potential users of a collection to be using.

Second, the ways in which people search in academic life are heavily (and increasingly) influenced by the strategies used to find information from the major web search engines, especially Google. The default tool for all these kinds of searching is the web browser. Many studies have been made of the ways in which people use the web in general, and searching generally, as well as in the academic context (Connaway, Dickey and Radford, 2011; Falciani-White, 2012; Janyk, 2014; Law, 2010). These are some typical behaviours (observed from user testing carried out by the authors as well as the referenced articles) worth noting:

- There is no extensive planning before searching; the preference is to use a relatively crude search term and then check through the results.
- But even then, if an appropriate item is not seen in the first few results (and certainly in the first page), the searcher will either just give up, or will make changes to the search term and try again.
- There is virtually no use of advanced search functionality, such as Booleans (to the extent that over the years the mechanisms for using these features in major web search engines have become more inaccessible or have even been removed).
- Information not immediately visible is not sought; in particular, the information needed to decide whether to access a result from the list must be in the short summary information provided as part of the result list.

Planning to improve exposure

The factors described above suggest that careful planning is needed before a project to expose metadata for discovery is carried out effectively. It is key to be clear about what is intended to be achieved, how this should be done, and how to measure success.

To do this, a baseline needs to be set, to know how easy it is to find the collection before doing anything. Various numerical metrics can be used, including:

- hit counts
- enquiries by e-mail or other means
- search engine ranking for selected queries
- social media metrics (Facebook likes, mentions on Twitter, etc.).

Bear in mind that the metrics may be seasonal. Many academic resources have different usage patterns during term and vacation, for instance; and activities which lend themselves to social media campaigns (newsworthiness for reasons such as anniversaries of the death of the subject of an archive, for instance) can skew the figures. Therefore the metrics should be monitored over a considerable period, if possible.

From the baseline, targets can be set. Choosing targets which are a percentage improvement on the gathered metrics is a sensible way to do this.

The middle section of the project is the actual work to improve the ranking. Work here can include:

- metadata improvements
- work to improve the usability from search engines
- social media campaigns
- linking to events such as exhibitions to generate exposure.

The remainder of this chapter discusses these options in more detail.

The final stage of the project is (obviously) to return to the metrics and see whether the targets have been met.

It is possible to repeat this a number of times, using different methods and targets. Some of the ways to improve the standing of the collection will bear fruit more quickly than others, so together with being mindful of the seasonal variation in the metrics, continued analysis and monitoring over a considerable period is needed to truly measure the success of the project. The luxury of time to spend a year (say) after the main work of the project to gather and analyse new metric data is not likely to be available, but at least this factor needs to be remembered by those reading the analysis.

Optimisation in metadata creation

From the point of view of discovery of a collection, metadata is the key (Schaffner, 2015, 85). If the metadata is incomplete or inaccurate (e.g. out of date), then potential users of the collection will fail to find it. Many unique collections are catalogued at the collection level only, or to a sub-collection level, rather than item by item. Where items are not catalogued individually, the metadata available needs to be especially well honed.

To describe something for discovery, it is necessary to have a profile of the intended discoverer. In most cases, this can be extrapolated from profiles of current users of the item, which is clearly the place to start. However, poorly discoverable collections have a skewed access profile, and it is likely that only local researchers and established researchers may have found it. Discovery in these cases is likely to be direct communication from a fellow researcher. If a paper has been published about the collection from a particular speciality, then it is likely that the paper will be read by others with the same viewpoint and not by others who may be interested in the collection for different reasons. An archive of early 19th century British army letters may have been analysed by a military historian and, therefore, become familiar to readers of specialist journals in that field, while remaining obscure to specialists in the establishment of British rule in India, even though several letters have information on that subject as well. Metadata editors need to think of how the collection description would allow discovery by all the subject specialists who might reasonably have an interest in some of its contents. This is especially difficult for a wide ranging collection, and it may be sensible to consider creating sub-collection-level descriptions to cater for different subject areas.

Where discovery has effectively been by word of mouth, the knowledge of the existence and relevance of the collection is determined by membership of social networks. This means that early career researchers are likely to be disadvantaged, as they have not had time to build up networks through participation in electronic communications and more traditional methods, such as conference attendance. Such individuals could be a key target audience of a project to improve discoverability, so the project managers need to decide how they can best be made aware of the opportunity.

Once you know what is desired for a campaign, you need to know where you are at the moment. This is where digital and analogue analytics come in. This can answer all kinds of questions about the use of your collection, including:

- Who uses it now? Does the breakdown by geographical location match access to the online information about it?
- Have people been mentioning it on social media? How frequently, and in what contexts?
- What search engines and which search queries are pushing people towards the collection?
- For common search queries, where does the collection rank in the results?

There are many books, articles and guides covering metrics and their analysis (e.g. Chowcat and Kay, 2014; Hughes, 2011; Stuart, 2014), and these should be consulted to see how best to use appropriate measures for the collection in question.

By looking at the current usage data, it is possible to identify gaps in the current exposure. If, for instance, search engine queries are not ones you would expect, then that is something to address. The curators of a collection should know it well enough to be able to suggest what sort of searches should bring it to attention. However, it is possible to know the collection too well, and to forget about generic terms which apply to the collection as a whole. 'Everybody knows that the Jane Doe collection is of nineteenth century ephemera' is possibly true for its curators, but if the words 'nineteenth century ephemera' do not occur anywhere in the description, it will either not appear in search results for that query at all, or will confuse users who see a search result which does not appear to be relevant.

Exposing your metadata

There are a number of studies that show that many users prefer starting their search with a search engine, rather than their home library (e.g. Education for Change, 2012).

There is also evidence that, in comparison with a decade ago, library heads are increasingly willing to recognise and embrace this change (Wolf-Eisenberg, 2017).

An obvious but often overlooked way of increasing your collection's visibility to search engines is to look at the collection's URLs and how they are stored in metadata records (Foulonneau and Riley, 2008). URLs are one of the main entry points for search engines. The Jisc 'Guide to Making Your Collections Easier to Discover' gives a useful list of reasons to invest in well structured URLs (Chowcat and Kay, 2017, 2):

- Improve durability or persistence.
- Increase ease of bookmarking.
- Avoid the appearance of duplicate content to web search engines.
- Make them easier for humans to read.
- Make them easier for machines to read.

Well structured URLs are reasonably short, logical and do not contain information that may change frequently (Wikipedia URLs are a good example). Consider using persistent URLs (PURLs) for dynamic web content that may change over time (www.purlz.org).

It is a good idea to create a sitemap of the library website. This is effectively an XML file that lists all URLs of the website, alongside additional metadata about each URL (e.g. when it was last updated), so that search engines can find them easier. Sitemaps.org offers a standardised XML protocol that is supported by Google, Yahoo! and Microsoft. The NISO report on the future of library resource discovery (Breeding, 2015) highlights the importance of adhering to the Open Archives Initiative Protocol for Metadata Harvesting (OAI-PMH) to aid discovery by search engines. However, special attention needs to be paid to the interoperability of unique fields, which is a particular challenge for special collections (Han et al., 2009).

Schema.org is another initiative to provide standardised schemas for structured data mark-up of web pages. This is a community-driven initiative, supported by Google, Microsoft, Yahoo! and Yandex. There are several validator tools that can be used to check data mark-up, e.g. the Google Structured Data Testing Tool (https://search.google.com/structured-data/testing-tool).

Users expect results ranked by relevance (Schaffner, 2015), so it is useful to understand how search engines rank their search results. This information is not easily available for a variety of reasons (see the section 'Understanding search engines' above for more information). There is a good explanation of relevance rankings for librarians by Jonathan Rochkind (2011).

Using a robots.txt file will allow you to control which parts of your website will be indexed by search engines (see www.robotstxt.org for a guide to the file). It is a simple text file that will prevent search engines from indexing unwanted content from your website. This will be good for the site's search ranking. It is a good idea to include a link to the sitemap to make it even easier for search engines to index your site.

While search engines are paying less attention to meta tags (Foulonneau and Riley, 2008, 134), it is still important to ensure that the <title>, <description>, <keyword> and <ALT image> tags are in order.

There are many tools available that help measure how well your collections get discovered by search engines, including advice and validators developed by the search engines themselves, as well as other resources (including the 'Toolkit for the Impact of Digitised Scholarly Resources').[1]

Using engagement and social media to expose collections

As mentioned earlier in the section 'Understanding search engines', social media campaigns are increasingly being used alongside search engine optimisation to maximise a collection's impact. While not every library can afford to employ a dedicated member of staff with special responsibility for social media engagement, there are a number of distinctive benefits that can be drawn from this effort, for example:

- improving the collection's reputation
- enhancing teaching and research
- improving the discoverability of collections
- increasing users' awareness of the collections and possibly of the library itself
- reaching a wider audience (or reaching out to a targeted audience, depending on the nature of the campaign)
- engaging with users in new ways
- using the same tools that users use as part of their daily lives
- promoting events and new initiatives
- providing instant help to users.

The social media platforms being used by libraries vary but often include Twitter, Facebook, Pinterest, LinkedIn, Google +, Tumblr, YouTube and Instagram. The Folger Shakespeare Library in the USA has a comprehensive and varied list of ways to engage with its target audiences at www.folger.edu/connect-with-the-folger. Undoubtedly, getting the best out of any of these (or any other) tools requires considerable time and effort but the rewards can be very substantial. A good example is a timely and effective use of social media to tell the story of a dead mouse that tragically found its end in a 155-old mousetrap at the Museum of Rural Life in Reading, UK. Within a few days, the story that had started as a tweet and a local blog post became a true news sensation

(BBC News, 2016). It is no good relying on an event like that to start your social media campaign: having a strategic approach is key here.

Increasingly, libraries develop a formal social media strategy, often as part of their overall marketing and/or communication strategy. The social media strategies of the National Library of Australia (NLA, 2013) the Baltimore University's Langsdale Library (Langsdale Library, 2013) and Columbus Metropolitan Library (Dodd, 2017) are good examples of social media strategies at a major national library, an academic library and a public library service, respectively. Burclaff and Johnson (2014) provide another overview of the process of creating a social media policy, from the perspective of a small academic library.

Without a clear understanding of the overarching purpose and long term goals, social media engagement has every risk of doing nothing more than promoting library opening hours and an occasional event, as library staff are increasingly required to do more with less. The social media strategy should reflect the library's overall mission statement and strategic goals. It is also important to think about the social media tools that would best support those goals, depending on the nature of the collection (e.g. Pinterest for images) and the human resources and expertise available. It might be better to choose fewer platforms but do more with them rather than trying to use multiple tools to very little effect. The choice of tools has to be regularly re-evaluated. Some careful thought should also be given to how and when the success of the strategy should be measured.

So, what makes a successful social media campaign to expose library collections? Below are some tips that may help with the planning process:

- Be clear about what you are trying to achieve and how this reflects the library's overall social media strategy.
- Define your target audience and identify how it can be reached online (enlisting the help of current users of the collection can be a key way to do this).
- Evaluate how the social media campaign fits in with other library initiatives, as seen in the section above called 'Planning to improve exposure'.
- Decide on the best timing and duration of the campaign.
- Choose your tools.
- Concentrate on quality, not quantity (e.g. make the text interesting to your audience, use images – with permission, make good use of humour, proofread).
- Act naturally but bear in mind that the campaign represents your library and organisation as a whole, so be mindful about how and what you say.
- Always link back to the original source.
- Social media platforms provide some powerful metric tools (Green, 2012) to measure and evaluate the impact of the campaign (e.g. number of page hits, likes,

shares) but bear in mind that metrics can be seasonal and so should be monitored over a period of time.

Alasdair Inglis, the Managing Director of Grow, a small UK marketing company, gives a good summary of how best to write for the web, stating that online writing should be more like terrible journalism (Inglis, n.d.). There are some interesting examples of how social media can be used to enhance the impact of a library collection, such as:

- effective use of Tumblr by the University of Iowa special collections (https://uispeccoll.tumblr.com) and the Getty Museum, USA (http://thegetty.tumblr.com/archive)
- data visualisation by Brown University, USA (Williford, 2014)
- use of Pinterest to promote the special collections at the New York Public Library, USA (New York Public Library, n.d.)
- use of Flickr and Twitter by the British Library Mechanical Curator Project (http://labs.bl.uk/Mechanical+Curator+Collection and @MechCuratorBot on Twitter) to promote 17th to 19th century book illustrations
- use of blogging by the Getty Museum, USA (Budrovich, 2017).

Social media and its use are still evolving, so it is important for libraries to remain flexible and experimental (McCallum, 2015).

Conclusion

While enhancing the profile of a collection online may seem to be an ideal focus for a project with a defined timetable, it is in reality an ongoing, long term process. The web is a dynamic entity, and search engine rankings depend not only on changes to metadata for your collections, but also on every other piece of accessible online information on the same subject (not to mention the effects of the frequent changes search engines make to their ranking mechanisms). Changes to Wikipedia entries may be masked or altered by later editors. Social media posts are even more ephemeral, few being accessed beyond a small number of days after their original appearance. On the other hand, continued interest can be generated by users of the collection, as they publish blogs or academic articles based on the contents of the collection. Continued analysis of relevant metrics should become a part of business as usual for collection management, empowering continuous improvement to the profile of the collection in its target audience.

It is hard to over-emphasise the importance of the web profile of a collection in the modern academic world. No matter how hard curators work on it, no matter how high is the standard of the metadata as an example of the art of cataloguing – it is all a waste of time if potential users of the collection are not aware of its existence.

Note

1 https://www.jisc.ac.uk/guides/toolkit-for-the-impact-of-digitised-scholarly-resources.

References

BBC (2016) Mouse Gets Caught in 155-year-old Trap in Reading Museum, BBC News, 5 February, www.bbc.com/news/uk-england-berkshire-35503613.

Breeding, M. (2015) The Future of Library Resource Discovery: a white paper commissioned by the NISO Discovery to Delivery (D2D) Topic Committee, NISO, https://www.niso.org/publications/future-library-resource-discovery.

Budrovich, N. (2017) 100 Years Later: the Hope Collection from London to Los Angeles, blog, 25 July, http://blogs.getty.edu/iris/100-years-later-the-hope-collection-from-london-to-los-angeles.

Burclaff, N. and Johnson, C. (2014) Developing a Social Media Strategy: tweets, pins, and posts with a purpose, *College & Research Libraries News*, **75** (7), 366–9.

Chowcat, I. and Kay, D. (2017) Making Your Digital Collections Easier to Discover, Jisc guide, Sero Consulting, https://www.jisc.ac.uk/guides/making-your-digital-collections-easier-to-discover.

CNN (1999) Lycos Market Share in Doubt, *CNN Money*, 26 April, http://money.cnn.com/1999/04/26/technology/lycos/.

Connaway, L. S., Dickey, T. J. and Radford M. L. (2011) 'If it is Too Inconvenient, I'm not Going after it': convenience as a critical factor in information-seeking behaviors, *Library & Information Science Research*, **33** (3), 179–90, doi:10.1016/j.lisr.2010.12.002.

Dodd, G. (2017) How to Use Social Media to Attract More Users to the Library, Columbus Metropolitan Library, https://princh.com/how-to-use-social-media-to-attract-users-to-libraries-columbus-metropolitan-library-insights.

Education for Change (2012) Researchers of Tomorrow: the research behaviour of Generation Y doctoral students, Jisc, https://www.webarchive.org.uk/wayback/archive/20140614040703/www.jisc.ac.uk/publications/reports/2012/researchers-of-tomorrow.aspx#finding.

Falciani-White, N. (2012) Understanding Information Seeking Behavior of Faculty and Students: A review of the literature. In Popp, M. P. and Dallis, D. (eds) (2012) *Planning and Implementing Resource Discovery Tools in Academic Libraries*, 1–21, IGI Global/Information Science Reference, doi:10.4018/978-1-4666-1821-3.ch001.

Foulonneau, M. and Riley, J. (2008) *Metadata for Digital Resources: implementation, systems design and interoperability*, Chandos.

Green, D. (2012) Utilising Using Social Media to Promote Special Collections: what works and what doesn't, paper given at the 2012 IFLA Conference, Helsinki, https://www.ifla.org/past-wlic/2012/87-green-en.pdf.

Han, M. et al. (2009) Metadata for Special Collections in CONTENTdm: how to improve interoperability of unique fields through OAI-PMH, *Journal of Library Metadata*, **9** (3–4), https://doi.org/10.1080/19386380903405124.

Hughes, L. M. (ed.) (2011) *Evaluating and Measuring the Value, Use and Impact of Digital Collections*, Facet Publishing.

Inglis, A. (n.d.) Why Your Online Writing Needs to be More Like Terrible Journalism, Grow, https://wearegrow.com/why-your-online-writing-needs-to-be-more-like-terrible-journalism/.

Janyk, R. (2014) Augmenting Discovery Data and Analytics to Enhance Library Services, *Insights: The UKSG Journal*, **27** (3), 262–8, doi:10.1629/2048-7754.166.

Langsdale Library (2013) Langsdale Library Social Media Policy, University of Baltimore, http://langsdale.ubalt.edu/about-us/policies-procedures/uploads/documents/social-media-policy.pdf.

Law, D. (2010) Waiting for the Barbarians: seeking solutions or awaiting answers? In McKnight, S. (ed.), *Envisioning Future Academic Library Services: initiatives, ideas and challenges*, Facet Publishing.

McCallum, I. (2015) Use of Social Media by the Library: current practices and future opportunities, a white paper from Taylor & Francis, *Australian Library Journal*, **64** (2), https://www.tandfonline.com/doi/full/10.1080/00049670.2015.1040364.

Mauldin, M. I. (1997) Lycos: design choices in an Internet search service, *IEEE Expert*, doi:10.1109/64.577466.

New York Public Library (n.d.) The New York Library Digital Collections, https://digitalcollections.nypl.org/.

NLA (2013) Social Media Strategy 2013–2014, National Library of Australia, https://www.nla.gov.au/policy-and-planning/social-media-strategy-2013.

Page, L., Brin, S., Motwani, R. and Winograd, T. (1999) The PageRank Citation Ranking: bringing order to the web, Stanford InfoLab, http://ilpubs.stanford.edu:8090/422/.

Ranganathan, S. R. (1931) *The Five Laws of Library Science*, The Madras Library Association.

Rochkind, J. (2011) Information Retrieval and Relevance Ranking for Librarians, blog, https://bibwild.wordpress.com/2011/03/28/information-retrieval-and-relevance-ranking-for-librarians/.

Schaffner, J. (2015) *Making Archival and Special Collections More Accessible*, Online Computer Library Center, www.oclc.org/content/dam/research/publications/2015/oclcresearch-making-special-collections-accessible-2015-a4.pdf.

Seymour, T., Frantsvog, D. and Kumar, S. (2011) History of Search Engines, *International Journal of Management and Information Systems*, **15** (4).

Statcounter (n.d.) Top 5 Desktop, Mobile, Tablet & Console Search Enginees [sic] Mar 2015 – Mar 2016, http://gs.statcounter.com/#all-search_engine-ww-monthly-201503-201603.

Stuart, D. (2014) *Web Metrics for Library and Information Professionals*, Facet Publishing.

Williford, C. (2014) Un-hidden Collections: CLIR's seven-year experiment in exposing scholarly resources and the question of digitization, Council on Library and Information Resources, http://connect.clir.org/blogs/christa-williford/2014/04/22/un-hidden-collections.

Wolf-Eisenberg, Ch. (2017) Library Directors and Discovery: A changing perspective?, *ITHAKA S + R*, 3 May, www.sr.ithaka.org/blog/library-directors-and-discovery-a-changing-perspective/.

9

Open source discovery using Blacklight at the University of Hull

Chris Awre and Richard Green

Introduction

Discovery tools and interfaces have emerged through a number of routes over the past 20 years: protocols to search across multiple sources (e.g. Z39.50) have had tools developed around them; library management systems have provided tools to bring to the surface the content they manage; specific library collection indices have been built and had tools developed to provide access to them; and the richness of the web has been surfaced through web search engines. The origins of these discovery tools have frequently informed how they have then evolved and matured, and how they have been adapted to meet changing needs within libraries and beyond. Blacklight is no different: because of its origin as part of a digital humanities project, it has been clear from the start that discovery had to be adaptable if it was to work across multiple types of resource and associated metadata. This starting point has enabled Blacklight to evolve to meet specific needs but always hold at its centre the need to be flexible with regard to what is being accessed and support the discovery needs of end-users.

Blacklight (http://projectblacklight.org) itself is an open source Ruby on Rails engine that provides a discovery interface for an Apache Solr index (Blacklight Project, 2019a). Its flexibility comes from two places:

- Apache Solr (http://lucene.apache.org/solr/), built on the underlying Apache Lucene search engine, offers a very flexible way of indexing the content to be searched. It is widely used around the world for many search applications. While

Blacklight's default Solr configuration settings will often be sufficient, there is real additional value to be gained from exploiting how Solr indexes resources to meet specific needs.
- Blacklight itself can be used to provide discovery across heterogeneous resources. It exploits Solr's capability of being able to index different types of metadata together (acknowledging the need for a mapping between them), and can also display different resources via different templates, allowing for specific views onto resources.

The flexibility is also inherent in the separation of the discovery interface from the underlying data. Blacklight operates by taking a feed from a data source (e.g. a library catalogue) and presenting it in a way that is not constrained by the underlying data structure: the Solr indexing and configuration of views can apply its own structure, so that discovery can focus on user behaviour and needs instead of database tables.

Blacklight also offers:

- stable URLs for individual resource records (and search queries)
- Atom, RSS (Really Simple Syndication) and JSON (JavaScript Object Notation) feeds for search results, plus support for OpenSearch
- faceted searching (with facets defined by how the index is configured)
- ContextObjects in Spans (COinS) support[1]
- export options for RefWorks, EndNote, plus e-mail and SMS.

This flexibility and capability has been put into good effect across a number of different implementations (http://projectblacklight.org/#examples). The University of Hull has applied Blacklight in three separate scenarios:

- as the discovery interface for its Hydra (now Samvera) digital repository (http://hydra.hull.ac.uk)
- as the search interface for the library catalogue (http://libsearch.hull.ac.uk)
- as the search interface for a combined archives catalogue at the Hull History Centre (http://catalogue.hullhistorycentre.org.uk/).

More recent Blacklight developments have allowed extensions to be developed to support specific discovery of geo-referenced resources (GeoBlacklight; http://geoblacklight.org/) and provide virtual exhibitions (Spotlight; http://spotlight.projectblacklight.org/), by making it more modular. Its platform provides a stable base on which others can develop their own extensions as required; for example, Stanford University has explored the discovery and presentation of archival records through its ArcLight initiative (https://wiki.duraspace.org/display/samvera/ArcLight). It has also proved possible to plug in other search application progamming interfaces (APIs) into Blacklight's presentation capability, allowing article discovery tools and other sources to be surfaced alongside the default catalogue search.

In describing Blacklight, as has been the case here, there is an instinctive emphasis on the technology that is being used; but what makes Blacklight's search offering better than others? Just as important in the development of Blacklight has been the open source community that has come together over time to continue its evolution. Blacklight has been actively developed for over a decade, and at the time of writing has seen the release of seven major versions of the software. Too often in academic libraries solutions have been created for specific purposes, which unfortunately has led to a limited shelf-life. The fostering of community effort to sustain these solutions can pay longer-term dividends, as Blacklight has demonstrated.

This chapter will explore the origins of Blacklight and its development, but mainly look at how the system has been used, focusing on the the implementations at the University of Hull as context for how Blacklight can be applied to different discovery use cases. It will also look at the future application of Blacklight and where it might evolve next.

Brief history of Blacklight

Blacklight has its origins at the University of Virginia. In 2006 the Library had reached a point of frustration with existing library catalogue interfaces, had taken on board a set of structured criticisms of such interfaces (Schneider, 2006a–c), and was looking at potential alternatives. In doing so the Library became aware of a digital humanities initiative at the University, Nineteenth-century Scholarship Online (NINES; www.nines.org/) and a Web 2.0 discovery interface staff were developing called Collex (www.nines.org/about/software/collex/). Following discussion with the team behind this a collaborative open source project was established to see whether the specific discovery solution created for the digital humanities resources could be adapted to more generic use for a library catalogue. This was explained in a book chapter written by the project partners at the time:

> Digital tools . . . originating in scholarly projects (that is, from the community the Library has typically served) can feed back into our most fundamental cataloging and retrieval systems in illuminating ways . . . the 2.0 versions of digital humanities and library science can (and should!) operate hand-in-hand in sharing novel approaches to issues of access and interpretation.
>
> Nowviskie, Sadler and Hatcher, 2007

Blacklight was the result of this project, and was pushed into production at the University of Virginia as its library catalogue interface in 2008. As the Library saw it, these were the key advantages and principles of this development (Sadler, 2009):

- *Relevance ranking.* Library catalogues had focused largely on exact searches and browse views of the contents of a library. But search on the internet, at sites such as Google and Amazon, was increasingly using relevance ranking to facilitate discovery of items. Blacklight and Solr applied this relevance approach to library catalogue collections to foster serendipitous access.
- *Faceted browsing.* Solr provides faceted browsing natively, and hence Blacklight has sought to take advantage of the ability to create and present different facets according to how a library wishes to index its catalogue records.
- *The ability to include siloed materials.* Through a range of projects the University of Virginia had created a wide range of standalone digital collections, described using Text Encoding Initiative, Encoded Archival Description (EAD) or specific metadata schemas. Blacklight was designed to allow metadata from them to be brought together and discovered through a single catalogue discovery interface and avoid the need to identify and use multiple individual discovery interfaces.
- *Customisable interfaces.* Standard views of a library catalogue focus on a standard set of fields to display. Blacklight development focused on how different material types and collections might be better served through tailored views so that specific metadata was appropriately presented.

In the years following the launch of Blacklight there was a flurry of explorations of so-called 'next generation discovery interfaces', and a number of other institutions adopted Blacklight for different purposes. Three examples highlight how Blacklight has helped to meet different library discovery needs:

- Indiana University carried out a review of open source discovery systems in 2011, resulting in the adoption of Blacklight to power searching on the library catalogue (https://iucat.iu.edu/) for two key reasons (Moore and Greene, 2013): the existence of a robust development community, which prioritises collaboration on a shared code base; and a scalable, flexible architecture that accommodates the multi-campus or multi-library structure of the university and has the potential to accommodate future needs.
- The Boston-based public service broadcaster WGBH has used Blacklight's flexibility for its online media catalogue (http://openvault.wgbh.org/) (Beer, 2010).

- The College of Charleston has used Blacklight as part of a digital content management and discovery system (http://lcdl.library.cofc.edu/) using Fedora to replace ContentDM (Gilbert and Mobley, 2013).

Recognising adaptations to meet evolving user preferences and developments in technology the original principles remain core to how Blacklight works and continues to be developed. They also help to place the library-specific discovery interface alongside general web discovery as an equivalent and feature-rich search experience.

Blacklight community development

The University of Virginia had been actively involved in the original development of the Fedora digital repository system (http://lcdl.library.cofc.edu/), in partnership with Cornell University, and fostered a community around its ongoing development based on the advantages it brought and the benefit of working together to meet a broad spread of needs. The success of this model and ethos for Fedora informed the initial Blacklight development, with Virginia releasing the Blacklight code under the Apache 2.0 licence (https://github.com/projectblacklight/blacklight). Outreach efforts brought on board a number of other institutions whose staff shared the same frustrations as Virginia over library catalogue discovery interfaces: initial adopters included Stanford, Johns Hopkins and WGBH, all of which made major contributions to ongoing versions. Blacklight's institutional home has now moved to Stanford and the system remains in active development towards a release of version 7.0 in 2018: contribution has come from a wide number of sources over time as institutional adoption and time commitments have allowed. See Open Hub (n.d.) for a review of development effort over time. There is a Google group discussion list, 'blacklight development', and Slack and Internet Relay Chat channels show what is currently ongoing and, if so inclined, can be used to get involved. Blacklight communication channels are at Blacklight Project (2019b).

Using an open source approach has benefited both Blacklight and other library initiatives. As Sadler (2009) explains in her article in *Library Hi Tech*, development on tools to index MARC records in Solr was carried out collaboratively with the VuFind team because of the mutual need for these, and the work on associated code libraries was released independently of Blacklight itself for others to use in related applications.

Although US based in its origins, there has recently been more activity of the Blacklight community in Europe as well. The University of Hull's adoption and use is described later in this chapter in the section 'Blacklight at Hull'. Broader interest was generated in 2016 through the adoption of Blacklight by Europeana (https://www.europeana.eu/portal/en), the European cultural portal providing access to digital collections from national libraries and associated collections. This adoption was based on the benefits that the Blacklight interface itself brought, as Europeana did not use Solr as an underlying index. The adoption was carried out in liaison with the Blacklight development community and resulted in an additional component, Europeana-Blacklight, which facilitates a link between Blacklight and the Europeana representational state transfer (REST) API. Following up on this European connection the 2017 Blacklight summit (http://projectblacklight.org/european-summit-2017), now becoming an annual meeting, was held at the Royal Library of Denmark in Copenhagen (a long-standing Blacklight adopter).

Blacklight and Hydra/Samvera

As Blacklight was going into production at the University of Virginia in 2008 the Hydra Project (now Samvera; https://samvera.org) was starting off, also at Virginia. Hydra was established as a collaboration between the University of Virginia, the University of Hull, Stanford University and Fedora Commons (now DuraSpace; www.duraspace.org/), and working with MediaShelf LLC, to identify and implement re-purposable repository solutions based on Fedora. Based on the principle of designing a set of individual component services that could be combined as required to create individual repository solutions, Hydra sought to provide workflow and interface services for use over a Fedora repository and enable practical exploitation of the flexibility that this system offers. The development of Hydra or Samvera has been documented elsewhere (Awre and Green, 2017), but key in this context was the decision very early on to develop the Hydra components using Ruby on Rails. The architecture for how Hydra or Samvera works is shown in Figure 9.1.

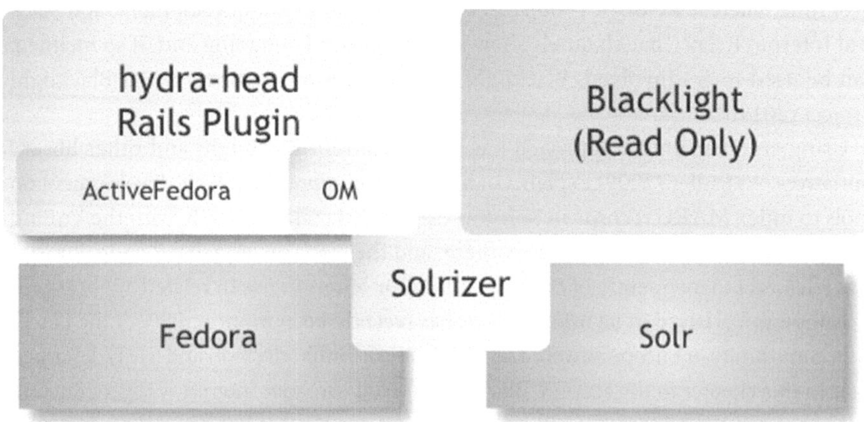

Figure 9.1 *Hydra or Samvera architecture*

The need for the management workflows was central to facilitating use of Fedora through configurable pathways. Once managed, the content needs to be made accessible. With the experience at the University of Virginia of developing Blacklight, and the aligned use of Ruby on Rails for its own development, the Hydra Project decided to adopt Blacklight as its primary discovery interface. This is not to say that other discovery interfaces cannot be used: Hydra or Samvera is designed to be modular and flexible as to the components that can be slotted into the architecture. But in taking forward the project's own implementation Blacklight met the technology requirements and also offered the benefits of being able to present access to the different types of digital collections that repositories are called to hold and manage. In many ways, adoption by Hydra or Samvera was a continuation of the original Collex software aims in serving up its own digital humanities collections.

The relationship between Hydra or Samvera and Blacklight has been a symbiotic one over the years, with what is now Samvera benefitting from an established and self-standing discovery component that can be bundled in with other repository solution parts, and Blacklight benefitting from a growing user base for a digital content management system to complement the library catalogue implementations that were its original use case. Over time, the Hydra or Samvera community has undertaken a number of reviews to determine whether Blacklight remains their preferred discovery solution, and to what extent they can continue to use it as a self-standing component without adaptation to best serve Hydra or Samvera's needs. But Blacklight remains a core component because of what it provides to digital content collection discovery. There is close alignment between the two software development communities, which ensures that any developments within each one that may impact on the other can be communicated to inform discussion on the best way forward for mutual advantage. The ability to create Blacklight extensions has been influenced by this, allowing additional functionality to be added without compromising core functionality. As Hydra now evolves to Samvera, Blacklight continues to provide the discovery into the rich variety of digital collections held within Hydra or Samvera repository solutions. See DuraSpace (2019) for a list of Samvera partners and implementations.

Blacklight at Hull

The adoption of Blacklight at the University of Hull has taken three paths, each of which has highlighted the flexibility that Blacklight can offer in presenting a discovery service:

- a digital repository interface
- a library catalogue interface
- an archives catalogue interface.

The University first became aware of Blacklight through its involvement in the Hydra Project in 2008 and while the primary use case for Blacklight was then for library catalogues it was in the context of providing a discovery interface to a digital repository that local activity first took place. The University of Hull had at that time already been involved in other open source communities, which had led to local implementation of the uPortal institutional portal solution (https://www.apereo.org/projects/uportal) and the Sakai virtual learning environment (https://www.apereo.org/projects/sakai-project). The Library had also been working with Fedora since 2005 as part of the Jisc-funded RepoMMan project and its successor, the REMAP project (Green and Awre, 2009). It was this ongoing exploration of open source solutions in the repository sphere, and positive experience of using open source solutions in practice, that led to the University's involvement in the formation of the Hydra Project.

The digital repository interface

While the development of Blacklight focused on providing a discovery interface to library catalogues and MARC records, it was the flexibility it offered in its use of Solr and internal configuration of views that suggested its value to the Hydra Project, as previously mentioned. In making a commitment as a project to using Blacklight as the discovery interface for the default implementation of Hydra the University became committed to using Blacklight in its own development of an ongoing repository solution. An initial implementation was developed during 2011 (Figure 9.2).

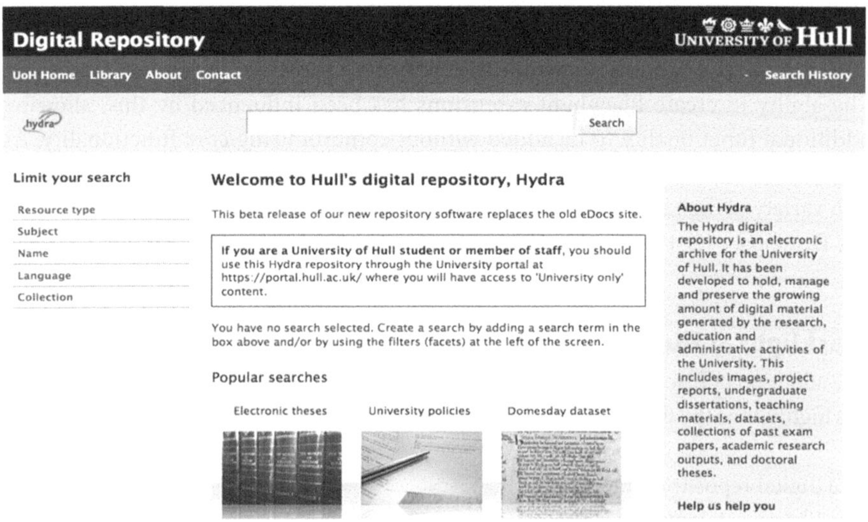

Figure 9.2 *Screenshot of initial Hydra at Hull interface*

Repositories based on Fedora, and by association those built using Hydra or Samvera components, are used for a wide variety of different digital materials. Many institutional repositories focus on research outputs, primarily journal articles, because of the association with the open access movement. Hydra or Samvera solutions are intended to help facilitate the management of many different types of digital content, and hence a metadata schema that was flexible enough to be applied to different use cases was needed. Instead of using MARC, repository objects were thus described using Metadata Object Description Schema (MODS; www.loc.gov/standards/mods), which was considered to have greater richness than Dublin Core and offered greater scope for future expansion of use. Other implementations of Hydra or Samvera use other metadata schemas, and Blacklight has been used to index these using the flexibility of the Solr index behind it.

The original implementation of Blacklight had a flexible interface insofar as it presented a default HTML template that could be edited and adapted to meet local needs, with the level of configuration dependent on the amount of work and maintenance a local site wished to carry out. In 2013 initial work at the University of Hull led to the Blacklight developers adopting the Bootstrap HTML/CSS/JavaScript framework (https://getbootstrap.com/) to build more adaptable and responsive interfaces for Blacklight. During 2013 Library staff had also decided to overhaul the local implementation of Hydra to make use of rapidly developing versions of the software and further develop local skills in maintaining Hydra. Building on the local Bootstrap work, and taking on board Blacklight's new capability when it was released, a fully responsive new version of the Hydra at Hull digital repository was released in January 2014 (Figure 9.3).

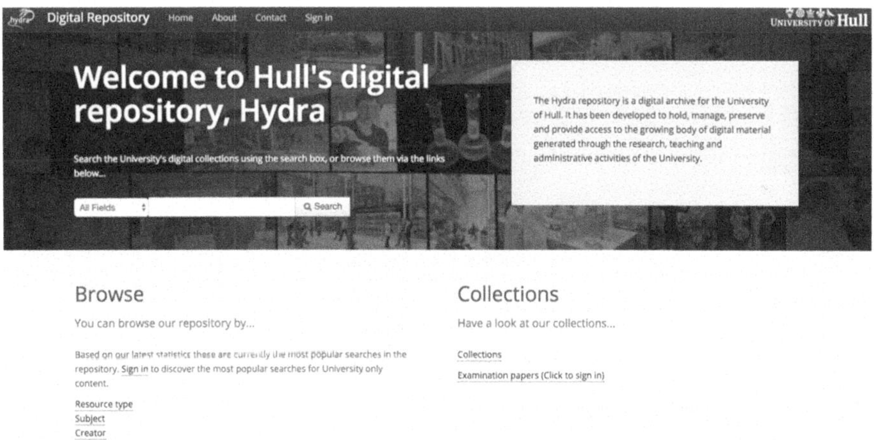

Figure 9.3 *Screenshot of current Hydra at Hull home page*

Within Hull's repository, different views have been configured for different types of material, to present these materials to best advantage. For example, Figure 9.4 shows the display of a thesis, while Figure 9.5 shows the display of a geo-referenced dataset.

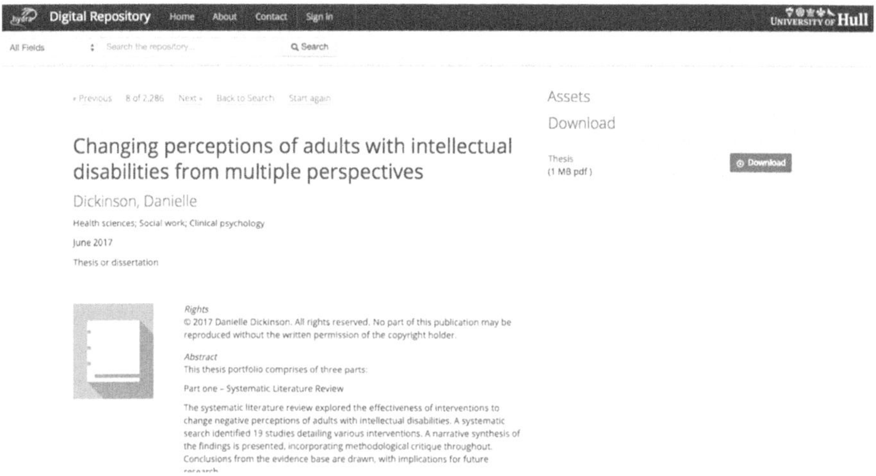

Figure 9.4 *Screenshot of thesis record display on Hydra*

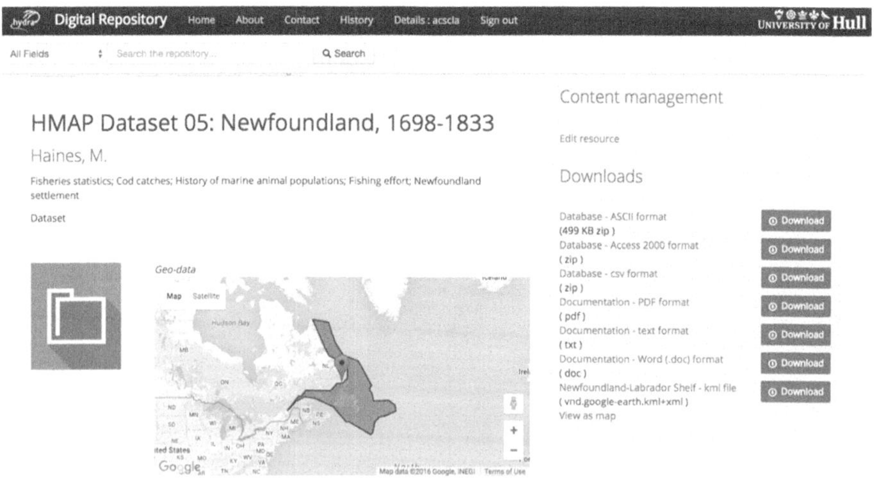

Figure 9.5 *Screenshot of dataset record display on Hydra*

The library catalogue interface

The Library uses the library management system Innovative (Millennium in 2008, Sierra since 2016) and in 2008 the Library had been re-designing its web OPAC interface using a new set of system-provided configuration options. This introduced greater flexibility in how the discovery options were made available, though the web OPAC interface was still very much just that, an interface onto the catalogue with access points built around how the catalogue was structured. There was much discussion in the literature at the time about next generation library catalogues (e.g. Singer, 2008) and the discussion about Blacklight in the context of Hydra or Samvera offered an alternative, which focused on discovery that aligned library discovery interfaces to more widely used discovery interfaces on the web. The cost of such next generation interfaces was not inconsiderable: Blacklight offered an open source option that required internal resource commitment to make it work, but gave us a solution over which we had complete control to address our discovery service needs. Because the University had committed to using Blacklight for Hydra or Samvera it made sense to explore the use of Blacklight as a library catalogue interface as well.

In parallel with ongoing Hydra activity, a trial implementation of Blacklight over the Library's Millennium catalogue was initiated in 2010 through a small Jisc-funded project, Blacklight at Hull (https://hydra.hull.ac.uk/resources/hull:3451). This created a proof of concept implementation of Blacklight using manually extracted catalogue records from Millennium. Usability testing was carried out on Blacklight implementations at Virginia and Stanford to inform further development and the project highlighted that Blacklight could be a success if implemented more widely. The focus of development attention following this then moved to Hydra@Hull and it was in 2012 when a longer-term pilot implementation was made available in parallel with our existing web OPAC for students and staff to provide feedback on. This ran for the 2012/13 academic session, during which the process of automating the extraction of records from Millennium was established, based on an overnight feed of additions, changes and deletions. The work concluded with a decision to move to using Blacklight as the primary catalogue interface from September 2013 (Figure 9.6 on the next page).

The timing of this development made it possible also to exploit the Bootstrap responsive interface, allowing for delivery of the catalogue to tablets and mobile devices (via its own shortcut app icon).

The archives catalogue interface

In the light of the launch of the new catalogue and repository interfaces in 2013/14, attention turned to how we may be able to use Blacklight for other discovery needs. The University Archives operate as part of a collaborative service with Hull City Archives through the Hull History Centre (http://hullhistorycentre.org.uk/). Both archives have their own catalogues, and these were complemented by entries in the public library catalogue for the Local Studies Library. There was an interest in

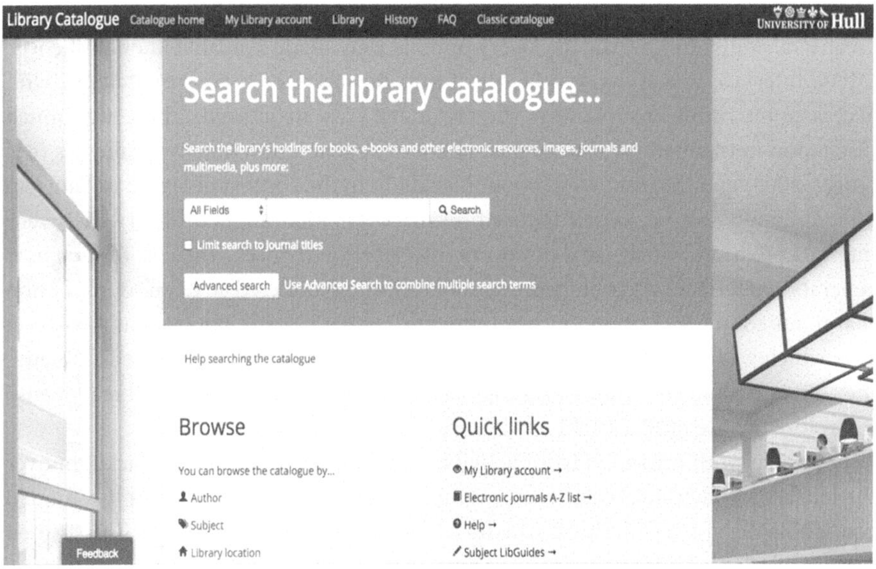

Figure 9.6 *Screenshot of library catalogue front page*

exploring how Blacklight could be used to help bring all these records together and make them available through a single interface. While the repository and library catalogue developments had focused on indexing a single source of metadata (MODS and MARC, respectively), this development required a combined index of EAD archival records (https://www.loc.gov/ead/) and MARC library catalogue records, to allow for discovery across these. The Library worked with the consultancy Data Curation Experts (https://curationexperts.com/) on this project during 2014, and the catalogue went live in the autumn of that year (Figure 9.7 opposite).

Updates are made to the host archive and public library catalogues and periodic extracts are manually taken for addition to the Blacklight index. The initial discovery interface enables access to both EAD and MARC records, but the facets expand, based on the origin, once a record of a particular type is chosen to allow for further depth of inquiry. On the archival side this encompasses navigation through the EAD finding aid from collection through to individual item.

Blacklight extensibility

While maintaining the core functionality of Blacklight, the community has occasionally looked at how Blacklight might be extended to serve additional purposes. In recent years a number of initiatives have been undertaken.

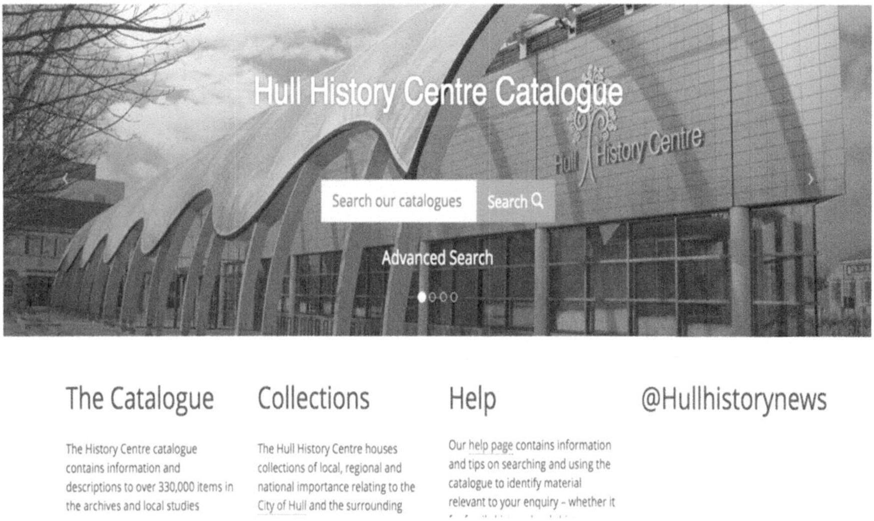

Figure 9.7 *Screenshot of Hull History Centre catalogue front page*

GeoBlacklight

GeoBlacklight is an extension to Blacklight to facilitate access to geo-referenced records, and enables discovery via a map interface as well as through more traditional routes such as search or faceted browse. Interfaces such as GeoBlacklight contribute to the exploration of how to make geo-referenced resources available via repository solutions: events such as Geo4LibCamp (https://geo4libcamp2018.sched.com/) are fostering collaborative partnership on such solutions, and represent an extension of the Blacklight community as much as an extension of the software itself. Figure 9.8 (on the next page) shows the VecNet portal (https://dl.vecnet.org/) of resources related to the eradication of malaria.

Spotlight

Providing discovery interfaces to catalogues and repositories enables discovery of the items held within these collections but do not necessarily provide a contextual guide to the collections, with users of the discovery interfaces often having to link up the items of interest for the specific research or learning being undertaken. The Spotlight extension to Blacklight demonstrates how a collection can have additional curated and contextual content added to it in order to provide added value. Online exhibitions are the basis of other technologies as well (e.g. the Omeka system; https://omeka.org/), but the advantage of Spotlight is to link this web publishing functionality with the

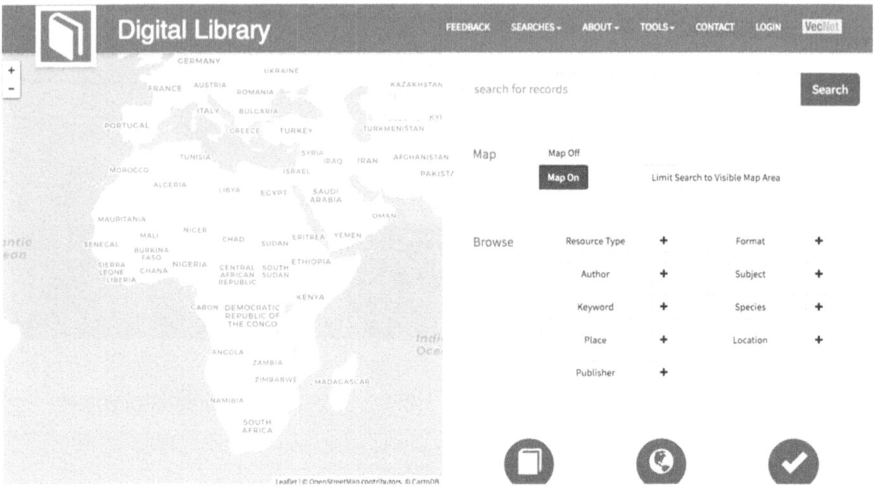

Figure 9.8 *VecNet portal of resources related to the eradication of malaria*

curated collection that sits behind it in Blacklight (or Hydra or Samvera). Figure 9.9 shows the Victoria to Vimy exhibition (https://exhibits.library.uvic.ca/spotlight/wwi) at the University of Victoria, British Columbia, Canada.

Figure 9.9 *Victoria to Vimy exhibition at the University of Victoria, British Columbia, Canada*

ArcLight

The development undertaken by the University of Hull in developing its archives catalogue was one example of there being widespread interest in how to best index and present archival records and support navigation through them. The ArcLight project at Stanford University has sought to bring interested parties together to explore this further. It is an ongoing piece of work, but again has benefited from multiple partners working together to best advantage.

Article searching

While Blacklight implementations have focused on discovery within an index built using the underlying Solr engine, Blacklight can also surface search results from other sources and exposed through an appropriate API. In developing next generation discovery interfaces further, a number of US academic libraries have explored a 'bento box' approach to providing multiple search results alongside each other, based on a single search or set of search terms. For a discussion of bento boxes, see Singley (2016). A bento box interface sends the search query to multiple services and displays them in a number of boxes in the web browser, named after a way of serving Japanese food. The Columbia Libraries Information Online (CLIO) service (CLIO; https://clio.columbia.edu/) at Columbia University in New York encompasses these two type of search, and enables access to the local institutional repository of research publications, dissertations, the Library website and any relevant geo-referenced data (Figure 9.10).

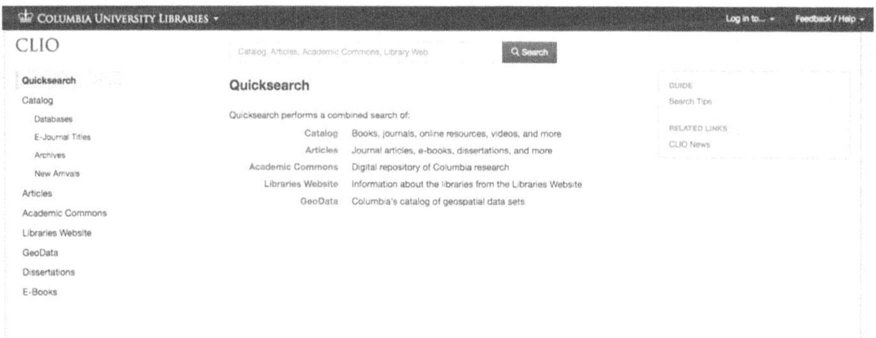

Figure 9.10 *Screenshot of CLIO bento box results page*

Future development and conclusion

The development of Blacklight since 2008 has resulted in a university-led open source collaboration building and implementing a general purpose discovery interface that can be used to surface any form of structured metadata in a way that provides access to library and related collections akin to generic experiences of search and find on the internet. To that end, Blacklight has successfully contributed to breaking the mould of how such collections are presented for discovery compared with prior library-specific approaches. As with all such developments there are always improvements that can be made, and Blacklight continues to take these on board and implement them. One of the key aspects of maintaining an open source solution is to ensure that the individual components that it uses are kept up to date. In this way Blacklight benefits from the work of related software developments as well as enhancements provided by the development community itself. For example, Blacklight Release 7 brings the Bootstrap 4 design library (Otto et al., 2018) into use and adds support for the latest version of Solr, as well as adding JSON-API support to enable richer manipulation of the search results and how they are presented.

Blacklight has also benefited from being adopted by other services to provide a discovery interface onto different underlying indexes. An initial focus on library catalogues provided a wellspring of interest based on the primary discovery interface that libraries serve; the adoption of Blacklight by Hydra or Samvera showed that Blacklight could be applied to non-catalogue use cases, emphasising its flexibility. If the pace of development for Blacklight, assessed by frequency of release, may have slowed slightly in recent years, this is in part because the institutions that have implemented Blacklight are also its developers, and demand for change progresses from within according to need. Blacklight does what it is intended to do, and does it well. There will always be ways in which the index for a collection can be refined and enhanced to facilitate better access to it (a factor that highlights the benefits of skills for working with a Solr index if using Blacklight to its fullest), but unmodified 'out of the box' Blacklight will provide a good basic search experience as a start, and has done this for many years. The maturity of the software is also evidenced by the increasing interest in enhancing not just the basic functionality but what can be done with Blacklight beyond it, through initiatives like GeoBlacklight and Spotlight, to improve the overall discovery experience.

To conclude, when implementing a software system it is important that it is flexible enough to accommodate the needs for which it is being used. Many systems require the implementer to bend to what the software can do, at least to some extent. Blacklight has evolved specifically to meet varied needs, and it continues to be a discovery solution that can be flexible to suit its limitations not within the software itself but in how we can imagine our discovery solutions should work and evolve over time.

Note

1 https://www.univie.ac.at/elib/index.php?title=COinS_Microfromat_Bibliographic_Metadata_for_Embedding_in_HTML.

References

Awre, C. and Green, R. (2017) From Hydra to Samvera: an open source community journey, *UKSG Insights*, **30** (3), 82–8, https://insights.uksg.org/articles/10.1629/uksg.383/.

Beer, C. (2010) Media, Blacklight, and Viewers Like You, Code4Lib, Asheville, 22–25 February 2010, https://code4lib.org/conference/2010/beer.

Blacklight Project (2019a) Home, https://github.com/projectblacklight/blacklight/wiki.

Blacklight Project (2019b) Support, https://github.com/projectblacklight/blacklight/wiki#support.

DuraSpace (2019) Samvera: partners and implementations, https://wiki.duraspace.org/display/samvera/Partners+and+Implementations.

Gilbert, H. and Mobley, T. (2013) Breaking up with CONTENTdm: why and how one institution took the leap to open source, *Code4Lib Journal*, Issue 20, http://journal.code4lib.org/articles/8327.

Green, R. and Awre, C. (2009) Towards a Repository-enabled Scholar's Workbench: RepoMMan, REMAP and Hydra, *D-Lib Magazine*, **15** (5/6), http://dx.doi.org/10.1045/may2009-green.

Moore, K. B. and Greene, C. (2013) The Search for a New OPAC: selecting an open source discovery layer, *Serials Review*, **38** (1), 24–30, http://dx.doi.org/10.1080/00987913.2012.10765415.

Nowviskie, B., Sadler, E. and Hatcher, E. (2007) Adapting an Open-source, Scholarly Web 2.0 System for Findability in Library Collections. In Cohen, L. B. (ed.), *Library 2.0 Initiatives in Academic Libraries*, Association of College & Research Libraries, https://books.google.co.uk/books?id=kQblvBoSIj8C&lpg=PA69&dq=blacklight%20project%20community&pg=PA58#v=twopage&q&f=true.

Open Hub (n.d.) Blacklight, https://www.openhub.net/p/blacklight.

Otto, M. et al. (2018) Bootstrap 4, The Bootstrap Blog, 18 January, https://blog.getbootstrap.com/2018/01/18/bootstrap-4/.

Sadler, E. (2009) Project Blacklight: a next generation library catalogue at a first generation university, *Library Hi Tech*, **27** (1), 57–67, http://dx.doi.org/10.1108/07378830910942919.

Schneider, K. (2006a) How OPACs Suck, Part 1: relevance rank (or the lack of it), ALA TechSource, www.ala.org/tools/article/ala-techsource/how-opacs-suck-part-1-relevance-rank-or-lack-it.

Schneider, K. (2006b) How OPACs Suck, Part 2: the checklist of shame, ALA TechSource, www.ala.org/tools/article/ala-techsource/how-opacs-suck-part-2-checklist-shame.

Schneider, K. (2006c) How OPACs Suck, Part 3: the big picture, ALA TechSource, www.ala.org/tools/article/ala-techsource/how-opacs-suck-part-3-big-picture.

Singer, R. (2008) In Search of a Really 'Next Generation' Catalog, *Journal of Electronic Resources Librarianship*, **20** (3), 139–42.

Singley, E. (2016) To Bento or not to Bento: displaying search results, blog, Usable Libraries, http://emilysingley.net/usablelibraries/to-bento-or-not-to-bento-displaying-search-results/.

10

A world of curated knowledge: leveraging the wider semantic web to enhance library discovery

Carl G. Stahmer

Introduction

Libraries have historically engaged computing technologies to advance two primary goals: to enhance user experience, and to improve the efficiency and accuracy of library work. The first decade and a half of the computerisation of libraries, which began in earnest in the early 1950s, was devoted almost exclusively to the first of these primary goals – to providing enhanced user search, discovery and access to materials (Kilgour, 1970). Attention to the latter goal of improving library efficiency was a secondary movement brought on by an economic imperative towards efficiency that 'must be an ultimate goal if libraries are to be economically viable in the future' (Kilgour, 1970, 219).

As Kilgour suggested, our present library landscape is heavily influenced by a pervasive economic pressure towards efficiency of operations. The two factors of shrinking budgets and an always increasing number of items that must be managed have required that, as a community, we focus on seeking ways to do more with less. Thus most of our attention and external funding in the area of linked data has focused on understanding the impact of linked data adoption on library operations. While migrating data to a format that would improve discovery may have stimulated the initial impulse to pursue linked data, this pursuit was quickly subsumed by a desire to leverage its capabilities to advance efficiency and lower the costs of library operations.

The Library of Congress report *On the Record* (Boehr et al., 2008) is a good exemplar of the tension between the two impulses of service and efficiency. The report is divided into the following titled sections:

- 'Increase the efficiency of bibliographic production and maintenance'
- 'Enhance access to rare, unique, and other special hidden materials'
- 'Position our technology for the future'
- 'Position our community for the future'
- 'Strengthen the library and information science profession'.

Organisationally, we see immediately that increasing the efficiency of library work gets top bill in the discussion and, when we get to discovery in the second section, we are presented with a limited view of discovery, which sees the conversion as presenting a moment of possibility for combining new disparate library data stores – something which could be accomplished just as easily using any number of non-linked data formats. The lower level organisation of the report reflects a similar bias. Each section of the report concludes with a section called 'Consequences of maintaining the status quo', followed by a recommendations section. Of the 27 consequences listed throughout the report, only six are even remotely related to the question of discovery as it relates to linked data implementation. Similarly, of the report proper's 17,398 words, only 2,808 are even remotely dedicated to discussions about discovery, just 16% of the report.[1]

This analysis is meant to be illustrative and not critical. *On the Record* is a report on bibliographic control and not on discovery, and it was produced in response to very real economic and bureaucratic pressures. Its bias towards discussion of efficiency over discovery should, therefore, be read not as reflecting some internal or theoretical bias, but rather as exemplary of an overall trend in the research. Institutional realities are continually redirecting our focus towards examinations of bibliographic effort, regardless of how we wish to prioritise our focus. Whatever our intentions, most discussions of discovery in a linked data ecosystem to date have positioned the need for the library to transition to linked data as one of necessity rather than opportunity.

This is true even of those efforts that have focused on the question of discovery. The various forays of the OCLC (Online Computer Library Center) into linked data represent the library community's most sustained effort to focus on discovery as a primary goal of linked data.[2] In contrast to the focus on workflows of *On the Record*, OCLC's *Library Linked Data in the Cloud*, a 2015 summary of OCLC's experiments in linked data to that date, focuses on the discovery opportunities made possible by linked data (Godby, Wang and Mixter, 2015). Noting that the majority of student and researcher information queries begin not in the library but in internet search engines, the report's authors conclude that the world wide web is 'the appropriate platform for the delivery of our standards' (Godby, Wang and Mixter, 2015, 13). They thus present a vision of 'library linked data in the cloud' where our data is transformed 'to a format that can be understood beyond the library community, where information seekers are increasingly more likely to find it' (Godby, Wang and Mixter, 2015, 8).

OCLC is not alone in its focus on world wide web search engines as the future of library discovery. The sinking suspicion that library information will be left behind if we don't align with the 'first gate that users approach when searching for any information' (Zeng and Quin, 2008, 233), what I like to call Google Anxiety, occupies most of our communal thinking about linked data discovery. If the mountain won't come to the library, then the library must go to the mountain, after all. But we should also be asking if it makes sense for libraries to build another, complementary mountain.

Major search engines will always do many things related to discovery better than the library ever could. For example, the library will never provide a better platform for directly searching the cloud of big data available on the web. And we will never provide the type of user-centric information delivery as the major search engines do, because we will never have at our fingertips the required amount of personal data on our users necessary to provide this type of smart delivery. But this does not mean that we should not also be looking at ways of turning this paradigm on its head and pulling the web into the library as a means of providing services that major search engines are ill equipped to provide. What discovery possibilities might we, as a library community, be able to provide by leveraging linked data that major search engines can't or won't? Do librarians have unique knowledge and skills that can be leveraged in combination with linked data to provide unique, albeit niche, discovery environments that major search engines could not duplicate? I believe that we do.

Libraries and linked data

Libraries provide a host of information-centred services that are only minimally connected to bibliographic control, if at all. For example, research librarians have a depth and breadth of knowledge of not only the quality and availability of resources in their area(s) of coverage, but also the major research foci of their patrons, as do librarians working in collection strategies and development. Regardless of the specific job description of individual librarians, most understand their work as advancing some form of quality control beyond controlling the quality of the bibliographic record itself. This is a point of pride for most library workers. Whether through the production of library guides, assisting patrons with research efforts, educating patrons on how to evaluate the quality of resources, or developing and curating collections, a core function of the library is to direct users towards quality information in a world of information overload. The need for this service function is made particularly acute as society grapples with the impact of fake news and social media's impact on the 2016 US presidential elections. Given this context it is neither surprising nor unreasonable that many librarians are concerned when linked data proponents advocate pushing our data out to the larger web, where it will be assimilated into a larger information context, which will place it at best in parallel, and at worst in the shadow of, unresearched blog posts, tweets and social media timelines.

The concern that linked data will obfuscate library data and render impotent the library's mission to direct users to quality resources is rooted in an understanding, perpetuated by linked data advocates as much as its critics, of linked data as a one-way information-sharing framework. It is not. Linked data both sets free library data to be consumed and repurposed on the global web, and allows libraries to consume and repurpose other's information that is available on web. The practical result is that information from our records appears in major search engines, Wikipedia and so on, and we can use others' information selectively in our own discovery environments to enhance records while ensuring quality control.

Prototypes for the future

We need to stop thinking of linked data as a stopgap framework designed to staunch the dilution of library work into the pool of the world wide web and see it as opening the door for librarians to capitalise on and add value to the ever-growing body of information available on the web. The idea of ingesting data to improve one's local discovery activity should seem neither new nor radical to most librarians. In fact, libraries were arguably the first data intensive organisations to work successfully towards this goal. WorldCat has been connecting data about hundreds of millions of records maintained by thousands of institutions since long before there was a world wide web, let alone a thought of anything like a semantic web or linked data. But by modern standards our current sharing universe is a closed universe. We can skip from one catalogue record to the next, either through searching or browsing, but the end result of any search is always another catalogue record.

For example, if I begin a search for the subject 'Horror fiction', I am a returned a list of partial catalogue records for books and essays catalogued under this subject. If I click on one of these, 'Frankenstein, or the Modern Prometheus', I am returned a list of partial catalogue records for books and essays catalogued under this title. If I click on one of these links, I am returned the full catalogue record for that book. If I am lucky, there may be a link to an electronic edition to which I may (or may not) have access, but in most cases the library catalogue as it currently stands is an incestuous collection of links to itself – an untenable situation in a world where our users are used to moving seamlessly from finding to learning, from identifying objects of interest to learning things about those objects. Linked data offers libraries a way out of this limited ecosystem. Using linked data, we could deliver a wider context of information about our users' objects of inquiry as an integral part of their search and discovery activity.

The experimental RelFinder linked data discovery interface (www.visualdataweb.org/relfinder.php) provides a good example of the type of functionality on which libraries could and should be capitalising. Self-identified as an interface for 'interactive relationship discovery in RDF data', RelFinder allows users to enter any two objects (authors, movies, books, etc.) and then traverses configured RDF gateways (SPARQL endpoints, specifically) and draws a network graph of all found relationships between the two objects.

Figure 10.1 presents a partial output of the RelFinder graph produced on the relationship between Mary Shelley and Frankenstein.

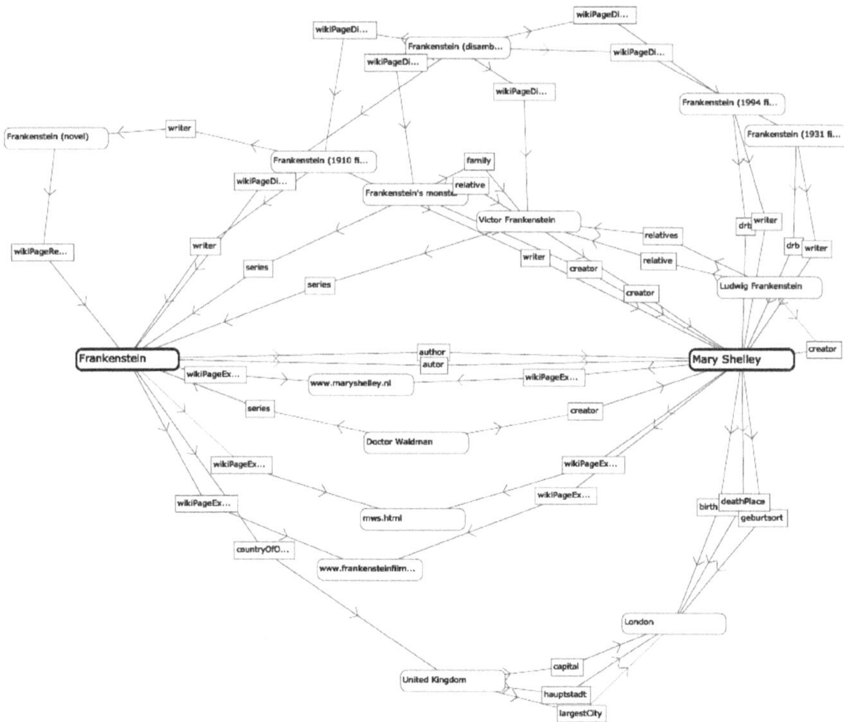

Figure 10.1 *RelFinder graph for Mary Shelley and Frankenstein. By permission from Visual Data Web*

Figure 10.1 immediately communicates to the user a host of information about the relationship between Mary Shelley and her fictional creation. Central to the relation is her authorship of the character, something easily seen as a catalogue record. But a large and important collection of other information is also present, some of which cannot be found in the closed catalogue, for example information on related characters and geographic data. Users necessarily have to leave our current, closed data world and seek elsewhere to find this information.

Allowing a mass of unedited, unfiltered and uncurated data into the catalogue is precisely the web effect that solicits so much anxiety among librarians. In early 2017, Jeff Edmunds of the Pennsylvania State University Library (PSU) launched a strong critique of linked data via an article published in PSU's ScholarSphere and much discussed on the Library of Congress BIBFRAME Listserv and in the Twittersphere (Edmunds, 2017).[3] In this 'Roadmap to Nowhere', which represents a wide, generalised anxiety among the library community, Edmunds asserts that, among other problems, 'libraries have effectively lost' the battle for information discovery in the age of the internet. In the face of this loss, he then asks the fundamental question, 'what of value do we bring to the ecosystem?' and responds:

> Is there something about the metadata created by libraries that makes it qualitatively different from the vast soup of data already available on the open Web? If yes, what is it? If yes, what happens to the brand of library metadata when it is liberally and freely admixed with that soup? Do we risk losing our data identity? Our reputation for neutrality and reliability? Do we become just another (minor) player in the dog fight of infotainment industries, one more (extremely minor) ingredient in the dubious information soup?
>
> Edmunds, 2017

The anxiety that lies behind Edmunds' rhetorical rejection of linked data is the fear that our well curated and carefully produced metadata will be lost as it becomes, 'one more (extremely minor) ingredient in the dubious information soup'. Most interesting in Edmunds' critique is the fact that he blames this dilution on linked data, whereas he, himself, admits, and I have argued here, that this is a battle that libraries have already 'effectively lost' and that this defeat was [inflicted?] under MARC's watch.

Most importantly, Edmunds' complaint, and I here rely on him as a proxy for a common concern among cataloguers, is the assumption that linked data necessarily degrades the quality of the catalogue. This is simply not the case. In fact, the singular benefit of linked data as it relates to providing service to our patrons is that it adds important context to the catalogue – and this context can be curated just as library information has always been curated. As an extensible framework, linked data bibliographic descriptions can grow to include an ever widening and supple amount of information about resources, and all of this information can be produced according to rules and standards of as high a quality as we currently demand of MARC.

There are at least two prototypical sites currently available on the internet that are specifically designed, each in its own way, to engage this potential directly: Big Diva and the English Short Title Catalogue (ESTC). The most developed is Big Diva (http://bigdiva.org), a nascent library discovery interface developed by the Advanced Research Consortium at Texas A&M University.

Big Diva

Big Diva was recently adopted by the Texas A&M University Library as a humanities research portal, and it is currently made available as a service to other libraries. Big Diva is built completely on an RDF-linked data backbone, and it uses this backbone to present a completely new type of discovery interface, which combines traditional search with network graph display and browsing capability (Figure 10.2).

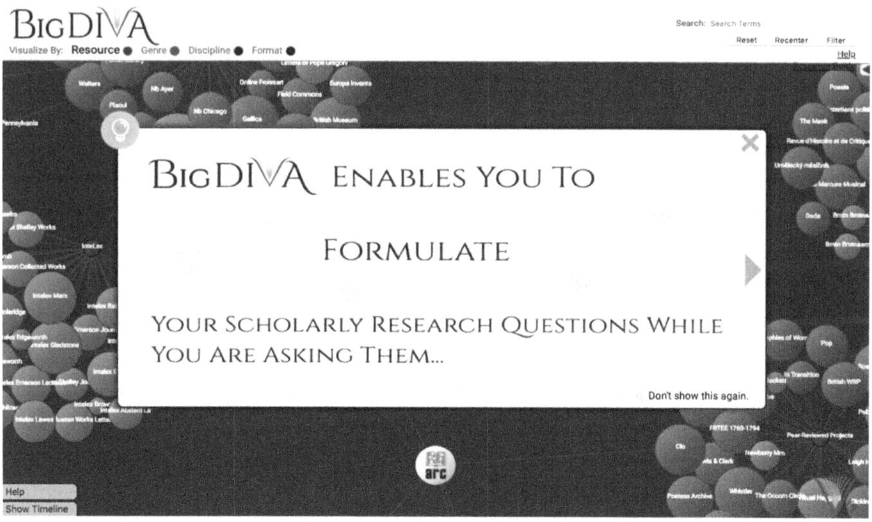

Figure 10.2 *Big Diva linked data search and discovery portal.* By permission from the Advanced Research Consortium, ARC

Using Big Diva, users can begin a session by searching or clicking through a network graph of related information that is organised and linked via a collection of traditional facets (fields) and then navigate results by using various tools such as a timescale slider to filter displayed nodes. A thorough discussion of the Big Diva interface is beyond the scope of this chapter. What is most relevant is the dataset itself on which the interface rests – an RDF-based triplestore, which combines traditional library resources and a large, carefully curated, index of non-library, peer-reviewed electronic resources.

While still nascent and somewhat limited in the breadth and depth of its catalogue, Big Diva stands as an important example of a curated linked data information gateway. Within its ecosystem, users move seamlessly through a single interface, between library delivered resources such as Early English Books Online (EEBO), Eighteenth Century Collections Online (ECCO) and the University of Michigan's Studies in Radicalism collection, and non-library resources such as The Poetess Archive, The Shelley Chronology and The Rossetti Archive. This approach provides a model of how libraries could and should leverage the vast quantity of information on the web to enhance our catalogues and, by extension, the services we provide to our users. Unlike turning our users over to major search engines that deliver information in either haphazard or unknown aggregations, Big Diva regulates the flow of information from the internet, ensuring quality and reliability, which would not be possible without linked data or trained and knowledgeable librarians and library staff.

The English Short Title Catalogue

The new, linked data version of the ESTC and the English Short Title Catalogue for the 21st Century (ESTC21) also exploits linked data capabilities in order to provide enhanced functionality to its users.[4] Founded in 1977 at the British Library and since expanded to an international team of librarians and scholars, the ESTC provides a union catalogue of over 480,000 short titles published in English or England and its colonies from the advent of the typeset press to 1800, representing a collection of the holdings of over 2,000 individual libraries, museums and collections. Originally housed in a MARC-based Cuadra STAR system, the current version of the ESTC is a MARC-based bibliographic and holdings catalogue housed in an Ex Libris Aleph integrated library system and made searchable through Ex Libris Primo.

In 2015, the ESTC received funding from the Andrew W. Mellon Foundation to implement a new version of the ESTC built on a linked data backbone and designed to capitalise on linked data information published on the web. Currently in its Alpha release, the ESTC21 seeks to capitalise on linked data in order to improve the quality and expand the content of its records. The ESTC21 interface allows users to suggest additions and corrections to the catalogue using an interface that provides behind-the-scenes uniform resource identifier (URI) look-up, through type-ahead querying of a variety of linked data endpoints, thereby ensuring that any information provided by users is aligned with controlled vocabularies when possible and that these alignments are linked data ready. For example, a user who wishes to supplement the record for ESTC Item N10013, 'The new dispensatory of the Royal College of Physicians in London. With copious and accurate indexes. Faithfully translated from the Latin of the Pharmacopœia Londinensis, publish'd by order of the King and

Council', is first presented with the option to select from a drop-down list of attributes that can be added to the record, such as author, noting the presence of a digital surrogate, etc. (Figure 10.3).

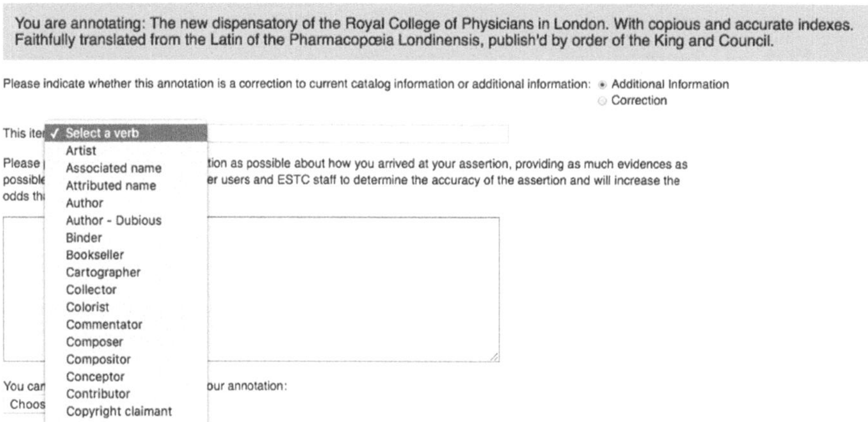

Figure 10.3 *ESTC21 linked data user annotation attribute selection.* By permission from the British Library and the Centre for Bibliographical Studies, UC Riverside

These attributes serve as predicates for a linked data triple that will be added to the graph for the object being annotated. Whereas the user interface presents the end-user with a string-based experience, the system captures the URIs associated with the attributes. For example, a user selecting the 'author' attribute is actually selecting the Library of Congress entity http://id.loc.gov/vocabulary/relators/aut. This same process is also applied to the selection of objects for the linked data annotation. Having selected an attribute, when the user begins to enter an object value for the triple, the system communicates with a linked data gateway appropriate to the selected predicate to provide type-head entry (Figure 10.4 on the next page).

Here again, the user is presented with string-based views of the data while URIs for selected items are captured in the background. The net effect of this process is that whereas the end-user is saying something like, 'Brand, Thomas was the author of ESTC Item N10013', the system captures the triple:

<http://estc.bl.uk/ N10013>
< http://id.loc.gov/vocabulary/relators/aut>
< https://viaf.org/viaf/19531061>

Unlike the RelFinder example discussed above, which mines an unfiltered network of information in web space, this feature provides a mechanism for users to connect

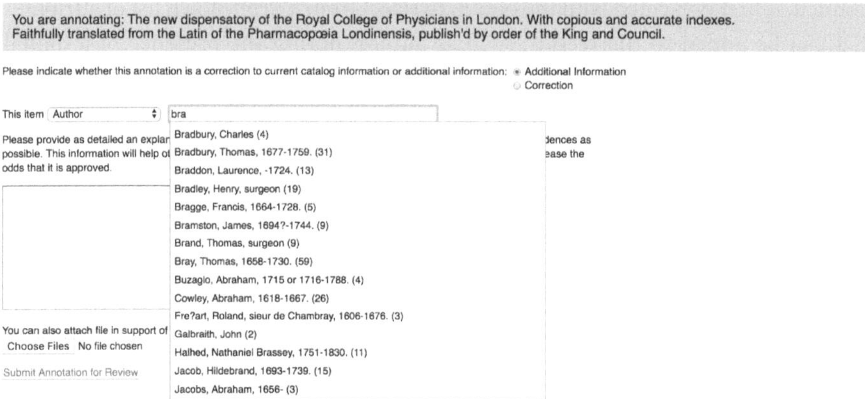

Figure 10.4 *ESTC21 linked data user annotation attribute value selection.* By permission from the British Library and the Centre for Bibliographical Studies, UC Riverside

curated graphs of content, exposing only those graph branches that are deemed to be of relevance and quality. This focus on quality is reinforced through the application of additional layers of quality control as part of the linked data record enhancement process. User annotations do not immediately become part of the official 'record' for an annotated item. Instead, they are added to a clearly delineated annotation history section of the item view as soon as they are created. Here they can be reviewed and voted on by other ESTC users, each of whom can provide documentary and narrative arguments about their responses (Figure 10.5 opposite).

With the exception of deletion of clear spam and inappropriate content, item annotations and their threaded histories become permanently associated with an item and are always viewable in the annotation history section of the item view, but do not become part of the 'record' until they are reviewed and approved by a librarian or other approved bibliographer. This ensures that data contained in the official item graph meets library quality standards.

Other possibilities for discovery and learning made possible by linked data

Big Diva and the ESTC21 stand as early examples of how discovery interfaces can be reimagined to provide systematic possibilities for capitalising on the depth of information available on the web while fulfilling the library mission of delivering quality, curated information to our users. But as is typical of 'first on scene' technology implementation, they only scratch the surface of the possibilities for discovery and learning made possible by linked data. As libraries and the information universe in

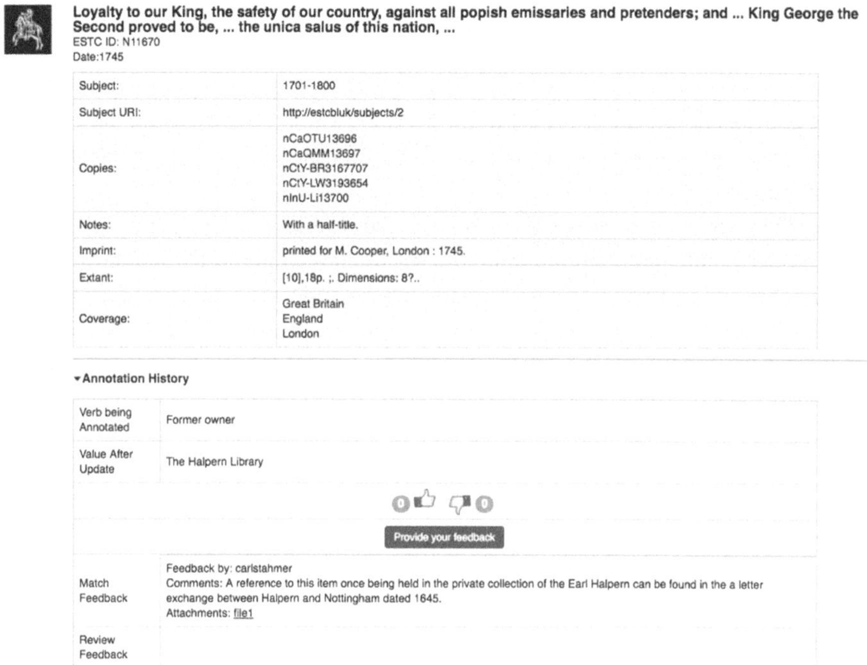

Loyalty to our King, the safety of our country, against all popish emissaries and pretenders; and ... King George the Second proved to be, ... the unica salus of this nation, ...
ESTC ID: N11670
Date:1745

Subject:	1701-1800
Subject URI:	http://estcbluk/subjects/2
Copies:	nCaOTU13696 nCaQMM13697 nCtY-BR3167707 nCtY-LW3193654 nInU-Li13700
Notes:	With a half-title.
Imprint:	printed for M. Cooper, London : 1745.
Extant:	[10],18p. ;. Dimensions: 8?..
Coverage:	Great Britain England London

▾Annotation History

Verb being Annotated	Former owner
Value After Update	The Halpern Library
	0 0 Provide your feedback
Match Feedback	Feedback by: carlstahmer Comments: A reference to this item once being held in the private collection of the Earl Halpern can be found in the a letter exchange between Halpern and Nottingham dated 1645. Attachments: file1
Review Feedback	

Figure 10.5 *ESTC21 annotation history.* By permission from the British Library and the Centre for Bibliographical Studies, UC Riverside

general move increasingly towards linked data, the complexity and functionality of such an interface will expand on multiple fronts. Returning to our RelFinder example of Mary Shelley's Frankenstein, imagine a library universe where a user searches for Frankenstein and is returned a graph of information pertaining to Frankenstein. A complete graph of all the information available on the subject would be extremely complex, and largely unreadable; but an initial view of this complexity, a dense, tangled web of information, lets the user immediately see that this is a well-documented subject. Now imagine that in addition to the graph our interface also provides the user with various controlled lists that define formats, subjects, etc. From this list, the user clicks on 'journal article' and the graph immediately re-draws itself showing only journal articles about Frankenstein, grouping the articles by publication and drawing edges (connecting lines) between publications based on controlled vocabularies. This reduced graph is more manageable, but still too large, so the user returns to the list of subjects that appear below the graph and clicks on 'Colonization'. The graph morphs again, and the user continues to drill down until the graph is manageable, leading the user ultimately to electronic editions of the articles. While this process seems to violate the 'fewer clicks' rule that states that the goal is to deliver content in as few clicks as possible, it provides an added value to users that is not present in traditional user interfaces: the search and discovery process is itself an educational process and not simply a means to an end. It is part of the actual research process, as the user learns something about the scope and depth of the subject as she or he navigates the information landscape.[5]

It could be argued that we could produce the same functionality by simply building new and better integrated library systems. But we haven't got to the magic yet. Now imagine that our user has read a few journal articles and has begun to understand the complexity of the research question. At this moment, the user un-checks the 'journal article' feature, and the graph re-draws to include a complex web of information from all over the web on the subjects, date ranges, etc. of her or his filtered universe. This will again be a very complex graph, but it is targeted complexity focused on the research question at hand. From here, the user begins another filtering process, but of a different type. From a list of options on the page the user selects 'Library Reviewed'. When this is checked the majority of nodes on the graph fade into the background, leaving highlighted only information nodes that have been culled from library-hosted linked data catalogues or librarian approved content, such as content vetted through the ESTC21 interface. This could include information about books, articles and films, and also reviews of extra-library information graphs that have been conducted by librarians, something akin to a linked data library guide.

At this point the user is looking at a graph of information that is either housed in or approved by librarians. From here she or he might choose to expand or continue to filter as needed. Perhaps she or he wants to include web-based resources that have been produced by non-academic but reliable sources, such as museums or institutes. At each stage of the process, the user learns more about the subject at hand as she or he moves across nodes of known quality. At times information sparsity will require the user to expand the search beyond the quality-controlled graph of library data, but the user will know that this is the case and treat the found results accordingly. Most importantly, the user does not have to leave the library interface to pursue investigations down other, non-library, paths. The user remains in library space where un-vetted information is always presented in the context of vetted information, where it can be more easily cross-checked and validated.

Both the ESTC21 and Big Diva are relatively niche projects, and neither could exist without tremendous support from external sources. But the linked data principles employed by each are scalable to library-wide operations. One can imagine, for example, ESTC21's annotation function in action in the library.

Conclusion

The scenario set out above is not wishful thinking. We have the technology. Certainly, much technological and institutional work needs to be done. Data must be migrated, new interfaces must be developed and tested, computational algorithms for connecting resources of like type and quality must be developed, and, most importantly and difficult, our institutional organisation and training must evolve to support this new environment. We must begin to think beyond simply retraining cataloguers to work in BIBFRAME or Schema and begin to think about what new kinds of library work will be required if we want to truly serve our customers in a linked data context. Are our current controlled vocabularies sufficient to capture librarian review of non-library resources available on the web? Who will do this work? Does it require a new skillset and node on the traditional library organisation chart? Or is it work that can and should replace some existing workflow?

We have been asking these and similar questions for quite some time. But our focus in doing so has been largely from the perspective of cataloguing and not from that of discovery. We have learned a great deal as a result of this focus, and abandoning it would be a mistake; but it is time to bring discovery fully into the investigation. And as we do so, we should think beyond our fear of being subsumed by the information universe and focus on the added value that we can bring not only to our own closed universe, but to the entire ecosystem. Packaging our information so that it can compete in the wild west of the world wide web and its search engine infrastructure is important; and we must pursue it. But we must also have the vision and tenacity to reverse the paradigm and implement systems that situate the information out there in the context of our deep knowledge and expertise.

Notes

1 The word count is the total number of words of the report proper. Introductory material (including title pages, tables of contents and executive summary) and closing pages (including works cited and acronyms and initialisms used in the report) were excluded. Word count for passages directly related to the topic of discovery were produced through manual reading, highlighting and subsequent counting of relevant passages by two independent readers.

2 The Library of Congress' BIBFRAME initiative is most likely the largest, sustained effort at linked data implementation in the library sector, but the effort is almost exclusively focused on back end processing and efficiency.

3 'Roadmap to Nowhere' (Edmunds, 2017) was first published in ScholarSphere, PSU's institutional repository, in April 2017 at https://scholarsphere.psu.edu/downloads/w9505064f. However, although according to the ScholarSphere 'About' page, 'through

ScholarSphere, PSU researchers – faculty, students, and staff alike – are able to share their work on a worldwide scale and be assured of its long-term preservation and thus ongoing access', the article was subsequently removed and is no longer publicly available (and this link is not live). A record of much of the discourse around it can be found in the archives of the Library of Congress BIBFRAME Listserv, however, at https://listserv.loc.gov/cgi-bin/wa?A1=ind1704&L=bibframe#5.

4 The English Short Title Catalogue can be found at http://estc.bl.uk. At the time of this printing, the experimental development version of the ESTC21 can be found at the non-permanent URL http://estc21.ucr.edu. Please refer to http://estc.bl.uk for persistent information about and links to the ESTC21.

5 The data format that makes this kind of discovery possible does not preclude more conventional search and discovery. A good interface would provide both.

References

Boehr, D., Clancy, D., Latham, J., Lynch, C. and Nadler, J. (2008) *On the Record: report of the Library of Congress Working Group on the Future of Bibliographic Control*, www.loc.gov/bibliographic-future/news/lcwg-ontherecord-jan08-final.pdf.

Edmunds, J. (2017) Roadmap to Nowhere: BIBFLOW, BIBFRAME, and linked data for libraries, https://listserv.loc.gov/cgi-bin/wa?A2=ind1704&L=BIBFRAME&P=39737.

Godby, C. J., Wang, S. and Mixter, J. K. (2015) *Library Linked Data in the Cloud: OCLC's experiments with new models of resource description*, Morgan & Claypool.

Kilgour, F. G. (1970) History of Library Computerization, *Information Technology and Libraries*, **3** (3), 219, doi:10.6017/ital.v3i3.5256.

Zeng, M. L. and Quin, J. (2008) *Metadata*, Facet Publishing.

11

Cultural discovery: trends and futures

Ed Fay

Introduction

It is well established already that 'discovery . . . happens elsewhere' (Dempsey, 2016) only sometimes, if ever, taking place within the walls – physical or virtual – of a traditional cultural memory institution (library, archive, museum, etc.).

Individuals' knowledge journeys, characterised only at times by explicit 'information seeking', are diverse, in the content sought and valued, and the discovery environment and search strategies employed. As digital technologies increase in power and sophistication, the design of tools and services takes an ever more subtle and nuanced account of user intention and behaviour, and the networked world makes it faster and easier to forge connections between individuals and information.

The downside of these advances is an ever increasing volume of information available globally and within specific communities or disciplines, and a diminishing understanding of the layers of mediation between an individual and the information they seek and consume. At the most basic level there is a common lack of understanding of the ways in which information is created, encoded, transmitted, preserved and retrieved, and a separation between individuals and the tools or technologies at their disposal to structure and navigate their information environment.

The most exciting example of technological progression is the advance in machine learning, which 'gives computers the ability to learn without being explicitly programmed' (Wikipedia, n.d.). Essentially, rather than simply following rules deterministically to solve a problem, machines are gaining the ability to determine rules for themselves. Previously, a machine was given data and rules, and produced answers. Now, machines can be given data and answers, and produce rules – which can then be applied to new data to produce new answers.

In the realm of discovery, this leads to an epochal shift in information retrieval, whereby machines can extract knowledge from documents (and other multimedia sources), and enable users to navigate knowledge graphs rather than lists of documents which they have to read themselves to understand. Knowledge graphs encode relationships between concepts, introducing more sophistication than the familiar citation graph (citations or cited-by links in article databases) to express any meaningful relationship between concepts. In this paradigm, users don't even need to know the question – machines can begin to uncover both known and currently unknown relationships, and open up new connections and hypotheses for exploration.

In this chapter, we will attempt to identify trends which affect resource discovery, from the increasing availability of information, changes in the discovery environment and formality of search strategies driven by the ubiquity of personal computing and the evolving digital social environment, the rapid advancement of digital technology, and the increasing focus on user-centred design to suggest possible futures – apparent and speculative.

Content sought and valued

To a large extent, the future of discovery depends on what it is possible to discover. Most information[1] produced today is supplied in formats already amenable to machine processing – it is 'born-digital' – and 'big data' studies suggest (Laney, 2001) that three dimensions emerge, from which we can identify influences on the opportunities and methodologies of discovery:

- volume: the amount of information produced or available is increasing
- velocity: the speed of production and availability is increasing
- variety: the variety of formats and encodings is increasing.

In the domains of scholarly communication and cultural heritage, we see these dimensions emerge in the availability of information supporting research and education.

We can observe some specific trends: increasing publication rate of scholarly literature (Bornmann and Mutz, 2014); increasing availability of and demand for open data (Digital Science, 2017); increasing granularity of published outputs (Groth, 2017) and fragmentation of those outputs across the scholarly infrastructure (Van de Sompel and Treolar, 2014); a spectrum of rights and permissions for access and reuse (Open

Data Institute, 2015), with an increasing emphasis on open access (Piwowar et al. 2017); the shifting role of traditional memory institutions and emergent services in facilitating access and ensuring long term preservation (Dempsey, Malpas and Lavoie, 2014); increasing digitisation of a broad range of cultural heritage collections (Nauta and van den Heuvel, 2015; Padilla et al., 2017), and preservation of contemporary born-digital culture through the Digital Preservation Coalition (https://dpconline.org/); and increasing demand from researchers for diverse sources of information (ProQuest, 2017).

Together, these activities and trends make available for processing vast stores of knowledge, increasing opportunities for finding, connecting and progressing human understanding. However, this deluge of information also makes discovering relevant sources and content increasingly challenging, as information publishing and availability exceeds the capacity of humans to discover and consume everything which might be relevant to a particular information need, and information is increasingly fragmented and scattered – 'silo'd' – across multiple sources with variable discoverability, interoperability and accessibility.

Faced with this volume, velocity and variety of information creation and dissemination, veracity is threatened, and trust is undermined. Digital media are notoriously fragile (Rosenthal et al., 2005), scholarly discourse takes places on commercial platforms with rights issues unsympathetic to traditional curation and preservation (Bilder, Lin and Neylon, 2015), and complex and expensive licensing regimes limit the ability of researchers to discover, connect and access all the information which might be relevant to a particular need (Willinsky, 2006). Understanding provenance and assigning authority, while maintaining access rights and permissions, becomes increasing challenging as online publication is unstable with long term preservation and availability often unconsidered or unplanned and the integrity of the cultural record under threat (Klein et al., 2014; Zittrain, Albert and Lessig, 2014).

In the face of these challenges, sustainable digital archives are emerging, which provide assurances about digital longevity beyond the commercial viability of the original creators or publishers of the information they curate. Local, national and international services ensure the preservation of scholarly literature (CLOCKSS [Controlled Lots of Copies Keeps Stuff Safe], https://www.clockss.org/; Portico, www.portico.org/), research data (OECD, 2017), web archives and digitised cultural heritage (HathiTrust, https://www.hathitrust.org; the International Internet Preservation Consortium, http://netpreserve.org; the Internet Archive, https://archive.org), the legal record (Perma.cc, https://perma.cc) and computer software (Software Heritage, https://www.softwareheritage.org; the UNESCO PERSIST programme, https://unescopersist.org). These efforts, although divergent in their missions and funding models, provide some guarantee of the future availability of the contemporary digital cultural record in its myriad forms.

Discovery environment

Historically, information seeking was an explicit undertaking, carried out in particular locations, using formally structured media, and employing formal and often mediated strategies – within a library or archive collection, using a catalogue, to carry out rule-bound searches, perhaps with the assistance of a reference librarian or archivist. While informal discovery is nothing new, for example the sharing which happens through networks of correspondence or collaboration among peers, the digital environment embeds discovery into the fabric of everyday life, driven in large part by the ubiquity of personal computing devices, and the advent of fluid and porous online academic social networks.

Informality of search strategy is driven by the increasing ubiquity of personal computing devices in the physical environment, particularly the 'mobilisation' of content creation and consumption, allowing discovery to happen outside a formal laboratory, office or library environment. This integration of information sources into the everyday lived environment results in increasingly informal discovery behaviours – an immersion within a rapidly evolving information environment of social feeds combining sharing, commenting, bookmarking and current news, accessed from anywhere, available for rapid or extended consumption, and complementing formal search strategies with a strong, socially influenced dimension (Cann, Dimitriou and Hooley, 2011; Gardner and Inger, 2018).

Despite superficially connecting machines and information, the digital environment increases opportunities for connections between people as academic social networks provide a range of different functionalities which support discovery, suggesting a trend towards 'more open, efficient and/or transparent ways of working' (Kramer and Bosman, 2016a, 2016b). Academics are increasingly maintaining online profiles (Nicholas et al., 2017), academic social networks are increasing opportunities for networking and impact on a range of researcher activities (Donelan, 2015; Noorden, 2014), and research itself is becoming increasingly interdisciplinary and collaborative (Bastian, 2015; Noorden, 2015). Altmetrics – such as user attention and social impact – are starting to be used to determine relevance and suggest recommendations in discovery services (Breeding, 2015), introducing less formal signals than citation analysis, which affects how relevance, importance and authority are presented during information seeking and discovery.

As personal identity and social networking become increasingly intertwined with discovery, trends in product development suggest there is an ever-greater focus on user-centred design and personalisation. User experience and user-centred design are increasingly ubiquitous in the library and publishing worlds (Botzer, 2015; EBSCO, 2019; Stohn, 2015) with systems vendors demonstrating that they are putting a nuanced understanding of users at the heart of their product design, based on an understanding of the diversity of personas and information seeking use cases that drive variance in discovery behaviours and functional requirements of systems and services. This increasingly nuanced understanding will drive products that closely match the specific requirements of an individual – 'the library in the life of the user instead of . . . the user in the life of the library' (Connaway, 2015) – with a decreasing expectation that users require expertise with obscure system interfaces and query syntax to be effective.

The trend is towards hyper-personalisation, where individual user context and intention can influence relevancy and discovery, and persistent identification of individuals drives opportunities for cross-platform personalisation (Grimes, 2013). This includes awareness of existing interests expressed in past behaviour (such as reading, referencing or bookmarking), or awareness of physical environment (enabling geo-spatial discovery), and represents a shift from a pseudo-objective description of a knowledge domain based on cataloguing rules to a dynamic information environment that presents different aspects to different users, based on an understanding of their interests and intent.

Taken together, these trends show a repositioning of the individual at the centre of discovery, presenting new opportunities for uncovering links between sources, new methods for maintaining current awareness, and for discovery without needing to know up front what it is you are looking for. At the same time, risks emerge from the tendency towards filter bubbles and echo chambers (manifested in popular culture through the emergence of fake news), and the loss of an objective sense of the boundaries of a knowledge domain – the risk of apparent completeness or comprehensiveness.

Current discovery technologies

Discovery technology began with physical catalogues, finding aids and index cards, providing metadata to enable exploration of a collection or archive and retrieval of documents or artefacts by describing their features including author, title and subject (Welsh, 2015). Early computerisation emerged from the pre-existing practice of exchanging record cards (Coyle, 2016) and mimicked these forms, enabling machines to process structured fields – such as authors, titles and subjects – and build indexes organised by standard terms or controlled vocabularies, which were populated through manual cataloguing (Furrie, 2009).

User interfaces gave individuals the ability to browse these fields, and use keyword searching to retrieve relevant results by locating metadata records which contained these terms – applying rules to data. Full-text indexing extends this ability to search for keywords directly within documents, complementing or bypassing the need for metadata. But in either approach, the onus remains with the user or searcher to use conceptual expressions and vocabularies which align with those of the author (or cataloguer, as an intermediary), and the formulation of a hypothesis about related concepts to retrieve documents which link keyword terms together.

Current discovery services build on central indexes of metadata and full text, compiled through direct relationships with publishers, to enable this kind of browsing and searching (Breeding, 2015). Displaying results relies on relevance ranking, which uses a number of indicators to prioritise results considered to be useful (according to user needs as expressed in the query) or important (according to the literature as expressed in citations or other altmetrics) with concerns being raised about transparency (Breeding, 2015) and bias (Reidsma, 2016) in these algorithms. Recommender systems adapt and extend search results by using insights into user context and behaviour, but with limited consistency or understanding of the impact on search effectiveness or user satisfaction (Beel et al., 2016).

The fundamental paradigm remains that of document retrieval, the end result being access to a set of documents or artefacts considered relevant, which the user or searcher must then consume (read) to understand. Only through this process can the user uncover the knowledge encoded in the documents. Discovery conceived as a keyword search for documents works when you know what you are looking for – you already know the answer, or you can formulate the question. It is not good at presenting the unknown, or for maintaining awareness within known or unfamiliar domains.

Emerging discovery technologies

Meanwhile, technological developments are advancing discovery in two dimensions, increasing:

- computing power (storage and processing) leading to the emergence[2] of artificial intelligence and machine learning
- connectivity (networking), leading to the emergence of linked data.

Machine learning enables the extraction of structured information from unstructured data through the identification of patterns – learning rules from data. Using these techniques, machines are gaining the ability to extract information from a huge volume and wide variety of sources, providing capacity for responding to the big data trends in scholarly communication and digital cultural heritage. Machine learning uses a number of different approaches, extending the use of manually curated ontologies and controlled vocabularies, to 'read' documents and transform multimedia (including audio such as speech and still or moving image) to extract identifiable features and 'reason' about their meaning.

Current applications in the fields of scholarly communication and digital cultural heritage include recognition of optical and handwritten characters (Transkribus, https://transkribus.eu/), image features (Somers, 2017), speech (Hinton et al., 2012) and music (Sturm, 2014); natural language processing, enabling the identification of language structure and meaning such as concepts (Gramatica et al., 2014; Juric and Rydahl, 2017; Xiong, Power and Callan, 2017), named entities (Manning et al., 2014) and embedded data (Clark and Divvala, 2016); reasoning about provenance and authority (Ceolin et al., 2016), author attribution (Stamatatos, 2009), sensitivity (Souza et al., 2016) or sentiment (Cambria, 2016); and translation between languages.

Of particular interest are the 'higher-level' applications which extract meaning, enabling documents and other multimedia sources to be automatically classified, and relationships between concepts to be identified from the locations where they are expressed. In the context of scholarly communication, such relationships might relate to hypotheses, arguments and assertions of scientific method or result which are present in the literature.

If machine learning enables the extraction of information from large-scale, multi-format corpora, linked data enables new ways of connecting information distributed at web scale across myriad sources or repositories. Linked data provides a way of identifying entities, making assertions about those entities, and providing links between entities and assertions held in distributed locations (W3C, 2015). Knowledge graphs built with linked data allow queries to be formulated not about the occurrence of keywords in documents, but about the semantic nature of relationships between concepts.

Together, these advances in artificial intelligence and linked data promise a revolutionary new paradigm of discovery and access.

The fundamental shift is twofold. First, there is no longer a reliance on the manual classification of every document within a corpus to find relevant information. Instead, the human effort shifts to the design and training of algorithms, which are then applied to vast corpora across silos and encodings. Second, the aim of discovery is no longer necessarily the retrieval of documents which have to be consulted. Instead, information itself is presented in the form of entities and relationships which the user can navigate, only if necessary referring to the document or source where the assertion is identified.

These approaches can be used not only to augment traditional retrieval by linking documents to concepts, automating the process of classification normally undertaken by subject matter experts, but also to provide new mechanisms for retrieval. Retrieval systems can link queries to documents via entity relationships, inferring with greater accuracy the user context and intent behind a query, and abstracting from a particular query formulation to transcend the need for shared ontologies or vocabularies between users and authors or cataloguers. Knowledge graphs enable new forms of interaction with information which no longer rely on linking a user to a set of documents selected from a larger corpus, but on providing a user with the ability to navigate the network of concepts and their relationships – aggregated knowledge from the entire corpus over which the artificial intelligence has operated.

Together, machine learning and linked data can start to provide mechanisms for uncovering new relationships without the information seeker even having to formulate the question or conceive the relationship, or be aware of all the collections around the world which might contain relevant information.

Implications

We have already described the issues of veracity which result from having privileged access to a corpus of information, and in the world of machine learning this is also true – the power of the artificial intelligence (AI) is limited by the corpus of material it has access to and can learn from, and the risks of accelerating production, fragmentation and silo-ing, and of long term fragility of digital information apply here too.

However, the advent of machine learning introduces additional concerns about the transparency of the algorithms that are mediating access to the corpus under investigation. In the same way that relevancy ranking informs perceptions of the boundaries of a knowledge domain and the relative importance of features within that domain (documents, authors, related topics, etc.), the machine-learning algorithms determine what is presented as a meaningful relationship. As these algorithms are the intellectual property of the AI owners, and the 'secret sauce' which drives their business model, companies are incentivised not to open their workings to outside scrutiny – workings which can be so complex as to defy straightforward explanation. The quality and ethics of an AI is ultimately determined by the materials from which it learns – any bias in its source material will influence the rules it learns and then applies in the future.[3]

At present, most semantic discovery efforts in the cultural heritage domain focus on transforming the results of years of manual cataloguing and metadata creation into linked data, to surface the cultural record into the contemporary linked data environment (Godby, 2017). In the future, we can imagine AI publishing the results of mining the cultural record into that web of linked data, surfacing connections across the entire sum of human knowledge, which may previously have been hidden.

Together, machine learning and linked data will present new opportunities in the breadth of connections and the depth in understanding of existing results within narrow fields. Researchers and students will be able to explore the use of concepts across disciplines, without relying on a pre-existing understanding of how language and practice has developed, or requiring item-by-item access to the collections of cultural heritage spread across multiple institutions. At the same time, information seekers will be able to cut through the deluge of information to find the exact piece of knowledge that is relevant to their information need at any given point in time, through a detailed and specific understanding of their individual context and the content of vast, aggregated collections.

In the semantic space of machine-learning extraction and linked data integration across vast corpora, new discovery opportunities emerge . . . for example looking at discourse captured in an archive collection of private correspondence between political activists, how the use of language and conceptual apparatus was influenced by thinkers and writers (some of which you may be aware they read, others not), how their activism influenced changes in legal statutes, how court judgements reflected a shift in social attitudes expressed in newspaper or web archives, and how that change was referenced by and influenced scholarly literature across different domains, and so on.

Conclusion

We can imagine a future where the vast majority of cultural heritage collections are published digitally and openly, with permissive licences or legal frameworks permitting reuse, allowing AIs to interrogate corpora at will, bringing with them questions and hypotheses from known or unknown domains, deriving their own views on the relevance and importance of 'your' collection to 'their' audience, publishing those connections as routes in from linked data knowledge graphs and connecting individuals to the breadth and depth of information, and driving new forms of consumption and reuse.

It is also possible to imagine a future where an AI faces in rather than out, to understand your (scholarly) life and trends and preferences in discovery, understanding as well as (or better!) than you do what your current and emerging areas of interest are – based on your reading patterns or references, ongoing research methods and data gathering, changing use of concepts and vocabulary in your discourse (anything from published outputs to conversations), and patterns of interaction in various social or disciplinary networks – and thereby configuring preferences from an awareness of more sources and links that a human could ever explore and distil by themselves, to surface new connections and content which have relevance to the activity at hand.

What if we imagine a future in which the goal of discovery is not content, or even knowledge, as AIs connect us not to information but to individuals, based on matching an understanding of a shared interest we may not even be aware of, through analysing the conceptual patterns in our lives, making visible connections we may never have uncovered, and even suggesting ground-breaking areas for collaborative research and study.

Such futures, or parts of them, may be in the near or distant future, or may never come to pass at all. No one predicted the powerful effect that social media would have on our democratic systems of government, as a technological utopia of openness and sharing turned to an echo chamber of fake news and sock-puppet actors, incentivised to drive attention and advertising revenue rather than progress social harmony or individual well-being.

Perhaps the same future awaits AI, a promising opportunity turned problem child. Or perhaps the promises and ambitions will come true. One thing is certain, the future of discovery will require the continuous reinvention and reimagining of trust, and presents new frontiers for library and information professionals.

Some suggestions of activities for future library services:

- Understand the information needs and behaviours of our communities in comprehensive detail, through partnership working and in-depth user research, using this knowledge to drive the design and application of AIs for information seeking
- Curate corpora for training AIs, advocating for a focus on ethical considerations and identification of the bias inherent in any cultural collection, and ensuring that provenance and authenticity drive the preservation of our digital cultural heritage
- Develop information literacy frameworks and programmes of training to build awareness of how to evaluate trust, not just in information sources but in AI and machine-learning algorithms that mediate discovery and access
- Assure the quality of AI discovery, based on understanding the scope of knowledge domains and being able to measure the impact of information seeking on the underlying motivation (e.g. research competitiveness or student outcomes, correlated against the use of AI discovery technologies)
- Continue advocacy for open collections and legal foundations for democratic access, to reduce the silo-ing of information and provide AIs with the greatest

opportunity to avoid bias and gain the ability to extract and link knowledge across the entire record and ongoing production of human cultural heritage.

In the future, libraries will add value by understanding the nuance of information seeking – its configuration across the broad and the specific – and be able to recommend and configure AIs which will serve particular use cases, tightly differentiated. This will move the skills required far beyond judgements about relevancy ranking, into a comprehensive understanding of user needs and behaviours, and a deep understanding of the content environment and technological mediations of AI. If successful, libraries will shape a future in which the vast and ever-expanding domain of human understanding remains responsive to individual navigation, multiplying the opportunities for linking the disparate and uncovering the arcane.

Whatever the future, it is clear that significant disruption has turned the corner and is approaching us head on.

Notes

1 Putting aside oral culture, or the direct transmission of information from one individual to another at a concurrent place and time. We are concerned with information encoded within a substrate for the purpose of transmission between individuals located separately in space and/or time.

2 Many machine learning techniques are based on computer science theory developed over 30 years ago, which are only now becoming practical due to advances in computing power (Somers, 2017)

3 It is important to remember, however, that humans are not perfect either, with some estimates suggesting that human indexers agree only 80% of the time (Upshall, 2017).

References

Bastian, H. (2015) Science and the Rise of the Co-authors, blog, http://blogs.plos.org/absolutely-maybe/2015/11/25/science-and-the-rise-of-the-co-authors/.

Beel, J., Gipp, B., Langer, S. and Breitinger, C. (2016) Research-paper Recommender Systems: a literature review, *International Journal on Digital Libraries*, **17** (4), https://link.springer.com/article/10.1007/s00799-015-0156-0.

Bilder, G., Lin, J. and Neylon, C. (2015) Principles for Open Scholarly Infrastructure, http://dx.doi.org/10.6084/m9.figshare.1314859.

Bornmann, L. and Mutz, R. (2014) Growth Rates of Modern Science: a bibliometric analysis based on the number of publications and cited references, Cornell University, https://arxiv.org/abs/1402.4578.

Botzer, M. (2015) Delivering the Experience That Users Expect, www.exlibrisgroup.com/files/Products/Primo/UserExperienceWhitePaper.pdf.

Breeding, M. (2015) The Future of Library Resource Discovery, NISO, https://www.niso.org/publications/future-library-resource-discovery.

Cambria, E. (2016) Affective Computing and Sentiment Analysis, IEEE, http://ieeexplore.ieee.org/document/7435182/.

Cann, A., Dimitriou, K. and Hooley, T. (2011) Social Media: a guide for researchers, www.rin.ac.uk/our-work/communicating-and-disseminating-research/social-media-guide-researchers.

Ceolin, D., Groth, P., Maccatrozzo, V., Fokkink, W., Hahe, W. and Nottamkandath, A. (2016) Combining User Reputation and Provenance Analysis for Trust Assessment, *Journal of Data and Information Quality*, **17** (1–2), doi: 10.1145/2818382.

Clark, C. and Divvala, S. (2016) Mining Figures from Research Papers, Allen Institute for Artificial Intelligence, http://ai2-website.s3.amazonaws.com/publications/pdf2.0.pdf.

Connaway, L. S. (2015) The Library in the Life of the User: engaging with people where they live and learn, OCLC, www.oclc.org/content/dam/research/publications/2015/oclcresearch-library-in-life-of-user.pdf.

Coyle, K. (2016) Catalog and Context, blog, http://kcoyle.blogspot.co.uk/2016/06/catalog-and-context-part-i.html.

Dempsey, L. (2016) Library Collections in the Life of the User: two directions, *LIBER Quarterly*, **26** (4), https://www.liberquarterly.eu/articles/10.18352/lq.10170/.

Dempsey, L., Malpas, C. and Lavoie, B. (2014) Collection Directions: some reflections on the future of library collections and collecting, *Portal: Libraries and the Academy*, **14** (3), www.oclc.org/content/dam/research/publications/library/2014/oclcresearch-collection-directions-preprint-2014.pdf.

Digital Science (2017) The State of Open Data, Digital Science, https://doi.org/10.6084/m9.figshare.5519155.

Donelan, H. (2015) Social Media for Professional Development and Networking Opportunities in Academica, *Journal of Further and Higher Education*, **40** (5), www.tandfonline.com/doi/abs/10.1080/0309877x.2015.1014321.

EBSCO (2019) User Experience, https://www.ebsco.com/technology/user-experience.

Furrie, B. (2009) *Understanding MARC Bibliographic: machine-readable cataloging*, Library of Congress, https://www.loc.gov/marc/umb/.

Gardner, T. and Inger, S. (2018) *How Readers Discover Content in Scholarly Publications*, https://renewconsultants.com/wp-content/uploads/2018/08/How-Readers-Discover-Content-2018-Published-180903.pdf.

Godby, C. (2017) *A Division of Labour*, www.oclc.org/content/dam/research/publications/2017/godby-division-of-labor-2017.pdf.

Gramatica, R., Di Matteo, T., Giorgetti, S., Barbiani, M., Bevec, D. and Aste, T. (2014) *Graph Theory Enables Drug Repurposing: how a mathematical model can drive the discovery of hidden mechanisms of action*, PLOS One, http://journals.plos.org/plosone/article?id=10.1371/journal.pone.0084912.

Grimes, A. (2013) ORCID as a Short Cut to Personalisation, Force 11, https://www.force11.org/presentation/orcid-short-cut-personalisation.

Groth, P. (2017) Are We Finally Ready For Transclusion?, https://www.slideshare.net/pgroth/are-we-finally-ready-for-transclusion.

Hampshire, V. and Buckley, L. (2017) Yewno Discover: discover what's been missing, http://fullstop.com/wp-content/uploads/2017/03/YewNo.pdf.

Hinton, G., Deng, L., Yu, D., Dahl, E., Mohamed, A., Jaitly, N., Senior, A., Vanhoucke, V., Nguyen, P., Sainath, T. N. and Kingsbury, B. (2012) Deep Neural Networks for Acoustic Modeling in Speech Recognition: the shared views of four research groups, *IEEE Signal Processing Magazine*, **29** (6), 82–97.

Juric, M. and Rydahl, M. (2017) *Comparing UNSILO Concept Extraction to Leading NLP Cloud Solutions*, https://site.unsilo.com/site/wp-content/uploads/2017/03/UNSILO-White-Paper-Benchmarks.pdf.

Klein, M., Van de Sompel, H., Sanderson, R., Shankar, H., Balakireva, L., Zhou, K. and Tobin, R. (2014) Scholarly Context Not Found: one in five articles suffers from reference rot, *PLoS One*, **12**, e115253, https://doi.org/10.1371/journal.pone.0115253.

Kramer, B. and Bosman, J. (2016a) *Survey 2015–2016*, Innovations in Scholarly Communication: changing research workflows, https://101innovations.wordpress.com/survey-2015-2016/.

Kramer, B. and Bosman, J. (2016b) *Academic Social Networks: the Swiss army knives of scholarly communication*, Innovations in Scholarly Communication: changing research workflows, https://101innovations.wordpress.com/2016/12/15/academic-social-networks-the-swiss-army-knives-of-scholarly-communication/.

Laney, D. (2001) 3D Data Management: controlling data volume, velocity, and variety, blog, https://blogs.gartner.com/doug-laney/files/2012/01/ad949-3D-Data-Management-Controlling-Data-Volume-Velocity-and-Variety.pdf.

Manning, C. D., Surdeanu, M., Bauer, J., Finkel, J., Bethard, S. J. and McClosky, D. (2014) The Stanford CoreNLP Natural Language Processing Toolkit. In *Proceedings of the 52nd Annual Meeting of the Association for Computational Linguistics: system demonstrations*, 55–60.

Nauta, G. J. and van den Heuvel, W. (2015) *Survey Report on Digitisation in European Cultural Heritage Institutions*, www.den.nl/art/uploads/files/Publicaties/ENUMERATE_Report_Core_Survey_3_2015.pdf.

Nicholas, D., Watkinson, A., Boukacem-Zeghmouri, C., Rodriguez-Bravo, B., Xu, J., Abrizah, A., Swigon, M. and Herman, E. (2017) Early Career Researchers: scholarly behaviours and the prospect of change, *Learned Publishing*, **30** (2), http://onlinelibrary.wiley.com/doi/10.1002/leap.1098/abstract.

Noorden, R. van (2014) Online Collaboration: scientists and the social network, *Nature*, **512** (7513), https://doi.org/10.1038/512126a.

Noorden, R. van (2015) Interdisciplinary Research by the Numbers, *Nature*, **525** (7569), doi:10.1038/525306a.

OECD (2017) Business Models for Sustainable Research Data Repositories, OECD Directorate for Science, Technology and Innovation, http://dx.doi.org/10.1787/302b12bb-en.

Open Data Institute (2015) The Data Spectrum, https://theodi.org/data-spectrum.

Padilla, T., Allen, L., Varner, S., Potvin, S. and Roke, E. (eds) (2017) Always Already Computational: library collections as data, https://collectionsasdata.github.io/statements/.

Piwowar, H., Priem, J., Larivière, V., Alperin, J. P., Matthias, L., Norlander, B., Farley, A., West, J. and Haustein, S. (2017) The State of OA: a large-scale analysis of the prevalence and impact of open access articles, *Peer J Preprints*, **5**, https://peerj.com/preprints/3119/.

ProQuest (2017) Content Diversity Survey, www.proquest.com/blog/pqblog/2017/Researchers-Demand-More-Diversity-in-Content-Sources.html.

Reidsma, M. (2016) Algorithmic Bias in Library Discovery Systems, blog, ProQuest, https://matthew.reidsrow.com/articles/173.

Rosenthal, D., Robertson, T., Lipkis, T., Reich, V. and Morabito, S. (2005) Requirements for Digital Preservation Systems, *D-Lib Magazine*, **11** (11), www.dlib.org/dlib/november05/rosenthal/11rosenthal.html.

Somers, J. (2017) Is AI Riding a One Trick Pony?, *MT Technologu Review*, https://www.technologyreview.com/s/608911/is-ai-riding-a-one-trick-pony/.

Souza, R. R., Coehlo, F. C., Shah, R. and Connelly, M. (2016) Using Artificial Intelligence to Identify State Secrets, https://arxiv.org/abs/1611.00356.

Stamatatos, E. (2009) A Survey of Modern Authorship Attribution Methods, *Journal of the American Society for Information Science and Technology*, **60** (3), http://onlinelibrary.wiley.com/doi/10.1002/asi.21001/abstract.

Stohn, C. (2015) How Do Users Search and Discover? Findings from Ex Libris user research, Ex Libris, https://pdfs.semanticscholar.org/fbae/90dabe01754ae55b6e8711790506f7be670e.pdf.

Sturm, B. (2014) The State of the Art Ten Years After a State of the Art: future research in music information retrieval, *Journal of New Music Research*, **43** (2), 147–72.

Upshall, M. (2017) Machine Learning and Academic Publishing: where are we today?, *UKSG eNews*, **405**, https://www.uksg.org/sites/uksg.org/files/Editorial405.pdf.

Van de Sompel, H. and Treolar, A. (2014) A Perspective on Archiving the Scholarly Web, https://hvdsomp.info/papers/Papers/2014/iPres2014_Sompel_Treloar.pdf.

W3C (2015) What is Linked Data?, W3C, https://www.w3.org/standards/semanticweb/data.

Welsh, A. (2015) Metadata Output and its Impact on the Researcher, *Catalogue and Index*, **178**, https://cdn.ymaws.com/www.cilip.org.uk/resource/collection/F71F19C3-49CF-462D-8165-B07967EE07F0/Catalogue_and_Index_issue_178,_March_2015.pdf.

Wikipedia (n.d.) Machine Learning, https://en.wikipedia.org/wiki/Machine_learning.

Willinsky, J. (2006) *The Access Principle: the case for open access to research and scholarship*, MIT Press, http://hdl.handle.net/10150/106529.

Xiong, C., Power, R. and Callan, J. (2017) Explicit Semantic Ranking for Academic Search via Knowledge Graph Embedding, http://ai2-website.s3.amazonaws.com/publications/Explicit_Semantic_Ranking.pdf.

Zittrain, J., Albert, K. and Lessig, L. (2014) Perma: Scoping and Addressing the Problem of Link and Reference Rot in Legal Citations: how to make legal scholarship more permanent, *Harvard Law Review*, **127**, https://harvardlawreview.org/2014/03/perma-scoping-and-addressing-the-problem-of-link-and-reference-rot-in-legal-citations/.

12

Discovering the future

Wolfram Horstmann, David De Roure and Simon McLeish

Preface: a resource discovery dystopia

David De Roure

> As long as the centuries continue to unfold, the number of books will grow continually, and one can predict that a time will come when it will be almost as difficult to learn anything from books as from the direct study of the whole universe. It will be almost as convenient to search for some bit of truth concealed in nature as it will be to find it hidden away in an immense multitude of bound volumes. When that time comes, a project, until then neglected because the need for it was not felt, will have to be undertaken.
>
> Denis Diderot, Encyclopédie (1755)

In the 2000s everyone was talking about 'information overload', fearing more data, more channels, more interruption. Discussion declined with the rise of personalisation – in search results, in social media recommendations. Filtering was the answer: 'It's not information overload. It's filter failure' (Shirky, 2008). By 2011 the risks of personalisation had been acknowledged, with the realisation that academics were living in 'filter bubbles' where algorithms gave them what they wanted – and sealed them off from new ideas. This led to community 'echo chambers' where ideas were amplified and self-reinforced by the penumbra of relevant information.

By 2015 the situation had deteriorated further. The digital marketing ecosystem had blurred with scholarly resource discovery. Algorithms made recommendations not just on reading habits but to maximise publishing corporations' income – purportedly to fulfil their legal obligation to shareholders' interests. In distorting information discovery, it corrupted the very process of research, bringing accusations of algorithmic censorship of scientific work. Universities were not far behind the publishers in privileging the academic outputs that would maximise their research income through optimising locations and citations, an increasingly automated process. A competitive ecosystem of algorithms arose – culminating in the infamous 2020 'Russell Algorithm' court ruling mandating transparency in search technologies.

Research was increasingly conducted in silico, and rising automation increasingly bypassed the human – especially as rewards went to those first past the post with research results. As machines became the predominant producers and consumers of research content, they became the primary users of real time resource discovery algorithms. While liberating for humans, this also denied critical reflection and challenge – they only got to see what machine-learning algorithms, and those who configured their behaviour, wanted them to see. Research methods had become built into our knowledge infrastructure, unchallenged.

A small band of academics and librarians started meeting in secret.

Editorial note: This extract was originally published as part of the report on resource discovery at the University of Oxford (Madsen et al, 2016), and is reprinted here with permission as a preface to the following chapter.

Introduction

Students, teachers, researchers and the public require comprehensive access to academic information and literature. Today, almost all literature, printed or digital, is discovered online, in library catalogues, search engines, dedicated academic discovery services, and many new forms to come. The cases of allegedly manipulating elections by placing information in the social web shows at least two directions of what we have to expect in the future of the discovery of information: that we will face completely new, complex, subtle forms of discovering academic information; and that we will require ever more access to information to be able to educate specialists and society at large to understand how to benefit maximally from the world of knowledge and be able to assess it critically.

In which future the discovery of academic information will develop is almost impossible to predict, but the following text provides several possible – at least thinkable – scenarios, including extreme cases, such as the upload of a human mind into the digital sphere. Some of these scenarios are utopian, some are dystopian – but all are based on technology for research that is in development at the moment, and are intended to provoke thought about the implications of the technology. The scenarios are written as short science fictional narratives and will not provide background information, explanation or discussion – they are rather to be thought of as an inspiration to think outside the box. Further reading is listed for each scenario, which is designed to provide fuel for the imagination rather than the standard style of reference for readers who want to investigate further. The overall purpose is to inspire interest in and thought about the future of discovery – and thus there seems to be no better way to end this book.

As an introduction – before the scenarios are presented – two possible directions in the future world of academic information shall be contrasted: one showing an open and transparent world of knowledge, the other a restricted and undisclosed one. Both seem to be possible outcomes of current trends in the world of academic research information, and these two extremes are presented to show just how different the future of research can be – and the future of the discoverability of research can be, in particular – depending on the outcome. By demonstrating the width of the difference between two very plausible scenarios, this section not only says something about the future of research and discovery, but also acts as a warning that the scenarios that follow are not to be taken as predictions. They can at most be possibilities.

We need to give a small procedural warning before you continue reading. The scenarios are presented in a mixture of first and third person narration, and this is deliberate. The purpose is to give either a more personal, first person, narration, as though the reader is being told something over a coffee or is reading a blog, or an apparently more formal, closed and impersonal narrative, as though the reader has access to a report. The narrative forms chosen were felt to the writers to be the best fits for what they wanted to say in each scenario.

Future of academic research and information: open or closed?

These are some possible characteristics of an open future of academic research and information:

- The public domain of scientific information is considered as international lore. Open access is the predominant form of publication.
- Academic information services work smoothly across borders, legally, organisationally and technically.
- Research data complies with FAIR principles: it is findable, accessible, interoperable, reusable.
- Sophisticated authoring and assessment tools allow researchers to dynamically and autonomously publish all research results.

- There is a global, freely accessible corpus of all scientific citations and usage data.
- Scientific impact is no longer measured by publications and citations alone.
- Reproducibility of research becomes so important that deception and plagiarism disappear.
- The boundaries between scientific expertise and general knowledge, such as in Wikipedia, dissolve.
- Scientific hypothesis formation is supported by machine learning.
- Start-ups on innovative forms of science communication and economic exploitation of scientific results grow on the grounds of public domain data.
- Digital skills are an essential part of scientific education. New degrees and scientific professions for digital science emerge. Data science is an independent discipline.
- By attributing academic digital services the same importance as buildings in budget planning, a sustainable, public global infrastructure is operative.
- High-performance digital libraries are created to distil all scientific information into the cultural heritage of the future.

These are some possible characteristics of a closed future of academic research and information:

- For scientific publications, publishers impose high fees as they are being created, and the cost of licensing magazines and e-books is growing at an unprecedented rate.
- There is only one single commercial platform for publishing scientific results and a single citation database decides on the evaluation of any scientific achievement.
- Deception and plagiarism in the digital world are increasing in numbers to meet the increased demands on rating systems.
- Digital research data is massively lost or disappears behind barriers to economic exploitation – publishers sell the research data back to universities and research institutions.
- The reproducibility of research using digital methods is worse than that of analogue research.
- The value of research for the economy and for societal and political legitimacy is dwindling.
- General knowledge on the internet is increasingly distorted and manipulative.
- There is a massive shortage of digital skills in science – digitally savvy researchers and the next generation migrate across countries.
- The interests of science are officially declared to be of less importance than economic growth. Academic freedom disappears as constitutional right.

- International law recognises that public domain content may be licensed and may be withdrawn from public access.
- Public budgets cannot justify the power consumption of institutional data centres, otherwise the cost will severely limit the quality of study.
- Large parts of the scientific information infrastructure are provided centrally by a single company.

Scenarios

Universal open access

Philip K. finds a recently deceased darkling beetle in the Namib desert. He stops his exploration of the dunes and puts a physical sample from its abdomen in his mobile analytics device. He tags the spectroscopic analysis process with the species name and geo-coordinates. The results display shows the organic and chemical composition of the sample, alongside choices of scientific literature relating to the beetle, vegetation and geology in the area, as well as biomechanical and engineering research that relate to the beetle's ability to produce water from fog that it gathers on its back. Philip is actually a meteorologist. To find clues about the origin of the water in the body of the animal, he enhances the spectroscopy to give clues about its composition. Literature about water and air composition in the area appears and a suggestion to upload the results of his sample to a data collection. 'Thank you for sharing your data' the display reads: 'Your sample has now been added to the database and linked to 13,456 scientific articles.' Philip is briefly thinking about the speed and efficiency of connecting scientific publications with each other and with research datasets since all research worldwide became open access. The display shows another message: 'Another dataset has been uploaded less that 10 km from your location.' Philip looks at the dataset and recognises the name of a Namibian colleague as author. 'Contact!' he speaks into the device. 'Dinner tonight?'

Further reading on the future of open access

Faye Chadwell and Shan C. Sutton discuss the changing role of the librarian in the next 20 years of a world where open access becomes the norm and where librarians have a very different role in academic life (Chadwell and Sutton, 2014). Meanwhile, Richard Poynder surveys where things are now, and how the current open access landscape differs from the expectations and ideals posited by its advocates (Poynder, 2018) – a warning for how the future may differ from the hopes of librarians planning for it now.

Run my thesis

The magic of using executable document tools from the start of my PhD is that I now have an executable thesis. This has made it a lot easier for me to perfect the science – as new data has come in I've been able to rerun and adapt the work. And as the thesis ideas developed in my head, I was able to incorporate them, hook the new text into the execution layer, and make sure it was firmly based on the data. I'm confident in the work I did, and the software underlying it – and what's more I know it's reproducible. My supervisor said it was the same for her generation when they first got their hands on digital tools – early on it feels like extra effort, but once you're doing it you get the benefits pretty quickly: the old Jupyter notebooks took off rapidly once researchers heard of them. I wouldn't work any other way now.

Next step is the viva, when my examiners will have run the thesis for themselves – not so much viva voce, more per machina. And then it goes in the executable library, and everyone can use it.

My colleague finished her PhD last year. She generated two new papers recently just by rerunning the thesis when she was notified of new data, which was great. But one of her friends wasn't so lucky – his thesis broke about six months after deposit. The data hooks still seem to be good, which is so frustrating, but the executable format is no longer compatible with the libraries on his institutional repository. Good thing my institution can afford the latest release of the autonomic software. Digital preservation is still an issue! Maybe one day the AI managing the library will get a bit better and the reproducibility robots will repair things. If that happens, the thesis can be rerun with the latest data, but for now, it is at least still possible to look at the ideas and conclusions from the data up until last January: back to the old world of fixed documents.

Further reading on executable documents

Project Jupyter aims to produce open source software, standards and tools for interactive computing, including a Notebook application to allow you 'to create and share documents that contain live code, equations, visualisations and narrative text' (https://jupyter.org). More theoretically Strijkers et al. (2011) discuss an executable paper concept aimed at improving reproduction and validation of computationally obtained results in scientific papers, and Montagano (2018) looks at the possibilities for research articles beyond the PDF format almost universal today.

Uploaded minds

Professor Anna Ng began her next task, catching up with the particle physics research literature. There were rumours yesterday that CERN were about to formally announce the confirmation that abnormal fragments from collisions in the Large Hadron Collider II conformed to one of the theories which extended the current version of the Standard Model. Her feed reader showed a new item, which was the expected news, with attached datasheets.

Immediately, she began to try to understand this new information, hooking part of her consciousness up to one of the physics department's data processing machines, while simultaneously looking up how the new announcement changed the relationships in the reference management system, and reading the suggested relevant papers.

Anna was able to see a three-dimensional animated model of the collisions, and work through them in ultra slow motion and ultra high resolution. She could see the yellow tags embedded by CERN researchers to mark features of interest, and the new green ones which were being added by research physicists around the world as they worked on it. Taking this data and adding the tags to her personal reference management system showed new connections, converging to an obscure paper from arXiv, one which had been written but abandoned without publication when its theoretical models had failed to materialise. Success! She appeared to be the first researcher to make the connection! The unique nature of her reference management, and the order of the import of the tags had given her a temporary advantage over other physicists across the world.

Assimilating the paper, noting that it was nine years since it had been read, she added a tag with a link to it at the crucial point in the collision model. Her ethical duty to the principle of shared scholarship done, she was able to relax and begin thinking about the implications, trying to formulate a modified Standard Model extension which would incorporate this paper and the new data. But even now she continued to communicate with the rest of the theoretical particle research community, as well as upgrading her Lie Algebra representation theory knowledge to incorporate the latest ideas. As this helper module loaded into her mind, she was able to see the flaw in the current version of the extension, and began to rebuild it, now acting as part of the university theory group as they pooled their knowledge. She did have time for an off-topic thought, that things had changed so much since this would have taken days of labour with discovery tools with their limited two dimensional lists of results, discussions and e-mails with colleagues, and, above all, coffee. Things were so much better for the onward march of science now that she had abandoned her physical body for the upload to the university research infrastructure, now that she could work as fast as their latest processors could manage, and now that anything on the internet was just a thought away. Even for her new way of living, this work was going to take a long time; already she had spent five whole minutes on it.

Further reading on uploaded minds

Quinn (2016) discusses immortality through uploading in an article based on an episode of the BBC's science magazine programme *Horizon*, quoting Russian millionaire and advocate Dmitry Itskov, while Jones (2016) is more sceptical. Hauskeller (2012) discusses the philosophical background to the topic.

Doing without my virtual assistants: blog post 1 from Charlie D.

I am one of a group of young cultural historians working on the 1980s who are taking part in, and blogging, a research project. Over the next week, we will be embedding ourselves in culture before the arrival of the virtual assistant. Apart from the connection to the blog, we will only use technology available before 1989. We believe that only by doing this can we properly understand the decade.

I have just said the words which start the experiment. 'Danni, start the live blog session. Now ignore what I say for the next eight hours.' Now I am what they used to call 'logged out'.

The plan is for me to do some research reading (on actual paper!), use an analogue telephone to order a pizza the old-fashioned way, and write a letter, which was still common back then. The day will end with a departmental seminar to discuss the experiment – and we will actually all be physically present!

My first problem is working out what to read. Danni usually makes suggestions based on my notes on the reading I've already done, and she can't do that, and I'm limited to the physical reading material in the campus library. Yes, there was a time when this was the only way to obtain research material. The project had used some of its budget to pay Mrs Culver (she insisted on the old-fashioned manner of address) to work with us. She is a retired librarian who had been working in the eighties. In those times, librarians acted as the gateways to knowledge.

So I tell her what I had read last week, and ask if she had any recommendations. Her response is strange: it was not her role to tell research staff what to do, she was there to make it possible for them to do what they wanted. This, then, will be my first big challenge: to organise my own research – Danni's job. I obviously have some idea of what I had read, but I couldn't list exact titles or anything like that. After thinking for a bit, I ask if she can find anything on the impact of computers on everyday life. After all, computers had been around for decades, there must be something I could read about how they were viewed in the eighties. Was there a famous study?

She leads me to a battered piece of furniture. 'All the information you need is in here.' I know eighties computers were big, but this did not look like a computer. No screen, nothing but wooden drawers full of small cards. 'There are a couple of books by Alvin

Toffler which you should read.' This is almost like Danni giving me a list of what to read next!

'The cards are sorted alphabetically . . . look at T for Toffler, not A! Then the cards will tell you where to find the books.' I shuffle through a few cards; this seemed easy enough. There are two for Toffler: Future Shock and The Third Wave. On the Future Shock card it said, 'HN17.5.TOF'. I ask, 'Is that a DOI?' Apparently, it's something called a 'shelf mark', and makes it possible to find items in a physical library. The shelves have plaques on them with part of the shelf mark, and you walk around until you find the aisle which has the ones you want, then the book is somewhere in that aisle. A lot more effort than clicking on a link! And the amount of work to find it was enormous: how did anyone ever get any research done, back in the day?

Further reading on virtual assistants

While not specifically about virtual assistants, the impact of technological change is the theme of the classic book mentioned in this scenario (Toffler, 1970), and digital assistants are likely to cause huge changes in how we relate to IT. Like the other topics in this chapter, virtual assistants have proponents, such as Brauer (2014) and Leetaru (2016), and sceptics, including Gonzalez (2017).

It can only be found if it is there

It is a big day for academic journal portfolio analyst Mark T., entering the HQ of KNO Publishing to present his new ideas on exploiting the publisher's search engine to the CEO. It's a general search engine that also includes journals that are not owned by them. It had started as a mechanism to inform KNO's journal acquisition strategy, analysing the whole world's research literature to identify journals that are strong and trending, using a machine-learning algorithm that detected hot topics in the world of research. If the algorithm detected the field of, say, solar energy panels as a trend, KNO started to acquire or develop the top journal in the field. This meant that researchers looking for articles about solar energy panels were likely to be directed to articles owned by KNO.

This has now led to criticism by academics because the search engine was suspected of favouring the publisher's own journal titles over foreign journal titles by putting them on top of the list of search results or highlighting them.

Mark begins his speech:

Academics are suspicious. They will detect the finest adjustments in ranking that are not complying with the principles of academic disinterestedness. Several attempts to rank journals that we own higher than journals that we don't own have failed. And this had detrimental effects on the reputation of the whole search engine, which, in turn, also harmed the usage and value of the journals that we own. We need to apply supposedly neutral measures for the ranking – such as citations. And we do. We have already achieved the position of the market leader by buying as many of the highly cited journals as we could. But now this development strategy is stuck because the residual competitive journals are in the hands of other publishers and too expensive to buy or otherwise not available. But there is a possibility that might help us to marginalise those competitive journals and secure our market leader position.

Now, how can we make use our analysis of research trends to secure our position? The software has been used for many years for informing our purchasing. Thus, our market position is based on the category system that we use. Take the example of climate research. There is an innovative but controversial research paradigm in glacier research that is mainly published in 'glacier theory'. The main journal in the field is 'Journal of Glacier Research'. We acquired the latter because it is the largest in the field of glacier research and we did not buy the former: 'Glacier Theory' never appeared to be on top in any category and thus was never a priority object for acquisition. It is categorised under geophysics, which, as a field, has other top-ranking journals that we already own. In general, we can only be as successful as our category system for research topics is. This is a risk for us.

What we need to do is to use our categories to define what is a research trend and what is not, rather than reacting to the emergence of trends. My proposal to do this is rather simple: we sell the research trends software to the leadership of universities and other research organisations to help them develop their institutional strategy. If an institution was to analyse its profile and, based on our research trends software, came to the conclusion that they should invest in climate research because big funding programs have recently been established there, they would seek to recruit in that field. If they now look for a professor working on glaciers, our research trends software will guide them to the researchers that perform best in both geophysics and climate research. These researchers are likely to publish in our journals and not in 'Glacier Theory'. When the same is happening in many institutions around the world, this would reduce the ranking of 'glacier research' and, eventually, could render it obsolete. As a bonus, we gain new profits by entering the sector of research trends with very little investment because we already have the software. All we need to do is to invest a little in user experience design and establish a sales team that specialises in institutional leadership. Actually, we could re-train our sales teams for libraries, since the library market is saturated. For us, it will be a zero-sum game.

The CEO sits back and exhales. He has listened very carefully. After a period of silence he comes forward:

Little investment and optimal use of existing resources: good. What about risks? What if this approach was seen as an attempt at manipulating institutional research strategies, similar to what we had with the boosting of search results?

Mark replies:

This risk is very low because the categorisation is not the main product being sold. Institutional leadership does not have the time and expertise to assess a deal with the philosophical question of how to categorise research fields. It is mainly interested in seeing the strengths and weaknesses of their institution. Scrutiny, if any, will be focused on how the research trends are being computed. And this method is transparent and robust.

And what if the algorithms constructing our category system were incorrect? It would mean that we steer global research to work in the wrong direction, correct? What if the controversial people publishing in Glacier Theory were right about the causes of climate change?

The algorithm that defines our category system has been developed by the leading researchers in the world. In other words, research itself does not have any better way to categorise knowledge.

Further reading on algorithm ethics

Ethics is an important topic in artificial intelligence. Some recent less technical discussions include Anon (2017), Beall (2018) and Mancha and Ali (2017).

Snakes and ladders

I was on the way to the interview, glad to see a notification that my last article had just been cited only last night – just in time for today. It seems crazy that not so long ago people used to print out their list of publications to submit with their application. Today's panel will use my citation graph and stats live in the interview. I wonder who cited me . . . Must remember to cite them back.

Waiting with the others to be called in for the interview, I take a closer look. Actually this is better than I thought – I've been linked into a really strong chain and it's pulled me up a notch. Even my Erdős Quotient is up by 0.01. And I can see more and more readers coming to the paper as we speak, the paper title flickering with darker hotspots.

I go in and the graph is up on the wall. Neat – they're using an animation showing it growing over time. Where's the new citation? Out of the corner of my eye I see a fragment greying out on the far edge but can't see what that is.

'Good morning. We have been modelling your outputs and projecting over the next 5 years. Could you talk us through your strategy around the outputs on the bottom right here?'

Outside the room, the next candidate put their device away. There's nothing like activating the strategic contracting bots once you've spotted the opposition.

JOBSEEKERS!

Looking to improve your career chances?

Our leading edge facial recognition app connects to the most advanced auto-authoring intelligence to rewrite your papers as you snap.

Further reading or viewing on manipulation of bibliometrics or clickbots

The *Black Mirror* episode 'Nosedive' (Wright, 2016) was an important inspiration for this scenario. Interesting discussions in metrics and manipulation include López-Cózar, Robinson García and Torres Salinas (2014), Neophytou (2015) and Rice (2012).

Data tripper

In the old days we had some good reputable archives of data and they told you exactly what they were and how to use them. That was more straightforward. Then we had the 'frontier society' of the new millennium with data everywhere, and the big problem was finding what we needed. In fact, it was knowing what it was we really had. These were dark days of data-centric research, especially in terms of the archive we left behind.

My favourite website (why do we still call them that?) used to be Data Tripper, especially when it all became about data streams rather than data archives. We used to rate data sources and see what everyone else thought of them, and the sources would do anything to get good ratings, encouraging us to review positively. Users meant credits and credits meant funding for the approved suppliers. Plus there was dBay for buying old datasets.

To an extent this helped us avoid the dis-data that was poisoning the ecosystem, and the side-effects of the illegal data trade. But the more data that was out there, the easier it was to find the data for the results you wanted. The appetite for results had overcome the appetite for truth.

Automation has helped a lot, and it was essential because it was the only way to deal with the flood of data supply. People, and machines, are now taking provenance seriously in the ecosystem, so at least we know where everything comes from, and trust is that much better with crypto-distribution behind the scenes.

> But now it's all automated I don't think we really know what it is we have. Who, or what, made the decisions and why? What is real any more?

Further reading on future or automated data curation
Two discussions on automated curation are by Ismail (2018) and Wade (2018).

Robots take over research

> *Software and Research News*
> **Lawsuit Over – Robots Can Research Too**
> *By our AI correspondent, 2042-02-15*

In a landmark decision, the US Supreme Court ruled last night that an artificial mind can be considered a creator of a PhD thesis, in a majority decision.

In 2035, psychology student Pat Schmidt submitted her thesis to the University of Northeast Michigan for her doctorate, not expecting to launch a lawsuit from A-Z Corps, who had developed the iJung digital assistants for psychology research. Ms Schmidt used a number of eJung modules, including the RJung research management tool and the wJung writing assistant. Her faculty adviser, Dr John Pellew, alerted the University to a possible case of cheating when he thought he detected that large parts of the thesis were not written in the manner he expected from Ms Schmidt. Dr Pellew, who died last year, commented when giving evidence as a witness, "Even when there is a suspicion that work is not original, it is vital to take it further. But in this case, several sections of the thesis were clearly not written by the same person as the rest of it."

Digital analysis software agreed, and Ms Schmidt was told that her thesis could not be accepted. The next day, 25 May 2035, her lawyer served a writ on the University. In it, the claim was made that the portions of her thesis – estimated at between 35% and 50% – which did not match Ms Schmidt's personal writing style, had been composed by eJung, which was a permitted writing and research aid. The University's lawyers countered by pointing out that the extreme level of use amounted to a collaboration rather than assistance, and that collaboration on a PhD thesis was not permitted.

This argument gained notoriety, and was the third fastest trending story of 2035 (after the British royal divorce and the Hollywood Walk of Fame murders). Interest died down as much of the case consisted of lengthy technical arguments, ironically produced in the main by artificial legal expert systems, conducted at a speed impossible to human advocates. Last night's ruling, by a majority of 6 to 3 justices, is widely expected by commentators to open the door to the acknowledgement of the role played by digital assistants and artificial intelligence in modern life.

Long time AI guru Maya Ingold, who was several times consulted as an expert witness, feels that this is inevitable:

> Over the last 35 years, since the early pioneering efforts of Siri, Cortana and Alexa, digital assistants have woven themselves into every part of our lives, from designing the perfect breakfast menu, to setting the optimal time to retire for the night. Since the first successful newsfeed produced without human intervention was unveiled in 2021, artificial intelligence has been taking on tasks previously thought to be the sole province of human minds at an increasing rate. While AI has helped in research for decades, it has until now seemed that the spark of manual intervention was needed to produce a creative new piece of research. That final bastion has now fallen, and it is only a matter of time – perhaps only a short time – before all research work is carried out by machines.

An opposing view was held by Professor Zachary Post, who has spent years campaigning for what he calls 'real work for real people'. To him, the advance of the machines is more a retreat from humanity:

> Since before the dawn of recorded history, the unique mark of the human species has been its questioning mind. We have come a long way since we were hunter gatherers, but every new technological advance has had its downside. This ruling, though, is taking things too far. We must stop our slide into dependency on machines. I call on all of you to turn off your assistants, to go back to finding your own way through life. Be inspired, be inspirational, and, above all, be human.

Who will prove to be right? This reporter is not able to decide, but as an electronic entity myself, I will fight to stay connected and not be switched off.

Further reading on AI creativity or journalism

Creativity is another hot topic in artificial intelligence. A general article can be seen in (Anon, 2015) while (Hall, 2018) and (Underwood, 2017) both discuss computer journalism.

Editorial afterword

Simon McLeish

to the chapter . . .

Other authors and I hope that the above chapter is a fun but thought-provoking way to end a book on discovery. Some of the ideas in it may seem outlandish, but even as we were writing them, we could see them resonate with current news stories (the coverage of Alexa laughing could almost have been another scenario, and there always seem to be stories about manipulating fake news and chatbots being led astray by human beings – or taking jobs away from them). Discovery is already changing fast, and the research and learning it underpins is also rapidly developing.

... and to the book

Discovery and the underlying data which supports it are closely allied, and the forms of the objects to be discovered are also important. While some of the scenarios in Chapter 12 may seem to be more about the evolution of research practice, such changes would have an immense effect on how the outputs of research are discovered. Recent suggestions on replacements for the academic paper (Andrus, 2018; Somers, 2018; among others) suggest that a more fluid, nuanced, multimedia – or even executable – format for scholarly communication will become prevalent. This clearly would not fit well with today's static indexes in bibliographic databases mechanisms for discovery: how would services need to change to keep up? Are artificially intelligent curation and personal discovery bots the answer? Or will future discovery use something else, not yet thought up?

As editor, working on this book has brought home to me even more just how important discovery is to teaching, learning and research, and thus how key the development of discovery services is to the future of academic endeavour. Perhaps because of my role as a facilitator of discovery services I am biased, but it seems to me that resource discovery is the purpose of existence for libraries today: there is no point to a library if its contents (and, nowadays, subscribed resources) are unable to be found by students and researchers.

It is an exciting and challenging time to be working in this field – and the one thing which is certain is that it will not stop being either for a while to come.

References

Andrus, S. (2018) Is the Research Article Immune to Innovation?, The Scholarly Kitchen, 3 July, https://scholarlykitchen.sspnet.org/2018/07/03/guest-post-research-article-immune-innovation/.

Anon (2015) The Quest for AI Creativity, *IBM Cognitive – What's Next for AI*, 11 September, www.ibm.com/watson/advantage-reports/future-of-artificial-intelligence/ai-creativity. html.

Anon (2017) When Algorithms Discriminate: robotics, AI and ethics, interview with Steven Roberts, Al Jazeera, https://www.aljazeera.com/programmes/talktojazeera/2017/11/algorithms-discriminate-robotics-ai-ethics-171117133216779.html.

Beall, A. (2018) It's Time to Address Artificial Intelligence's Ethical Problems, *Wired UK*, August, https://www.wired.co.uk/article/artificial-intelligence-ethical-framework.

Brauer, C. (2014) Virtual Assistants Are the Way Forward, CNN, https://edition.cnn.com/2014/10/03/business/virtual-assistants-are-the-way-forward/index.html.

Chadwell, F. and Sutton, S. C. (2014) The Future of Open Access and Library Publishing, *New Library World*, **115** (5–6), May, 225–36, doi:10.1108/NLW-05-2014-0049.

Gonzalez, R. (2017) The Real Problem with Voice Assistants like Siri is your Brain, *Wired*, https://www.wired.com/story/multitasking-problem-with-virtual-assistants/.

Hall, S. (2018) Can You Tell if this was Written by a Robot?: 7 challenges for AI in the media, World Economic Forum, 15 January, https://www.weforum.org/agenda/2018/01/can-you-tell-if-this-article-was-written-by-a-robot-7-challenges-for-ai-in-journalism/.

Hauskeller, M. (2012) My Brain, My Mind, and I: some philosophical assumptions of mind-uploading, *International Journal of Machine Consciousness*, **4** (187), doi: 10.1142/S1793843012400100.

Ismail, N. (2018) Three Ways to Automate Content Creation and Curation, *Information Age*, 5 January, https://www.information-age.com/3-ways-automate-content-creation-curation-123470237/.

Jones, R. (2016) Could We Upload a Brain to a Computer – and Should We Even Try?, *Independen*t, 5 July, www.independent.co.uk/news/science/could-we-upload-a-brain-to-a-computer-and-should-we-even-try-a7120451.html.

Leetaru, K. (2016) How Automated Curation and Chat Bots Could Restore the Human Touch to Online Commerce, *Forbes*, 19 September, https://www.forbes.com/sites/kalevleetaru/2016/09/19/how-automated-curation-and-chat-bots-could-restore-the-human-touch-to-online-commerce/.

López-Cózar, E. D., Robinson-García, N. and Torres-Salinas, D. (2014) The Google Scholar Experiment: how to index false papers and manipulate bibliometric indicators, *Journal of the Association for Information Science and Technology*, **65** (3), 446–54, https://doi.org/10.1002/asi.23056.

Madsen, C., Hurst, M., McLeish, S., Emsley, I., Stacey, R., Garibyan, M., Abdul-Rahman, A., Khan, S. and Chen, M. (2016) *Resource Discovery @ The University of Oxford 2015*, https://www.bodleian.ox.ac.uk/__data/assets/pdf_file/0009/197118/Oxford-Resource-Discovery-Final-Report.pdf.

Mancha, R. and Ali, H. (2017) The Unexamined Algorithm Is Not Worth Using, *Stanford Social Innovation Review*, https://ssir.org/articles/entry/the_unexamined_algorithm_is_not_worth_using.

Montagano, P. (2018) Guest Post: transforming the research paper into a functional tool, The Scholarly Kitchen, 15 November, https://scholarlykitchen.sspnet.org/2018/11/15/guest-post-transforming-the-research-paper-into-a-functional-tool/.

Neophytou, J. (2015) Anomalous Citation Patterns in the World of Citation Metrics, https://hub.wiley.com/community/exchanges/discover/blog/2015/09/09/anomalous-citation-patterns-in-the-world-of-citation-metrics.

Poynder, R. (2018) The Open Access Big Deal: back to the future, open and shut?, blog, 28 March, https://poynder.blogspot.com/2018/03/the-open-access-big-deal-back-to-future.html.

Quinn, T. (2016) The Immortalist: uploading the mind to a computer, BBC News, 14 March, www.bbc.co.uk/news/magazine-35786771.

Rice, C. (2012) How Journals Manipulate the Importance of Research and One Way to Fix It, London School of Economics Impact Blog, 12 July, http://blogs.lse.ac.uk/impactofsocialsciences/2012/07/12/journals-manipulate-research-one-way-to-fix/.

Shirky, C. (2008) It's not Information Overload. It's Filter Failure, keynote address, Web 2.0 Expo New York, September 19. https://www.youtube.com/watch?v=LabqeJEOQyI.

Somers, J. (2018) The Scientific Paper Is Obsolete, *The Atlantic*, 5 April, https://www.theatlantic.com/science/archive/2018/04/the-scientific-paper-is-obsolete/556676/.

Strijkers, R. et al. (2011) Toward Executable Scientific Publications, *Procedia Computer Science*, **4**, 707–15, doi: 10.1016/j.procs.2011.04.074.

Toffler, A. (1970) *Future Shock*, Pan.

Underwood, C. (2017) Automated Journalism: AI applications at New York Times, Reuters, and Other Media Giants, *TechEmergence*, 22 June, https://www.techemergence.com/automated-journalism-applications/.

Wade, M. (2018) 5 Ways Chatbots Are Revolutionizing Knowledge Management, *AtBot*, 12 February, https://blog.getbizzy.io/5-ways-chatbots-are-revolutionizing-knowledge-management-bdf925db66e9.

Wright, J. (2016) *Black Mirror,* Series 3, Episode 1, Nosedive, aired 21 October, https://www.imdb.com/title/tt5497778/.

Index

The manufacturer's authorised representative in the EU for product safety is Logos Europe, 9 rue Nicolas Poussin, 17000 La Rochelle, France (contact@logoseurope.eu, www.logoseurope.eu)
GPSR Authorized Representative: Easy Access System Europe—Mustamäe tee 50, 10621 Tallinn, Estonia, gpsr.requests@easproject.com
Printed and bound by CPI Group (UK) Ltd, Croydon, CR0 4YY
28/07/2026
02179479-0005